Wilbut,
may all your
dreams come true!

Sister-in-Christ

Allene [signature] 02/23/00

I Am Not Afraid to Dream

Joen Seale DDS

I Am Not Afraid to Dream

((((((((((((( ))((((((((((((())))))))))))))))))((((((((((((( ))((((((((

BY

Dr. Joe N. Lester

JOEWOLF PUBLISHERS

Editorial and Sales Offices:
Joewolf Publishers
P.O. Box 80127,
Conyers, Georgia 30013
email to joewolf@bellsouth.net
Fax 770-388-0521
Phone 770-922-6655

03 02 01 00 99 5 4 3 2

Library of Congress Cataloging-in-Publication Data

Lester, Joe N., DDS
    I Am Not Afraid to Dream :
    Inspirational / Joe N. Lester, DDS
        p.   cm.
        ISBN 0-9671344-0-4 (alk. paper)

This book is printed on acid-free recycled paper meeting
the requirements of the American National Standard
for Permanence of Paper for Printed Library Materials.

((((((((((((((¡

Manufactured in the United States of America

This book is dedicated to my parents,
Allene Battle Lester and Raymond Lester, Sr.

To Mother for loving the ten of us unconditionally. We will cherish
your memories forever.

To Father for never abandoning a ship that the world believed
was too crowded.

The ten of us were blessed to have you both.

Contents

Preface

It has been said that, "life is a short trip." With this in mind I have tried to live life to the fullest, always letting my life become a testing ground for spiritual growth and development.

In a struggle to survive I have spent most of my time and energy in somebody's school or slaving at one job or another. I was a "professional" but was in imminent danger of becoming a spiritual wreck.

In 1992 after the loss of my sister, my life took a turn for the better. Taking a couple of steps backward and realizing my sole purpose of living, I started to do what I loved. I started to write. And as one thing led to another, very soon I found myself in the bookstore buying books to read. In due course, I found myself enjoying the two oldest and simplest skills known to mankind, reading and writing. It's amazing how often we can find joy in life's simplest pleasures.

I must truly say that there are some things in life that one must do just for the sake of plain old unadulterated pleasure. Writing this book has been just that for me, a real pleasure.

It has never once crossed my mind who would read or buy this book. From the onset my intentions were to start it, finish it, print it, and if need be give it to someone as a Christmas present. Smile, and I hope you enjoy "I Am Not Afraid to Dream."

Acknowledgments

First and foremost, I would like to thank God for giving me the courage to step out on a limb and spill my guts in front of the entire world. It is truly amazing, with a spoon full of faith and God as my chief navigator, mountains have been moved to make my dreams realities.

A major thanks must also go to my loving wife Kimberly and my three daughters, Denise, Jarvia and Tiffany who read and continued to read my manuscript, rewrite after rewrite until it became boring. I appreciate you guys and the sacrifices that you made on my behalf.

Thank God for my mother, Allene Battle Lester, whose greatest dream was to see all of us grow up and become respectable self-supporting adults. Her teaching left the ten of us with a wealth of knowledge, love and traditions that will be cherished forever. To my father, Raymond Lester, Sr. who taught us to stay focused, to never fade nor falter. Daddy, you were right, "a little work ain't never hurt nobody."

To my friend Arlene Robinson, "I salute you." You were the captain of this ship. You believed in my story as much as I did. Thanks for forcing me to dig deep within my soul and capture the true story, when I only wanted to dance at the tip of the iceberg. Thanks for helping me. Only you and God know what my story really looked like before you jumped in.

A very special thanks to my friend Peggy Morris who constantly reminded me to keep this book both spiritual and inspirational. Thanks to Ross West and Marc Bailey for helping me transform my story into literary form.

Last but not least, to my siblings, Nell, Ray, Robert, Mary, Leonard, Nancy, Allene, Jack, and especially Gwyn (in your memory), this is your story as much as it is mine. Let us all continue to dream.

My 2:00 A.M. Question

I stare at the clock as it blinks 2:00. My foggy brain reminds me that it's Saturday morning. It's another sleepless night. My body and soul are simply refusing to shut down. I've tried lying on my right side, and then my left, but neither option will soothe my troubled, restless soul.

I've tried very hard not to look at the clock. That's a mental trick I've used to keep me from worrying about just how much sleep I'm losing. But I finally look. That old clock is always reminding me of something, and it usually has something to do with what I haven't done and what I won't have time to accomplish anyway.

But this night God had other plans for my insomnia. I finally gave up trying to sleep and laid there wide awake, resigning myself to the crook in the neck or spine that would definitely follow me around tomorrow. My mind rambled on in a kaleidoscope of half-formed thoughts and impressions, as the night moved at a snail's pace toward a relentless dawn.

I could think of no reason for my restlessness. I was exhausted, but my exhaustion was not physical. Many times before, I had lain awake, too tired to sleep, exhausted physically after long hours of work as a dentist at the prison or at my private dental practice.

Tonight's weariness was different. My brain was jammed in a thought process and would not shut down. "If only I could just disengage or jiggle the wires in this old skull, sleep would surely follow," I thought.

As it usually happens on a restless, sleepless night, I quickly imagined myself back at the prison, in the health services unit—my full-time job located twenty minutes away on Atlanta's east side.

After almost ten years of the "voluntary incarceration" of prison work, my subconscious had no trouble recreating my workplace—even hearing the sounds that are unique to this institution. The clacking sound of that prison gate was unforgettable. The pathos created by the sometimes anguished sounds of the women incarcerated behind that gate can be transcended only by the pitiful cries heard in a funeral procession.

"I'll have to charge them for this overtime on my time sheet tomorrow," I thought wryly, wondering just how quickly that request would be disallowed.

As if my subconscious was attempting to clear my mind's palette with more wholesome thoughts, a quick interlude superimposed itself over that sorry scene. I am a child again, back at home on the farm some two hundred miles south of Atlanta. The air is fresh with the smell of pollen from the blossoming fruit trees, a visual treat with their bright white blossoms and blood-red veins.

That thought was enough to dispel the distasteful image of prison but in a more palatable manner. And so I went with the image, and the thoughts that followed.

"The bees parading in the nectar of those blossoms know precisely their purpose in life. No thought, no indecision. Their actions are instinctive, no thought is required for them to fulfill their life's plan." In contrast, here I lay, ordained by God to have dominance over all creatures, but a slave to a thought pattern that is constantly hammering within my skull. You might call this tension. Still others would say it's stress. I know it now as the silent voice of my spirit and soul—a voice not welcome at this early hour, but beneficial nonetheless. I had come to accept these sleepless nights as God's manner of clearing my soul.

I came to the realization that night that God was trying to communicate something to me, something that I had all but ignored since my imaginary pal, Bubba, started to watch over me as a child. It occurred to me that it was possible that Bubba had actually been my guardian angel. This feeling grew quite strong, and reminded me of the same experience I had when I prayed to be accepted into dental school. Too, the sense of warmth that I felt about that memory was identical to the one I felt when I prayed for a way to pay the tuition at Meharry Medical School in Nashville. I truly believe that this was and is now, the still, small voice of God, and that He is watching over me even when I carelessly deny His presence within me.

Perhaps God attempts to reach me in the wee and vulnerable hours of the night because I am not always receptive to him in other, less-protected circumstances. To illustrate: Old Minister Hollywood kind of got to me last Sunday with his sermon and altar call. He played a trick on me that I was still unwilling to forgive.

Of course, Old Minister Hollywood doesn't know I call him that. That's just my name for him. Hollywood was not really old. I suspect he was about forty-nine years old, which would make him about ten years my senior. He refrained from telling people his birth date. If you asked him about his birthday, he'd answer in this way: "My spiritual rebirth was in June. The Lord spoke to me as plain as day. And I have been saved ever since."

You can rest assured that any conversation with him would be centered on the Lord. I could always sense that he had been burned with the fire of the Lord. It was obvious that he positioned himself close to the Lord in fear of slipping back into the hands of Satan, who had probably singed his coattail a few times.

This doesn't mean that I lack respect for him. I have always respected ministers. Back home, in Hawkinsville, Georgia, a visit from the preacher was a special occasion. The preacher always sat at the head of the table. Mother would put out the best silverware, and a good home-cooked meal from the wood burning stove would be in the making. We kids were cautioned not to get dirty, and to be on our best behavior. In exchange for this, we were treated to an extraordinary meal by our mother and treated like grownups by our guest. We were made to feel both special and unique.

Even with these positive memories and feelings about church, I wasn't enthusiastic about going to church. But I went. My reasoning was simple, if a little heathenish. I rarely got to see my wife and children. On Sunday—my only day off—they went to church—with or without me. So I would go to church with them.

The church itself was a tiny industrial building that had been recently renovated into a sanctuary. This particular Sunday, the congregation was packed together like sardines in a can. The air was tainted with every perfume you could imagine. The result was a confusing smell that I still cannot figure out or describe. Oddly enough, this is the same smell I remember from the church of my youth, a church that was much larger, much older, and a couple of hundred miles away. I can definitely associate that sweet aroma with social gatherings where people put on their Sunday threads.

Today, I was acutely aware that Old Hollywood felt quite comfortable in his position behind the podium. He literally pranced from one end of the pulpit to the other, all the while working the crowd like a performing artist. Truly, he was in his element.

I, too, felt very comfortable from where I sat—something that Old Minister Hollywood, with those bright, shrewd eyes of his, would soon notice. Sitting there in my favorite seat, minding my own business, I clapped when the rest of the members clapped; I even sang along with them when they reached a verse of a song that I knew. Otherwise, I just hit a word here and there to keep my lips moving, never singing loud enough to be heard.

My mind took in only bits and pieces of the sermon until Old Minister Hollywood's question touched a nerve that left my soul burning. I suppose that my sleep-deprived mind dwelled on his last sermon because of the effect it had on me that past Sunday. At the end of the sermon he did as he did every Sunday, his booming yet persuasive voice "opened the doors of the church" for new members. None came this Sunday, and Old Hollywood wasn't satisfied with that.

I thought I knew why. He was building a new congregation. This new congregation, the one I was sitting in right then, was only about ten months in existence, and he indeed needed new members. So, Old Minister Hollywood continued wheedling, trying to lure someone, anyone, to the altar—all in the name of Jesus.

I was surprised that no one had responded to the "call." Hollywood surely had the congregation on fire this morning. During his sermon, one sister kept clutching her fists incessantly and shouted, "Say it Preacher! Say it Preacher!" Periodically, she would gently remove her glasses in order to wipe the tears from her eyes. It was a shame—at least from Hollywood's standpoint—that this lady was already a member! She wasn't the only one so affected. The lady in front of me stood and pointed at Old Hollywood, waving her handkerchief like a flag.

The Holy Ghost was truly in that place today. And Old Hollywood seemed the perfect embodiment. His smooth, dark skin glistened as the sweat rolled from his forehead, mostly unnoticed by him. When he did finally notice the deluge that was threatening to blind him, he whipped out his large white handkerchief, wiped the sweat from his face, brought his fist down on the podium, and shouted rhythmically, repeating his plea, "Is there any person here today (pause) who is not sure what his real purpose in life is?"

His voiced trembled with emotion as he spoke those words. His teary-eyed gaze roamed slowly over the congregation, looking for prospects in need of prayer and salvation.

I was not overly impressed by this display. "Oh, look at him," I thought. "Does he know his real purpose in life? Maybe he's asking that question of himself."

With that thought, my sarcastic nature got the better of me. "He has probably got a lot of skeletons in his closet. I wouldn't mind taking a look in there. Let's open up that Pandora's box of his and see what flies out."

But I never got the chance. Suddenly our eyes met, and he looked a little startled for a moment, as if he had seen someone he didn't expect to see. It was a cold stare that sent chills running down my spine, despite the warmth of the room.

I became instantly irritated. He had touched a nerve with me. Of course he didn't have to search all over the church to find me. He knew where I sat almost every Sunday. I sat to the left of the pulpit, third row, first seat. If anyone was in "my" seat, I'd sit behind him or her, a silent reminder of my disapproval of their "borrowing my space."

But even knowing where I sat, he acted quite surprised to find me there. "Is there anyone here today that does not know what God has in store for them? Would you please come now?" Old Hollywood issued this final call with even more force. He opened his arms as a sign of his humbleness and receptive heart.

Before I knew it, I was making my way to the altar, my gaze still locked with the minister's—a very brave and big step for me, I might add. I usually do not go up there unless my wife Kim or one of the girls gives me the eye to go with them. I still don't know what force compelled me this day.

It was tight in that little sanctuary, but slowly I made my way to the front. Old Hollywood smiled with gratification (and perhaps relief). "Let us all join hands with our neighbor." He quickly signaled for the other minister to come over and join him for prayer. As in a well-rehearsed play, the assistant minister reverently walked over to join Old Hollywood.

"Touch and agree," prayed the pastor. "Let us bind off any hindering forces. Let's pray that this lost soul comes to know you, Lord Jesus."

To use the common term, my first thought was, "Excuse me?" My eyes instantly peeled open in astonishment. That's not what he said the altar call was for! He had asked for members to come forward if they did not know their purpose in life. I had fallen victim to this sly old fox's game. I had been had!

I now knew why I had trepidation about going before the altar! The whole church was staring at me like I was a lost soul in need of salvation. I imagined I could feel the congregation's collective eye boring into my back. Later Kim told me—to my relief—that everyone had bowed their heads and closed their eyes in prayer.

I managed to hold back what I wanted to say, but just barely. What I wanted to say was: "Hollywood, I am a firm believer in Jesus Christ and am NOT 'lost' in my faith. I can NOT, for the life of me, see what not knowing what my purpose in life has to do with this prayer!"

Nevertheless, I closed my eyes and continued to pray. And to plot my retaliation!

But no matter how I felt at the time, it was apparent to me at this wee hour of the morning that Old Hollywood's performance served its purpose. It accentuated the question of what my real purpose in life was—or should be. I have puzzled over this many times; I am still no closer to an answer at 2 a.m. tonight.

If nothing else, I did gain some reassurance by going to the altar. I know I am not alone with this issue. God is with me. If I continue to ask for His help in answering this question, I know He will ultimately give me the solution. But accepting that I was a "lost soul" was not the answer! I would have to search elsewhere. But where?

Uncovering the Family Secret

My childhood memories are a mixture of events that actually happened, fantasies I imagined, and stories of events related to me by others. Whether experienced personally, imagined, or learned through others, these memories are part of what has made me what I am. I began to feel, too, that exploring these memories would help me get a perspective on my purpose in life.

What I set out to do that one day, I discovered more, much more, than I had bargained for. I unearthed a family secret that could have destroyed me but instead gave me powerful insights for overcoming obstacles.

Driving down I-75 south from Atlanta, I slowed only to exit onto the Golden Isle Parkway in Perry, Georgia, and drive east toward Hawkinsville. That is where my memories began and the family secret was hidden. As I drove, I recall trying to see my childhood home as you might see it if you were visiting there for the first time.

The Golden Isle Parkway, the main artery through this rural part of Georgia, soon took me into the small town of Hawkinsville and its six thousand residents. Some things have changed since my growing-up years, of course. In Perry I noticed the newly built state fairgrounds and agriculture exposition center. Besides this new building and the new road on which my wife Kim and I were traveling, what I saw that day was essentially what I saw, however, as a young man traveling home from college from the nearby town of Fort Valley. In about thirty minutes I had zipped pass the red brick department stores of the Hawkinsville town square and its three traffic lights and was traveling south on Highway 247 to Blue Spring Road. As I approached the narrow, two-lane blacktop road that descended to my family's home place, fluffy clouds drifted lazily above me, like heaven's version of cotton candy.

Spring and summer are the epitome of life in the country. Where I grew up, all that can be seen for miles are the corn fields and the bright green of the cotton and peanut fields. From the road, the fruit trees in the yards seem to be accented by tiny dots of color. A closer look would show these dots to be the various fruit the trees bear. There are many apple and peach trees, but Blue Springs Road was lined with plum trees of many kinds. Behind these trees were acres and acres of watermelon, cantaloupes, and wild grapes. We called these grapes "bullets," but the real name is muscadine. These grapes make a heady, musty wine that is much enjoyed by all—even though this area rests in the heart of the Bible Belt.

Almost every house in this rural area has a small garden, which some call a "kitchen" garden because of its close proximity to the homeowner's kitchen door. These gardens grow sweet potatoes, Irish potatoes, turnip greens, mustard greens, tomatoes, squash, butter beans, and other tasty vegetables. In the summer, all the lucky owners of such gardens need to do is step off their porches to harvest a wonderful lunch or supper. This is the ultimate health food!

In plots that are larger than the kitchen gardens, but much smaller than the cotton and peanut fields, are the purple and green cane fields. Although some of the cane is sold, my hometown's art of making cane syrup and molasses is alive and well even today.

Most of the frame houses around the fields and gardens remain un-painted. White seems to be the favored color of the few houses that are painted. This sight got me to thinking about the old home place, and re-minded me of little things, like how unique we thought we were when our parents decided to forego the norm and chose green siding for our home. We felt like big news in our little town because of our unconventional choice!

As I had hoped it would, rekindling that memory led to others. Still driving down Blue Springs Road, I thought about my grandparents, who surely served as the sturdy roots of my family tree. I couldn't help wonder-ing whether the person named Joe Lester is that person because of the solid foundation they provided for the little branch I became.

Not to say that my grandparents were perfect; no one is. But even now their influence affects how I think and how I conduct my life.

As I had planned, I passed up the opportunity to visit with my father at the home place. Instead, I drove to my Uncle Jesse's house just across the county line in Wilcox County. His house sits about three or four miles off the main highway, down a long narrow lane that turns into an impassable sea of mud in inclement weather. Large pecan trees border this lane, and a rusty barbed-wire fence surrounds the whole eighty-acre property.

I smiled as I turned off the main road, partly in relief because it had not been raining, but also because of the sign hanging off one of the fence posts: "Forget the Dog, Beware of the Owner!"

I scanned the fence quickly, looking for dead chicken hawks. When Uncle Jesse catches a chicken hawk trying to eat his chickens, he kills it and hangs it on the fence. Sort of a warning to all the other chicken hawks, I suppose!

Uncle Jesse is pretty handy with a gun. In his younger years he could strike a match with a .22-caliber rifle from a distance of twenty paces. Any chicken hawks flying over this yard were in big trouble.

Jesse's house is painted white and trimmed in red. It's a large, rambling structure, built to no particular architectural standard. Perhaps unconventionality is a family trait. You might think that red trim on a house is an odd choice, but not for Uncle Jesse! As he puts it, that is his "thang!" The white truck parked near the house also has red trim. I do not think I have ever known Uncle Jesse to have a car or truck that wasn't painted these colors. If they weren't red and white when he got them, they soon were!

If you go to my Uncle Jesse's, you will see chickens running in the yard—all kinds and all colors. A goose lives in the yard, too. That goose has been there for thirty-five years. The mate died, but the goose has apparently found enough companionship among the chickens to be happy. It honks and flaps its wings as I pull up in front of the house. A barn out back is supposed to house Uncle Jesse's livestock, but mostly the animals roam where they please.

Uncle Jesse walks out on the porch as I get out of the car. He shoos away the goose, which is trying very hard to defend its territory. Uncle Jesse beckons me in, and we take up where we left off, just as though no time had passed since my last visit. I notice that his hair is now quite thin, balding on the top. His light complexion has darkened with age to a paper sack brown. My heart tugging painfully, I also notice that his usually swift pace has been slowed by his recent triple-bypass heart surgery, yet his wide smile that extends far beyond even his eyes is as youthful as ever.

My Aunt Pearl, Uncle Jesse's wife of fifty years or more, is working at the stove in their kitchen. She is a short, petite woman with a round face made for smiling. As quiet and reserved as Uncle Jesse is talkative, she shows her pleasure at my visit in a characteristic manner. She wipes her hands on her apron and gives me a gentle hug, which I return even more gently, fearing that I will break the fragile bones of her shoulders with my affectionate gesture. Without speaking, she returns to the stove, leaving Jesse and me to sit at the kitchen table.

Jesse wears his pants loose and baggy, always looking as if they are in danger of falling off. He has been wearing his pants this way long before the rappers made it stylish. A born jokester like me, I know that when I have to leave, he will bid me farewell with his usual parting shot, "Anytime you want a little bit of truth mixed up with a whole bunch of lies, come back and see me!"

I have forgotten to bring my tape recorder today, but I have no worries about forgetting any of his words. These words are about our family, and I am not likely to forget them. Since Uncle Jesse knows why I have come, we sit down and got right to work.

"Well, where do you want me to start, Joe?" he asks. I had already told him what I was trying to do.

"Anywhere you want, Uncle Jesse."

"Well, I guess I'll start as far back as I can remember, then." And he proceeds to do so.

It wasn't long before Uncle Jesse had me firmly in his spell. But I must admit that I occasionally regretted what I was hearing. Even so, no memory-regression therapist could have done what Uncle Jesse did for me that day, unlocking memories as a key unlocks a well-oiled door.

Listening to him, I remembered the emotionless stare frozen across my Daddy's face with the mention of Grandpa Buford's name. Even now I could hear Daddy's strained voice as he spoke to my brother Jack and me the day we all visited his mother's grave site. I don't remember the words, but I do remember wishing I could just lock down into silence the words Daddy was using to describe my infamous grandfather. I wanted to run away.

This grandfather's life gave my family the rattling skeleton that many families seem to acquire. His life had always been closed to conversation in our household. His life, particularly one incident in it, was our family secret. Even Uncle Jesse, so forthcoming with other family information, hesitated to enlighten me on this subject.

Jesse is quick to point out that he was named after his uncle Jesse Ache, who was a Cherokee Indian. He also is quick to point out that his grandpa, Matthew Ache, was a Cherokee Indian. And he has pictures that he's kept for years and years of his uncles and his grandpa.

He carefully pointed out to me that the most beautiful thing in the world is to grow old with someone you care for. Uncle Jesse's wife Pearl—

my Aunt Annie Pearl—is a very petite woman, similar in stature to my mother. Aunt Annie Pearl generally sits quietly and reads or fiddles with some chore as my uncle goes on and on telling jokes and stories continuously. Although my Aunt Annie Pearl is short on words, her facial expression lets you know when she really means business. Aunt Pearl's facial expressions are the same as my mother's. A stare means that you knew you were wrong, a frown means that you are in big trouble, and a smile means you are okay for now. I think my Uncle Jesse knows by her facial expressions when she means business too.

Uncle Jesse has been married only once—to Aunt Annie Pearl, my mother's sister. Throughout most of my childhood and adult life, I have always looked to Jesse as a role model and as a father figure. He's always believed in a sound family foundation, and he passed those values down to his children.

Jesse's children and my family grew up very close. Although my parents had several other brothers and sisters, Uncle Jesse's wit and humor somehow distinguished him among all the rest.

Ninety-five percent of the time, Uncle Jesse is busy telling jokes, going about life in his humorous and witty way. He sometimes says, "The only way you can get someone to believe a lie is to mix a little lie with the truth." He has a way of making his stories funny and exciting by mixing fact and fantasy. The listener can sometimes get caught up in the mental game of sorting out the two. Today, however, for my sake, he seems to realize how important it is to me to get to the heart of things.

The effort of doing this seems to trouble him. He seems tired, or perhaps he feels we should be out of Aunt Peal's hearing before he begins telling me much.

He says, "Com'n, Joe, into the bedroom, I thank I want'ta lay down a spell." We settle down in there, me in a wooden chair and Uncle Jesse lounging on the bed. He begins to tell me, as he puts it, "Everthin' there is to know—even what's not fit to print."

Uncle Jesse left home for a short while in his youth. He lived in Delaware briefly, moving there soon after he married some fifty years ago. He must have been happy to leave. He and his new wife were young, and they must have looked forward to the opportunity that living in a Northern state represented to most colored people back then.

While Uncle Jesse and Aunt Annie Pearl were away, the event occurred that became our family secret. I was hearing about it for the very first time that day. As much as I anticipated having my long-held questions answered, I dreaded finding out just what a person of my own flesh and blood was capable of doing.

But Jesse wasn't going to tell that story right away. He wanted to begin somewhere else—with his mother. There was much to tell about her, and the manner of her death was less important to him than telling what his mother was like.

"Joe, I wish you coulda' seen her—a lil' ol' short Geechee woman. Momma's hair was long and straight, cause her own grandpa was a Cherokee Indian. She was so purty. Now, she could spit fire when she was mad! Uh-huh! Maybe that's where our temper came from, cause she shore had plenty of temper to spare!

"Her own Ma was a slave, but she was freed before my momma was born—so my momma was born free." Uncle Jesse spoke this last comment with special emphasis, which I understood. Most black families took pride in an ancestor who had been born free of the bonds of slavery.

I could see pain in Uncle Jesse's eyes, even as he struggled to hide his deeper, joyous emotion over the memory of her beauty. "She was a little Geeche slave woman; she only stood about forty-eight inches tall. Grandpa Ache stood 6'11." They say he had to get on his knees to kiss her when they got married." He stopped for a moment, eyes tilted toward the ceiling, appearing lost in some memory from the long-ago past. The silence lasted far longer than was characteristic of him, and I wondered whether he was having some pain that was preventing him from speaking.

At this moment, I wondered too if perhaps I should never have asked him for the "whole story," but my curiosity prevented me from stopping him. Even the livestock in the yard seemed to feel the tension; there was, for once, no sound from them.

Without warning, Uncle Jesse began speaking once again of the background of his mother, my grandmother, Mary Bell. "Mary Bell's own mother was sold into slavery. She lived at a plantation in Savannah . . . dang it, I wish I could remember the name! But she didn't live there long. Her master sold her to a landowner in Blakely County"

"So the generation before Mary Bell's saw the end of slavery, Uncle Jesse?" I asked with wonder. The visual image of what it must have been like to live then astounded me, as did the thought of the massive changes that were wrought in the aftermath of the Civil War. To think that my own grandmother lived during that time! I was instantly sorry that she passed before I got to know her. I regretted this of course because of the tragic manner of her death, but also for the stories she herself could have told about her life during these troubled and turbulent times.

While this thought was still swirling in my mind, Jesse brought me back to a later time, the period right after Mary Bell's death. After his mother's death, Uncle Jesse did what a loyal child would do. He came back to Georgia, moving back to the farm to take care of the children still living at home. It was difficult for me to discern whether he regretted this necessity.

The homecoming to Georgia could not have been very joyous. When Uncle Jesse returned to the old home place, he discovered not only four of his own brothers and sisters there, but four more siblings, his father's "outside kids," all living in the same household.

Only twenty years old, with an eighteen-year-old wife, by this time he already had one child of his own. (He would go on to father six more.) Simply because there was no other way, Jesse and Pearl took on the task of raising these youngsters, four of whom he knew about and four of whom he could never have imagined in his wildest dreams.

Uncle Jesse and Aunt Pearl did have some help. Our great-grandfather, Matthew Ache, did what he could, advising and supporting them on occasion when the farm and Uncle Jesse's own efforts to keep body and soul together failed. Even though quite burdened with responsibilities of his own, Grandpa Ache came by weekly to check on them, and to offer what little he could.

Jesse continued with difficulty to tell the story and reveal the family secret. I could see my dear uncle's emotional struggle with the details of this tragic story. I understood his angst in revealing this secret. Jesse had, contrary to his nature, respected the confidence of the family about it. After years of keeping the secret, it took great effort to break the code of silence.

Although I could have stopped him at any point, instead I sat patiently, allowing him to meander through this sensitive subject at his own pace. With reluctance, I finally admitted to myself that this was the focal point of my visit.

Even with his discomfort, Jesse's voice gradually settled into a comfortable Southern dialect as the story unfolded. Never one to be excluded, Aunt Pearl had come into the room. She sat comfortably in her rocking chair, appearing to read a newspaper. This subject belonged to Jesse, and she had no desire to participate. She realized how difficult it was for him, however, and perhaps wanted to serve as a silent sentinel.

"Joe Nathan," Jesse continued, "My Pa, y'all's Grandpa, was a rough man—a rough man! Ever'body in town knew that. He wanted to buy this land here—wanted it bad. He had even got up the money to buy it. But you see? Those white folks told him that they were not gonna sell him anything until he got his house straighten' out.

"By that I mean, you see, Pa had two sets of children. There were the eight of us including your daddy, and then there were Miss Irene and her four children. All Miss Irene' children belonged to Pa too, you know? Miss Irene and her children live out back of our house about one-half mile in a black and white shack—practically in our back yard. Why, we could see his mule and buggy park down there, tied around the fence pole at Miss Irene house every time he drove down there."

More at ease with the subject, Jesse continued, "I don't know how our Ma put up with his flaunting another woman right in her face. I do not know. I sup'ose 'cause there was a lot of that "promiscuity"—you know, "a-catting around"—going on then. You see, these were post-slavery days. Black men were free, black women were supposed to be, but that wasn't so. Women depended upon their man for ever'thin'. Most found themselves easy prey for this dilemma.

"When my oldest sister, Ethyl, left home," Jesse explained, using his hands to magnify his expression, "Well, Pa moved that woman right into the house with us! He gave her Ethyl's bed and moved it into the room with him and Ma. He faced one bed to each wall. I guess he thought that give him enough privacy to handle his business. He slept in one bed and Mama and Miss Irene slept in the other, right there in the same room. And neither woman ever complained, not even once. I guess they was too scared. Pa's gun rack, the same one you see right now, hanged over his bed. And I guess they figured he'd get a gun out of it and use it on them if they complained."

Uncle Jesse pulled himself up from lying in the bed to a sitting position. "Pa was crazy about that yellow woman called Irene. Do not let anyone tell you differently! When we killed hogs, Pa would send one of us over to Miss Irene's house to take her some meat too. That was before she moved in with us. Every chance he got after working us in the fields all day he was on that wagon with that bull whip to those horse's backs, headed to Miss Irene house.

"That right! That right!" Jesse said twice, looking me straight in the eye to see my reaction. Right now he had my full attention, eagerly anticipating what came next.

I had never heard this story in its entirety, only snatches of it—bits and pieces overheard from adult conversations during my growing-up years. Now I understood why. My ears felt as though they were bulging with the effort of listening. I was actually trying to suppress my breathing. I couldn't help sneaking an occasional glance at those guns hanging on the wall. My skin grew cold with goose bumps when I envisioned the terror that must surely haunt this house, Irene and Mary Bell living like hostages to the will of my grandfather. As my uncle spoke I entertained a brief thought that this love triangle possessed all the ingredients that men continue to use today to betray women and children in the name of love.

Uncle Jesse said, "Pa loved our Mama Mary Bell, but he was torn with lust between the two. Back then, black men had their way with women.

"Indians did too for that part. You see, my Grandpa Ache was part Cherokee Indian." Jesse said this with great pride, not an unusual thing, because it was felt that having Indian blood in one's ancestry made one superior. But in this instance, I wasn't so sure!

Jesse continued speaking, telling me about his own "Pa's" "catting" ways. "My Grandpa could not say much to his son-in-law Buford, because he himself was the biggest bigamous' in Wilcox county. Why, Grandpa Ache married four times before he jumped the broomstick with our grandma. He fathered children by four of the marriages. I remember him telling once that the wife that could not have children, he just let her clean up around house. He had that kind of power over his women, the kind that made them believe in their own unworthiness.

"Ma did not like what Pa was doing, but Pa was a powerful man. He was farming three-hundred-and-eighty-four acres of land for the white folks. He was running eighteen plows with over a hundred people working for him. But that wasn't all of his power, you see. He was a big man, riding around on those dirt roads with a cloud of dust gushing behind that horse and buggy.

"In that time, Joe, any man who could manage a farm that big was a great asset, important and powerful. So the white people took good care of Buford—at least till he wanted to buy his own land. Then they laid down the law!"

Jesse rambled on briefly but came immediately back to the subject at hand. "Polygamy was against the law in the state of Georgia. This law had gone somewhat relaxed until the early 1900s. Nonetheless, this law was now standing in Pa's way of becoming a landowner. To get around this, the sheriff left the kids with Pa and took Miss Irene away from here up to somewhere up in West Georgia—Dawson County I thank. Just took her away in a wagon pulled by mules."

"You see, chil'ren was considered to be an asset—free labor for the fields. And Miss Irene—well, Miss Irene, she was just considered a loose woman. Even worse, a loose colored woman! And that was the trade-off for Pa gettin' to buy this here land.

"That right! That right! You see them white folk in Georgia didn't play during this time. No matter how powerful my daddy was, he was still colored, and he wadn't doin' right. All them white folk, they all belong to the Klan. You had to do what they said or you were forced to leave Wilcox County with only your bags. Hell, they castrated Mr. Henry Jackson because they thought he was steering up the black folk about segregation in community!"

I smiled, because I actually remembered Mr. Jackson—a withered-up old relic by the time I came along. My amusement deepened as I tried to imagine him as a rebel activist. But I knew Jessie was telling the truth. I had heard this story from others in my neighborhood.

"Mr. Jackson was a Sunday School teacher then. He was an educated man, a good talker, and he could read and write very well. There was jest a few who could read and write back then, and even those few didn't admit to it, 'cause a black man that could read and write was a threat. So when the Klan heard about him talkin' like that at Sunday School, they didn't do nothin' but take care of business. And he learned his lesson, that right, cause he backed off from that kind of talk after that!"

Unable to stop my meandering thoughts, I mused, "I knew he always talked with a high pitched voice. Boy!"

Jesse's mind became fixated on the Klan, the source of his biggest fear growing up—and perhaps even now. "The Klan was all over this place, and the Indians were too. The Cherokees who stayed here after the Trail of Tears took citizenship and were living right around here."

Warming to the subject, he continued, "Where the hell do you think all the Indians went? They got breed up with all the other races around here, mostly black folks. We all mixed up. Some black, some Indian, and some white. That is why our minds are mixed up sometimes. We got too many different people in our head."

Suddenly Jesse started smiling, realizing that he was starting to mix some lie into this story. Nevertheless it added some flavor to a difficult subject.

With some sadness, he continued, "Nobody's heard from Miss Irene since they took her and the littlest one away from here. The baby was no more than eight months old. Hell, she had to steal her own baby because Pa was gonna keep that baby girl too! That was his child also. I just do not know where that child and her Ma ended up. Lord help them," he groaned clenching his hands together with anxiety.

"She did not have a man besides Pa. Even if she'd wanted to, she didn't dare. Most men in the community feared him. He had muscle like a body builder and was as strong as an ox. His look was intimidating, to say the least! Everyone in the county knew about his temper and took care to avoid riling him.

"He was willin' to have all them children in one house for my mama to raise. He didn't care, 'cause this way he got to buy this land." Jesse paused, looking down at the floor and shaking his head as if he could not make sense of it even fifty years past his event.

He took a few minutes here, to rest and regroup before continuing.

"Now, my mama did the best she could with all the children. She bathed them, she fed them, and they worked in the fields right along with everybody else. They were all little—I think the oldest wasn't over twelve or thirteen years old. But Ma did the best she could to treat them like her own."

"Pa was just devastated after Miss Irene left. He got to buy the land, but it just seemed like he had lost his own soul in the deal. He got even meaner, angry all the time, unreasonable, and he raised hell with Ma Mary Bell daily. Partly, I believe, because he was going mad cause Miss Irene had left.

"Pretty soon he got so feeble-minded that nobody could do nothin' with him. That's when we had to put him in a mental asylum. He was physical healthy, but we was scared of him. The only way we could get him to go was to trick him. He had been fussing 'bout a toothache that he constantly picked at with his finger. We told him that they was gonna' check out his teeth. He was complaining of that when we put him in that asylum.

"But after a while, he got better. Or maybe he pretended to get better, you see? Anyways, he came home one weekend."

He stopped again, clutching his chest. Aunt Pearl laid down the newspaper and made as if to rise from her rocking chair. But he waved her back down. "I ain't hurting, Pearl, leastwise nothing physical. I was just thinkin'."

I dropped my eyes to the floor, seeking to conceal the anguish that was surely on my face, not wishing to cause him any more discomfort than was necessary. And he continued.

"When he was home that weekend, he killed our mama, right here in the kitchen with a skillet while she was cooking." While saying this slowly and ponderously, he pointed to a room in the back of the house where he now lived. "She was dead at age 43 at the prime of her life and beautiful as ever."

"February 14, 1946, Valentine's Day, a day to cherish your loved one. My mama would not bring harm to a flea," Jesse, said shaking his head in sorrow and anger. "Your mother, Allene, was the only adult witness."

I looked up at him quickly, startled, as my ears captured this newfound knowledge. It took a few more moments to understand what he'd just said.

"Oh God, not Mother," I gasped inwardly. Years of memories raced though my head. It all started to make sense. Mother never provoked an argument with anyone and saw to it that we didn't, either. A fight in our household meant severe punishment. Now, perhaps, I knew why.

My mind reeling, I could barely hear the suppressed mutter of Jesse's voice. "Your mama had her two babies over here, Raymond Jr., and Annie Nell. Raymond was just talkin', and Annie Nell was barely walking, so I guess they was about one and three. Mary Bell's baby, Jay Henry, and Miss Irene's two babies, Martha, and her sister, were there too. I don't think any of 'em was over five years old."

"This had happened before the eyes of babies?" I simply could not fathom this; it was too much to try to think of!

"Yes! Your mother was the only adult witness, but the children were witnesses, too. I always thought that those who were old enough to remember would be scarred for life."

"Mother, too," I thought with deep remorse and misery. I grieved her death more than ever. My blood boiled within my veins and rushed to my head. I was stunned, perplexed, and overtaken by a nagging feeling of anger and sorrow. I was starting to hate this man that I had never known.

Oblivious to my sorrow, Jesse continued, "After it happened, Allene told us that it was she and your daddy who went and signed him out of the asylum for a weekend pass. I remember hearing that Pa had been constantly pleading to come home, saying how much he wanted to visit his family. Raymond and Allene went weak with pity, and drove over to Milledgeville pick him up in Raymond's green Mercury. You remember that car, Joe?"

"No, Uncle Jesse, Daddy probably sold it before I was born," I replied absently, not really able to think right then about cars or anything else, because of the tangle of other, more sinister thoughts in my head.

"I am sure that your mama and daddy didn't see what was coming, or they would never have done what they did next. Your daddy dropped your mother and Pa off at the house with our mother and all the children. As soon as he got home, Pa quickly changed into his overalls and boots and commenced cleaning one of the skillets that he kept outside. The skillet was in bad shape, all rusty, and actually had holes in the bottom. But he scoured that skillet like a surgeon preparing his tools for an operation. When he finally got all the rust off of it, he started turning it over and over, staring at it.

"Your mama got uneasy when she saw Pa acting like that. She asked him what he was planning to do with the skillet that he was cleaning. She said later that he got all shifty-eyed and wouldn't look her in the eyes. He finally replied. Quietly, too quietly, he said, 'I am going to cook some pancakes for my children. Y'all go on home, ya hear? I would not harm a strand of hair on your head, Allene.'

"Then your mama really got uneasy. She was close to Grandpa. What I mean is that she was the only daughter-in-law living nearby. So she knew him pretty well. But she sure didn't recognize the man standing on the porch.

"Allene was too scared to try to get in the middle of what happened next, and I don't blame her. It was just her and Ma and Pa and all those children. There was nowhere close to run to for help, and no child old enough to send for help. If she had tried to interfere, she might not have come out of it alive. So all she could do was stand there, afraid to look directly at him."

By this point Uncle Jesse wasn't really talking to me anymore, or to anyone. He seemed simply to be relaying the story as it unfolded.

"As it was, even if Allene had been able to run for help, I just don't think it would have got there in time. Next thing Allene knew, Pa went straight into the house and picked a fight with Ma about the food that she was cooking. Then he started tormenting her about having eyes for Mr. Jerry Allen. You remember him, Joe? His property bordered ours. I guess he lived about two miles away."

With a note of disgust in his voice, he mused, "Pa ought to have know better than that. Ma wouldn't have mess with Mr. Allen any more than she would have messed with the man in the moon!

"The way Allene told us later on, she was afraid to know what was going on, but she was more afraid not to know, you see? So she stepped up a little closer to the screen door, trying to see out of the corner of her eyes.

The fight got worse. Pa was shouting that Ma had been unfaithful to him while he was locked up. Ma tried to calm him down; Allene could hear her trying to calm him down by makin' her voice real soft and soothing. But she said that with every second that passed, Pa's just got madder. Without warning, none at all, Pa grabbed Ma Mary Bell by the throat. Ma Mary Bell tried her best to get away from him but he was just too strong. Gasping for air she screamed, 'Run for your lives Allene, take the children and run!'

"As Allene ran off the porch, she said she could hear the thud of the skillet along with my mama's screams. And she did run, then. She was so frightened by that point, all she could do was run for help. She ran toward home with the babies in her arms, calling for Raymond. The rest of the children struggled behind her, crying in panic, not knowing what was going on, just knowing that Allene was scared for her life.

"Your daddy heard her screaming as she approached the house. 'He is killing her,' she cried. 'It's Ma Mary Bell! Yes, it's Ma!'

"As well as they could with all the babies in tow, the two lunged into the car, intending to get the sheriff. You see, your daddy was afraid of Pa, too, and he was not going to that house without the sheriff. In his haste, he flooded out the engine. Said it turned but refused to crank. Raymond jumped out and started to push it, with her and the children in the car. He pushed that car so fast that it started, flooded or not. Off they went speeding toward town.

"As soon as the sheriff could make out from them what was happening, he came out here right away. What he found when he got there was a charnel house. The entire kitchen was painted with the Ma's blood. He had beat her repeatedly over the head with that skillet. He musta' kept on beating her long after she passed out. After she collapsed, he grabbed a butcher knife from the table and stabbed her in the chest, back, and anywhere that he could land a blow.

"And Pa was just setting there in the kitchen with her body lying on the floor, waiting. He gave no resistance. The sheriff arrested our Pa without a fight.

"A couple of weeks passed while Pa was locked in jail in town awaiting his trial for murder. When his trial started, the courtroom was packed; I ain't never seen nothing like it. All that could not get into the small courtroom waited outside. Your mother Allene was the only witness, but she couldn't testify. After she told the sheriff what had happened, she just couldn't speak of it again, I suppose. She started crying the minute she sat down at the witness stand. She never spoke a word; every time the lawyer asked her a question she just started crying harder. The others knew what she had told the sheriff, but they couldn't testify, cause it would have been hearsay. So the lawyer had to keep asking her about it. Raymond said it seemed like it went on forever."

I sat, still stunned, shaking my head in disbelief over what had happened to my dear mother, long before I was born. I would have given my life to be able to warp back in time to comfort her for just one moment. To think that, in all this time, not once had anyone ever mentioned that my mother was the sole witness to my grandmother's murder! The incident that had been too traumatic for her to talk about had also been too sinful for her innocent eyes to witness.

"The judge saw that your mama couldn't take any more of that. He ruled Pa criminal' insane and had him put back into the asylum. This time we left him there to die. I know he was crazy, that he didn't have his mind. But none of us wanted to have anything else to do with him.

"But, you know, Joe," he said, with a mischievous gleam in his eye, "I still have that butcher knife he killed her with in the kitchen to this day."

The room fell silent, the breeze through the pecan tree outside the only sound. Uncle Jesse stared at the floor, his hands shaking nervously. My heart raced as I took in a deep breath. In his way, Uncle Jesse had released years of mourning and anguish. I, too, felt some sort of release. It seemed as if I was undergoing the same transformation as my uncle. I felt sorrow for my mother. I never knew that she had witnessed such a violent act.

But hearing this made me aware of so much, so much that had happened in my parents' lives that I could never fully understand before. Somehow this anger of my uncle's had been passed down to me. Although subdued, it was alive and well inside me. I had been anxious to know the reason our family history had been such an avoided subject with my father. Now I knew. And it hurt. More than hurt—it bore right through me.

But the family secret was now out. The secret was terrible to hear and know. However, terrible as the secret was, the secret also opened me up to a cauterizing ray of light. Only with this knowledge could I bring resolution to my own existence, understand more about my purpose, and commence the healing process.

Jesse ended by saying, "This is what Mama and I found," referring to Aunt Pearl, "when we were summoned home from Delaware. I had heard that they were going to get him out. But I begged them not to. He was a madman. He had gotten even crazier after Miss Irene left him."

To which I replied, "Jesse, you have nothing to feel guilty about. You did the best you could."

When I said that hearing this increased my understanding of my parents' lives, I refer particularly to something that happened the winter I was fourteen. In February of 1972, the saga that had tormented Daddy's life all these years came full circle. Buford Lester, the man that Daddy had grudgingly called his Pa and who had murdered my grandmother, died thirty-six years later in the very same month that his wife met her death at his hand.

I had often wondered why Daddy never showed us his Pa's grave at the cemetery. We had visited there often, to "see about" Mary Bell's grave, but not once had my Daddy ever indicated that my Pa was buried there too.

The death of Buford unlocked years of silent memories for the adults in the family and created new woes for the virgin ears of the young. I had not heard the name of my grandpa mentioned in our household until the day that brought news of his death. I will never forget this day, because that is the first time I ever heard my Pa mentioned in our house.

My mother answered the phone. Her voice immediately became nervous, trembling, thus giving the first warning of bad news. Since I didn't know about my Pa, my first thought was, "Has something happened to one of my siblings living in Florida?" But I hesitated to ask, even though I could tell by the fear and sadness in her eyes that this was not news of small substance. She held the phone so tightly that the knuckles of that hand had turned white against the phone's black receiver. She fidgeted with the tail of her work shirt, something that worried me more. I had never seen Mother do that before.

Daddy was at home and, seeing my mother's obvious discomfort, became alarmed and made his way quickly down the tiny hallway to the phone. Mother saw him coming and whispered as he approached, "It's about your daddy."

He surely knew this day was coming, but no amount of preparation could have readied him. Daddy paused, reluctant to take the call, but eventually he did accept the receiver from Mother's hands. He listened intently to the person on the other end of the line. We kids listened to Daddy's end of the conversation, and our whispered questions started to flow.

"Who is that Daddy is talking to, Mother?" we asked.

"Y'all be quiet; your daddy is talking business."

"But, who is Daddy talking to?" we persisted.

She could say no more. Her eyes tearing up, she could only shake her head. But even though we didn't know what was wrong, we picked up on her tears, as children do. As Mother cried, we cried along with her.

Finally Daddy hung up the phone. I then witnessed something that was not characteristic of him at all. This invincible man who had stood emotionless at the helm of our household sobbed openly, still sitting in the chair next to the telephone. Not until my Mother's death years later would I ever see him display such open emotion.

Evidence to my parent's shock was that they made no attempt whatsoever to move into another room before Daddy started speaking to Mother. "Pa just passed; they want to know if we want come get the body. They said that we could just sign some papers and donate the body to science and bury him over there."

We had been well trained to know where our boundaries were when it came to adult business, and so we struggled to control our curiosity. From the intensity of the conversation, we dared not interject any questions now. We felt privileged merely to be allowed in the room.

My siblings and I listened intently to our parents' conversation. We knew they were talking about someone named "Pa," and yet we had no explanation of who "Pa" was. Perhaps this was our parent's way of informing us about the history of Pa. My parents never gave us any clear answers, but they still allowed us to stay around. Whoever this "Pa" was, though, he must have been important, I deduced, because his death had obviously upset my parents.

Another clue to "Pa's" importance was that Daddy actually spent some time on the phone. The phone lines were soon humming, with a call to Uncle Jesse first. Mother dialed Uncle Jesse's number and gave the phone to Daddy. That day I only heard Daddy's end of the conversation, but now, after talking to Jesse about it, I'm able to put it all together.

Jesse took the news of his father with no remorse. He told my daddy, "I washed my hands of Pa many years ago." When my father told him about the asylum's offer of burial, Jesse's reply was angry.

"Preacher [referring to my father], let's just let them folks bury him in the asylum where he died. We won't even have to call and tell the others that he dead."

Daddy replied, just as angry, "Jesse, that's not the right thing to do!" Then the conversation really heated up.

"You brought him home that last time, and he killed Ma. I don't give a damn what you do with him now!"

Daddy listened quietly even though these words intensified the guilt that had been haunting him like a ghost for thirty-six years. Daddy blamed himself for the death of their mother. Jesse knew this and knew that this would be a damaging blow to our father. Too, this was his way of striking back at him for not agreeing with his suggestion.

But Jesse had confidence that Daddy would do the right thing, no matter how angry he became. So, angry and hurting himself, Jesse punched in a couple more blows.

Jesse remembers shouting into his receiver, "Raymond, if you bring that man home, do not bury him next to our mother, because if you do I promise you that I will dig him up and move him! Don't bother looking for me at any funeral, either! The only way that any of my children or I would be at his funeral is if I was dead and someone carried me there, and that's the God's truth!" Jesse can't remember whether he hung up on Daddy, but, as he puts it, "I prob'ly did. I was sure enough angry!"

After this took place, a discussion ensued between my parents, with Mother at the helm. Daddy was having a hard time deciding what to do with the body of his father. Daddy wanted to do right by Pa, but he didn't want to break friendship with his brother. So he naturally turned to the only person he knew for advice—Mother, who had stood by him through this entire tragedy.

Mother had always known the right thing to say, and her words were appropriate now. How she kept her head about her, I don't know, because she must surely have been dealing with some harsh memories herself.

"Raymond, he is your daddy and will always be. We have no choice of who brings us into this world or what they do when we get here. What we do have, each and every one of us," here she faltered for words for a moment, " . . . that is, God holds each of us responsible for our own sins. Go on and call your sisters and brother in New Jersey. Y'all give your daddy a proper burial. Forgive him and save your soul and souls of our children. 'Vengeance is mine, said the Lord.' It is not up to us to punish him, Raymond. That's for the Lord to do, if He wills it."

Daddy listened quietly, and this was the support he needed. It seemed to make the rest of those phone calls easier, if only a little. Soon the entire family was informed of our grandfather's death, and funeral arrangements were in process.

I related my parent's side of the conversation to Jesse, and he responded as I thought he might: "I suppose, I suppose," he said quietly, as noncommittal as I have ever heard him.

Pretty soon I found the two of us slipping into a more pleasant conversation. This story had been a lot to bite off. I would chew on this information for months to come, and even with the passage of time, it was still hard to digest. Feeling confident that I had heard the story in its entirety, I welcomed a change in subject.

My uncle was feeling better after a while, and he and I walked the farm, chitchatting about some things of insignificant value, such as how his kids were doing and who had visited last. He gave me a tour of the livestock, calling most of them by name. He pointed out a new homemade irrigation system that he had invented and constructed. Uncle Jesse had trenched out an underground water system so that all the animals could be watered at the same time.

"All you have to do is turn this knob right here, and this job of watering the hogs and chickens is done," he boasted, smiling broadly. I could tell that he was well-satisfied with his system.

Uncle Jesse had one other new toy to show me. He had had the phone company put him a phone in a box that he constructed on the side of the barn.

"I need this just in case one of them young things call me while Mama's at home. You see. Out here I got some privacy, you see." I saw.

Maneuvering his hands to help express himself as he talked, he was forever smiling, happy to get some visitors back here in these woods. While he spoke, I turned to thinking about what I already knew about my favorite uncle.

Jesse by trade was a skilled mechanic, who worked on industrial equipment. In fact, his reason for moving to Delaware so long ago was to help to do construction on the Delaware Bridge. Different homemade gadgets around his home showed that he maintained a deep love for his work. His mechanical skills came naturally for him. Even after retirement, he continued to fix up things around the house and dream up new mechanical inventions.

To see my aging uncle bright-eyed, full of youthful vigor, and dreaming up new ideas was uplifting. I felt sure that I was observing a carbon copy of what I would be like in thirty years. I, too, love to work with my hands and dream up inventions.

As we drove away, Kim and I talked about how friendly and loving my uncle and aunt are. I think that they never meet a stranger. Anyone who comes to visit is considered a friend and is usually greeted with a big grin and, "How are you doing?" When the greeting is returned, they respond, "Pretty good."

And they would be quite correct in saying this. They are doing "pretty good." My Uncle Jesse and my Aunt Pearl could write a book of their own, outlining the steps to a long and happy marriage. The closeness of this couple seems to be unmatched, unparalleled to any other couple I have ever known. The two of them have set and exemplified an astonishing example of marriage. They are willing to work hard, for each other and for their family. Generous to a fault, they would share anything they have without any expectation of anything in return. They have endured many ups and downs, but they have taken their marriage vows seriously: "Until death do us part."

The two-and-a-half-hour drive up I-75 seemed a short trip that night. I barely noticed any other cars on the road. My wife and I were silent for a long time as we made our way home, my mind firmly fixed on what Uncle Jesse had shared with me that day. I could see why this had been such a closed subject in our home. Mother and Daddy probably felt that this nightmare was just too grave for our young minds to hear.

Mental illness was very poorly understood in those days, and the stigma attached to it probably helped keep my parents mute. I didn't blame them, not really. Even today, a shame is attached to the condition.

Perhaps Pa could have even been successfully treated for it had he developed those behaviors today. Of course, I mused, Pa could have killed our Ma simply because he was low-down, mean, and angry. But I didn't think so. The way Pa acted carried all the hallmarks of madness. In my mind, there was no doubt. But perhaps the shame of mental illness was so strong that my family actually preferred to think of my Pa's actions as evil and mean, rather than as the product of a sick mind. Although our parents never discussed this incident with us, the firmness with which they reared us possibly stemmed from this tragedy.

So now I knew our secret. Now that I had uncovered the details of the family secret, though, for me the next question was what I was going to do about it and how I would let it affect me and my purpose in life.

An Idea Takes Shape

The information gained about my family's past during the visit with Uncle Jesse gave me a better understanding of what had haunted my family for years. It also compelled me to examine myself and search my very soul. Was I making full use of all the gifts and talents with which God had blessed me? Had I let pride or fear of failure confine my dreams and ambitions to mere mental fantasies?

One night, as my wife and three children slept peacefully, I entertained those questions once again. I thought I had fulfilled my every ambition by completing dental school and becoming a practicing dentist. But now I felt these goals were somewhat lacking in substance and importance.

I enjoy the practice of dentistry. It is rewarding to be able to cure a patient's pain or to restore a lost smile. In tandem with this professional satisfaction, my chosen vocation has afforded a comfortable middle-class lifestyle for my family. Some would say that I have reached a rather luxurious plateau in life: I own an above-average home, my wife and I drive luxury cars, and I've even been able to provide cars for my two oldest daughters as soon as they obtained their driver's licenses. More importantly, I've been able to provide my children with a choice of public or private schools, a choice that not many children have, and a choice we've used to enhance their education. They've attended private school whenever we felt they would benefit from the experience.

It felt good to be able to provide my family with the extras of life, having grown up with only the essentials and sometimes without the essentials. Still, I felt the need to achieve more. I came to the realization that God wanted me to continue to strive to fulfill an as yet unknown plan.

As the glinting of a new day peeked through the two windows facing my bed, my eyes struggled to adjust to the sun's rays. "Life is a struggle," I thought. "Some things in life we have control of, but there is always the unknown, those things that are uncontrollable." I glanced over to

Kim's sleeping form. "We've talked so often about her parents' life strug-gles directly influencing her personality today. My own parents gave me their lives to learn from, too. What would we have done if we had been forced to raise ourselves? We wouldn't have been half the people we are today."

"I wish that I could take all the things I'd learned from my family and teach them to my children, and other children," I mused in that early morning haze. "My family saved me so much pain, so much needless grief, by sharing their experience with me. So many kids don't have that advan-tage. I wish I could give it to them."

Boom! God's hand must have been directing me, because my next thought was, "You can do that! You can write it down. Write a book!"

Then that old devil Doubt reared up and said, "Huh! With your writ-ing skills? You barely passed English in college! You ought to be glad you're a better dentist than you are a writer, or you would have probably killed a patient by now!"

Not wanting to be left out of this conversation, I said (to God and myself), "I may not be able to write like Maya Angelou, but I can speak! And I can find a way to make what I speak into a book!"

I had the sudden and overwhelming feeling that this was the great plan God had for me, and I intended to spread the word. I wasn't wor-ried about my lack of writing skills. As Scarlett O'Hara said, "I'll think about that tomorrow." Instantly, I banished that old devil Doubt from my head.

That decided, I had a burning desire to talk to someone about this good news, right away. Hesitant to wake Kim, I resorted to the next person in line to pick a good conversation with, my sister Nancy.

The hour was a little early for her, even though I knew her to be an early-riser by nature. So I waited, a delicious agony considering the extra-ordinary nature of my mission.

Soon as I thought it was reasonable to call, I reached my hand out from under of the covers and grabbed the bedside phone. I had no reser-vations about calling at this early hour, because I knew I was only return-ing the favor from all the times she had awakened me to make, as my mother would have said, "little-to-do about nothing."

Nancy lives only about a fifteen-minute drive from me. So I briefly pondered the idea of driving over and started to get up, but the chill of the November air seeping into the room quickly changed my mind. My children complain frequently about my habit of sleeping with the heat off, but it feels natural and reminds me of home in South Georgia. Fortunately, waking up in a nicely chilled room is now by choice. But getting up, dressing, and then cranking a cold car will never become a willing choice for me.

Tucked snugly beneath a load of blankets, leaving only my head exposed, I waited for my sister to answer. Nancy and I talk frequently on the telephone. We still manage to keep in close touch, even though we have gone though some difficult times.

I'd intended to get to the point of my call right away, but Nancy, who is the pivot of our family, wanted first to know all the usual news about family happenings, and to tell me some news from our other siblings. But finally I was able to steer the conversation to my own news. Soon we were talking about how we grew up, about how we not only survived but achieved a level of success many people only dream about.

Nancy said, "It's funny, Joe. None of us are wealthy. None of us are well known to anyone other than our family and friends. But here we are, all settled into respectable and comfortable positions in life."

Nancy had just given me my break. I said, "Nancy, I've been thinking about that very thing for a long time. I suppose we must finally have lived long enough to realize how unique we are."

But before I could get around to the idea of a book, Nancy once again took the reins, delving deeper into why we succeeded when so many others in the same situation failed. I'm glad she forced me into this detour, because it reminded me once again that this was God's plan and not my own. It also reminded me of the many influences that had contributed to our achievements. First and foremost was God's sustaining strength, followed by Mother's encouragement. Even the negative aspects of our home life contributed, because they forced us to aim at a better education and future.

Notwithstanding the force of God's design for me, I suddenly realized that my own achievements could have been instrumental in intensifying the drive within each of us to succeed. Now I felt that I could delay no longer; I had to tell her my plan!

Using one of the oldest tactics around, I intentionally angered Nancy by acting puffed-up about my newest realization. I knew this ploy would gain her full attention. Taking what I hoped would sound like a serious but sarcastic tone, I said, "Nancy, it seems to me that most of our sibling's academic success came after I earned my doctorate degree. In fact, I feel that I have been the major driving force in taking our family to a higher plane of academic achievement."

I was pretty sure Nancy would remember quickly that it was our brother Raymond and our sister Mary who had earned their masters' degrees first. They had inspired me. And that our other impetus for achievement was that Daddy was strict as hell, and none of us could wait to get out of his house and into a life of our own. Furthermore, he took full responsibility of being the head of the household and provided us with the basic necessities of life. That was a stabilizing factor that many black households lacked.

Another very important factor was that Mother had taught us that God will not give us a free ride in life. We have to do the work.

I paused for a moment, and for an hour-long second I could hear only the ominous hum of the phone line. Nancy was my elder and was before me in the family hierarchy. So I listened in respectful silence, awaiting her certain rebuttal.

Finally, the sister who is never at a loss for words spoke. "Well," she said, seeming more curious than shocked by my sudden outburst of emotion. This meant trouble. I knew full well that the fewer words Nancy uses, the more intense her feelings, and so I hastened to explain my seeming pretentiousness.

"Nancy, do you remember that 'day-dreaming at night' thing I used to do? Well, I was up half the night, wondering what God wants for me. But about 3 o'clock, I believe God spoke to me, He really did."

I could imagine what was going on in her mind about then, but not willing to be interrupted by anything negative, I rushed on, saying, "Nancy, I strongly believe someone needs to document our family's struggles and accomplishments and, girl, I am taking on the challenge!"

When she was finally able to speak—another ominous sign—she said in a baffled tone, "Whatever do you mean, Joe Nathan?"

Now I knew I'd better do some fast explaining! So I began to lay out my plan and my dream. "I'm going to write a book about all of us, and I will probably go on Oprah, Montel, or Rolanda to promote it." At that point, the impish raconteur in me took over. "Girl, one day you're going to come home to relax in front of your TV and see Montel sitting up there wearing a nice pair of slacks, turtleneck sweater, and one of those little old vests he wears. He'll have his legs crossed, making those funny little gestures he usually does with his head and hands as he introduces his guest for today as 'a very distinguished gentleman accompanied by his lovely family.' I can see it all right now. The audience will applaud spontaneously, while the cameras zoom in and there I'll be—shoes shined, new suit, looking all prosperous. I'll be nodding my head modestly, cheesing around, thanking the audience for their warm welcome."

I didn't have to have psychic powers to sense that Nancy was now wide awake and had the telephone clutched to her ear in slack-jawed silence. And that she was winding up to speak—or perhaps throw a bomb at my teasing. Even so, I felt it was now safe to explain to her just why I was the catalyst behind the family.

As I started to justify my claim, I felt my voice change spontaneously from its usual slow Southern dialect to a more serious, professional tone. I felt as though a deep spiritual feeling had fallen upon me as the words rushed off my tongue in the attempt to explain my feelings. "Nancy, you remember what it was like back then. Graduating from high school was beyond the expectation of anyone in our little world. Especially us—the Lesters. We were the 'stair-step children.' All that we owned were rags and hand-me-down clothes.

"I never even dreamed that I could go farther in life than Hawkinsville until I saw what Raymond and Mary accomplished. I decided at sixteen that I was going to become a professional, that I was going to go a lot further than Hawkinsville, and you know I did. We all did! I want to tell about my life, of course, but I want to do more. I want to tell about how and why I reached that point. I want to tell about all of us!"

As I continued to ramble on in my dream land for a little bit longer, Nancy sighed. I thought she was still reacting to the picture of my family and me on the Montel Williams show. Jokingly, I told her, "Please don't worry, Nancy. The whole family will be in the book, and you all might get on TV, too!" It was killing me to try to keep a straight face.

Suddenly I could not restrain myself any longer. I started to laugh until tears rolled down my cheeks. At this point, Kim awoke with a start. As she peeled back the cover from over my head she saw me, phone in hand, laughing with tears in my eyes, she just sighed, turned over, and went back to sleep, knowing I was on another early morning palaver. That woman of mine really understands me!

I could tell from Nancy's answer that she had not appreciated the story as much as I had. She said, "No, Joe, my sigh wasn't about your dream. I'm just so glad to see you haven't changed, and I know that if anybody in the family can make that dream come true, it will be you! You've always been a person who managed to do the impossible."

She knew that even though I was laughing, I was dead serious. And indeed I was. I knew I would not have to make another phone call to convince her that this idea was real. Also, I was sure that the rest of the family would know in short order. Nancy keeps secrets like a bucket with a hole holds water. Everything somehow seems to leak out.

Nancy paused, then continued. "It seems like you were always wanting to be the one who beat the odds, even when we were little."

After assuring Nancy that I would keep her updated on the book's progress, we hung up. I was certain Nancy would begin her round of phone calls to the rest of the family, telling the news. And I would reflect on our lives and on our hard-earned achievements, gained by overcoming many obstacles.

《《《《《《《《《《《《 *4* 》》》》》》》》》》》》

Getting a Good Start

It's 1974, and a sixteen-year-old black kid living in the little podunk farming town of Hawkinsville, Georgia, suddenly announces he is going to be a dentist. To become a dentist! My announcement was a topic of discussion among all the town's residents. They wondered whether that "boy" might just do it. In fact, some of them kept wondering that even after I returned to Hawkinsville with my degree!

Their bewilderment and surprise shouldn't have surprised me. High-school dropouts were not uncommon. Of the young people who overcame that attitude and graduated, only a small number expected to go on to college. College was usually reserved for two types of high-school graduates—those whose families had a little money and those who were high achievers. I didn't fit either category.

Most boys in my town stayed on after high school to help their fathers on the farm. They later became farmers themselves. But sometimes the rules were broken, and a child from a poor family like ours made it to college. The first to do this in our family was my oldest sister Mary Ann. By the time I made my shocking decision, Mary Ann had graduated from college with a degree in math. Her achievements inspired me.

Mary, though, was a serious student and earned good grades. Me? I was just a "C" student. In fact, I had to struggle to keep that "C." This wasn't the only tide I was swimming against with my plan to go to college and become a dentist; I was short in a lot of areas. The only thing I had a lot of was the ability to talk. I may have been a "C" student, but I did an "A" job of keeping my lips bumping all of the time.

So, I had more than my share of critics of my bold announcement to be a dentist. In fact, the people who weren't critical laughed at the idea. I even laughed along with them sometimes.

In spite of all this, and with the bold faith the young sometimes seem to possess, I vowed to make those who smirked and criticized have to eat crow. I trusted myself enough to know that I could beat the cards stacked up against me.

There were reasons for this belief of mine. When I was born on June 3, 1958, the eighth child of a family of ten children, on a small cotton farm in Pulaski County, Georgia, my mother named me Joe Nathan. She told me she named me Joe because it was easy to spell and she anticipated it would give me a substantial advantage in school over other students my age with long names like Shakawanna and Demarius. Mother was right, and I thank her for her foresight. As things turned out, I needed every advantage possible to get by in school.

In fact, I can trace much of my decision to go to college and become a professional to her. From early childhood, I remember my mother as being the most beautiful woman I had ever seen. By looking at her body, no one could ever guess she had given birth to ten children; she showed no sign of aging. She wore her medium-brown complexion as if it were a crown of glory. If she had not had physical beauty, she would still have been beautiful, because her demeanor and her faith overshadowed any physical beauty. She lived every day in the Christian spirit of humility and modesty.

Mother was a very smart person even though she did not have a formal education. She attended high school completing perhaps the tenth or eleventh grade, but she never stopped learning and striving to improve herself. She motivated my siblings and me because she placed a very high priority on making sure we learned everything we could.

And I do mean everything! Unlike many parents today, mother did not depend solely on schools for our education. In fact, the lessons she taught us about work, play, and staying close to the family could not have been learned in any school. The Bible was her textbook and her life.

No tenured professor could have outdone her in the lecture department, either. If I close my eyes and listen to the silence, I can sometimes hear her famous speech: "All y'all children, just remember I am working day and night, going without, sewing up holes in my draws! I have bent over backward to make a better life for y'all."

Her idea of a better life for us embraced more than material gain. Her vision was of college and a profession for each of us. She spent many hours on her knees petitioning God for his help in keeping our feet on the pathway she'd chosen for us. Following the crowd and peer pressure could so easily have turned us down the wrong pathway, but a caring mother, her prayers, and God made the difference in our lives.

Mother was the needle and thread of our family. She used her skills to maintain and, when necessary, repair the bonds between us. Just by being who she was, she laid a firm foundation for who we are as adults. God used a simple black country mother, whose heart was full of the love for God and her family to guide us in the direction God wanted us to go.

My mother seemed to be a perfect complement to my father. In my earliest memories of him, he is a medium-built man with dark complexion. Daddy was muscular, built like an athlete, except his muscular build came from the sweaty, backbreaking work in the fields of south Georgia. He didn't tolerate a lot of foolishness either. He possessed a very stern and forbidding expression and rarely displayed humor in the presence of us children. We sometimes would see him laughing with adult friends, but I don't ever remember hearing him initiate a joke. Although I never saw my father on his knees in prayer, except at church, I know his belief in God was strong.

My daddy was not an educated person, but he was ambitious. He had a burning desire to own his own business. As a young man, too, he had been a very good baseball player. Daddy never spoke of this himself, but others—mainly Uncle Jesse—told us he had played for the Pineview, Georgia, team during the time of the American Negro League. He could hit a ball so far that people would come out to measure just to see what the distance was.

When we children knew him, though, Daddy didn't play games. Short on patience and high on temper, he could go off like a fire alarm, suddenly and without warning. He believed in strict discipline. Daddy rarely administered any physical discipline, but he was very verbal even when we thought we'd done nothing wrong. When Daddy was really steamed, what he said would make us want to grab the broom and beat ourselves.

Even with his temper, he was a good, honest, hard-working man, a dedicated father. He and mother formed a team that encouraged and challenged their children to set their sights high and strive for the best. They gave me a good start.

((((((((((((*5*)))))))))))))

Life in a Sharecropper's House, Our Family's Home

Daddy sharecropped for Mr. Freeman, a tall lean white man whose skin was tanned from working in the sun. Sharecropping was a common arrangement among farmers who did not own land and could not afford a house. Sharecropping meant that the owner provided us a house to live in and gave my father, in return for his work, a portion of the crop he planted and harvested.

My daddy may well have fudged a little on the deal, perhaps keeping a little in excess of what Mr. Freeman granted him. It's also possible that Mr. Freeman, a shrewd businessman, was aware of this. Since Daddy was a good, hardworking tenant, perhaps Mr. Freeman just chose to look the other way in an unspoken agreement between the two men. Whatever the case, this arrangement added to Daddy's savings for the future purchase of his dream farm of one hundred acres.

Buying a one-hundred acre farm was no small dream for my father. He spoke of it every day, and he intended most absolutely to make it a reality. He wanted to own his own farm and be more than a sharecropper.

Though my father hoped and worked for more, I have many fond memories of the sharecropper's farm. My parents and my older siblings moved there in 1955, and I was born in that sharecropper's house a few years later.

The simple beauty of the house has been frozen in my memory forever. At age five I did not realize our lack of material things, or how hard the family had to struggle to make ends meet. To me, our home was grand and luxurious.

The house rested in the shade of two giant oak trees. The house had three bedrooms situated one after the other, "shotgun" style. A house was called a "shotgun house" if you could shoot a shotgun through the opened front door and have the shell pass through the house and out the opened back door without causing damage. An advantage of this design is that opening both the front and back doors created a breezeway, an essential in the blistering hot South Georgia summers.

Our house was situated about 200 yards off a dusty dirt road. The driveway consisted only of a large bed of sand that spread out near our mailbox. This bed of deep white sand made steering a car over it tricky, so tricky that Daddy eventually moved the mailbox because out-of-control cars and trucks were constantly banging into it.

Brown tar siding covered the outside of the house, a customary building style for rural homes in that area. Winter's cold caused the siding to become brick hard; summer's heat transformed it into scalding putty.

A huge wood-burning stove presided over the kitchen. This stove was central to both the kitchen and our daily lives, because it did double duty as the cooking apparatus and as our main source of heat in the winter.

I remember that stove well. As a child, I quickly learned that playing in the kitchen was dangerous business. One day when I was no more than a toddler, I followed Mother around in the kitchen, listening to the clanging of pots and pans as she prepared supper. By that time, the stove was glowing almost red-hot as Mother prepared to cook our daily bread. I stumbled and bumped into the stove. The flesh on my arm sizzled as the stove popped a stinging blister on my arm.

Mother ran over and swiftly rubbed my arm with butter and some salve she had bought from the Watkins man. My screaming and thrashing about quickly subsided, but the memory has stayed with me.

In the middle of Mother's kitchen sat a small wooden table with a wooden bench at its side. Mother' chair was at one end of the table, and Daddy's was at the other. Their chairs were curiously designed, with two poles that extended up each side of the chair. These poles made the chairs resemble a chair made for a king or queen. All the family knew that the end where Daddy sat was the head of the table; he sat there as proud as a king on his throne.

While Daddy was never an overly religious man, each meal he led us in our thrice-daily ritual of family prayer. "We're thankful for the food that we have prepared before us. May it go toward the nourishment of our bodies and for the betterment of this family, dear Lord. Bless the hands that prepared it. In your name's sake, Amen."

Not only did we eat our meals at that table, but this was also where plans were drawn for each day. Even as we were all passing food and picking up our forks, Daddy began going over the progress being made in the fields and talking about other work-related events. He spoke mostly for the benefit of the older boys, Raymond Jr. and Robert Louis. This was the time, too, when Daddy relished giving his daily financial update on our savings for the purchase of his hundred-acre farm.

The younger ones (me included) pretended to listen politely, but our sights were set on a more immediate goal—eating. Mother consistently outdid herself in preparing our meals, especially supper. Our meals may not have qualified as banquets, but they were delicious, with food prepared from the bounty of our farm. So as Daddy talked, we rushed to snatch our favorite piece of crisp, fried chicken, always leaving room in our bellies for several slices of Mother's moist homemade pound cake.

It would be difficult to forget her pound cake or to explain adequately the depth of our anticipation of it. Mother made her cakes rich in flavor by using twelve eggs and six cups of sugar, with a couple of teaspoons of vanilla extract she purchased from the Watkins man. On special occasions, she made the cake even more delicious. She would heat some lime juice and sugar and let it simmer in a pot on top of the wooden stove until it made a thin creamy white syrup. She would then pour this over the cake, letting it cool to form a frosty glaze that dripped down the sides of the cake.

Whether the cake was plain or fancy, I usually rushed to finish supper to get to the dessert. Knowing my family's appetites, I often hid a slice or two of cake underneath the table for later.

However unimportant Daddy's discussions were to the younger children, good news on the family's financial status was always an incentive to work harder. This good news brought smiles to the faces of the older siblings, but it was boring to my young ears.

To my discomfort, we were not permitted to leave the table until Mother dismissed us. I usually passed the time by staring at the bare, unpainted walls of the kitchen and counting the pots, pans, and other cooking utensils that hung from nails hammered into the wall. But even though I chafed at having to sit there, over time I matured enough to become interested in this grownup talk and eventually even to participate.

It is fortunate that the rooms in this house were large, for there were plenty of people to fill them. There was one bedroom for our parents, one for the five boys, and one for the five girls. Each room was equipped with only one full-size bed. I remember sleeping comfortably in spite of the crowded conditions, though. The oldest three slept at the head of the bed, and the two youngest slept at the foot. In the boys' room that meant that Jack and I had the honor of sleeping at the foot.

Our parents' bedroom had a fireplace, and this room became the central sitting area of the house during the winter months. We also used this fireplace to boil water, heat the iron, and roast sweet potatoes. That fireplace made some of the best roasted sweet potatoes I've ever tasted. The heat from the ashes of the fireplace changed the juices of their hulls into nectar as sweet as honey.

As was common then, the house's roof was made of tin, and it leaked like a sieve. We often had to place a large tub in the middle of a room to catch the water from the leakage. If rain filled the tub with water at night, the older boys Raymond, Jr., Robert, or Boot would take turns emptying the water out over the railing of the back porch. Jack and I were too small to lift the tub, and so we usually slept uninterrupted. I have many fond memories of being put to sleep by the soothing sound of the rain drumming on the tin roof.

Mother said that when it rained God was pouring out His dishwater. She also said that when it thundered His angels were bowling. For the life of me I could not understand why God poured His dishwater on our house, since He should have known there was a hole in our roof. Mother came to God's defense by saying that God is always right and that we should never question His work. Trying to follow her logic, I reasoned that maybe God did this in an effort to get my daddy to repair the roof.

We lived primitively by today's standards, of course. We had an outhouse that sat some distance from the house. One day our "city cousins," Daddy's sister's children, came to visit us from "up north." Shortly after dark, one of the boys asked to use the restroom. I didn't really care for this cousin, and neither did Boot. This cousin had haughty, "Yankee" ways. His northern brogue was so thick you could slice it with a knife, and he enunciated every syllable he spoke, sounding very prim and overly-educated in doing so. But that wasn't the primary reason Boot and I disliked him so. His scornful eyes and supercilious manner made Boot feel inferior.

Boot was not inferior to anyone, though. On the contrary, he was sharp as a tack when it came to math and science, and he could repair anything he put his mind to. He also had a way of his own with words.

To this cousin's arrogant request about the restroom, Boot replied, "You gonna' haft to go outside to pee," and, more ominously, "or if you a' sissy you can use the girls' slop jar, which is unda' the girls' bed." Our cousin's haughty smirk turned into a long frown. Astounded to learn we didn't have an inside restroom, he said he'd just wait until morning.

Unable to resist coming to my brother's aid, I told my cousin, "If you're afraid of the dark, you don't hafta go all the way to the outhouse, you can just pee off the back porch like I do!"

But our cousin declined our "helpful" suggestions. Morning, though, turned out to be too long in coming. After a short but miserable wait, nature took its course, and our cousin peed right in his pants! Mother threatened us with dire consequences if we laughed, but to no avail. We fell to the floor, kicking our legs and laughing so uproariously we cried. "Served him right," Boot smiled, reminding us that our cousin had once called us "little stair-step children" and said that we lived in a "pea-patch shack."

When our aunt heard what her son had said about us, she took him straight out on the back porch. As soon as she scrubbed him down, she washed out "that dirty mouth" of his with some lye soap. Adding to his chagrin, since we didn't have running water, he had to be bathed in one of Mother's aluminum wash tubs. Now, every time he visits us from "up north" in New Jersey, we can't resist reminding him of that night, calling him "Pee-the-Pants," the name we'd christened him with shortly after the incident.

Our main source of water was a well located at the rear of the house. Mr. Jet, a tall, razor-thin black man, had drilled the well. We named him Mr. Jet because he was the blackest black man we'd ever seen. Of course we didn't call him Mr. Jet to his face. In fact, we were scared stiff of Mr. Jet, because he had an extra stubby little finger on each of his hands. In addition, his nose was so wide and flat it gave him the appearance of having three nostrils. He looked creepy to us children, and well-digging seemed a fitting profession for him.

Whatever his appearance, Mr. Jet had done his job well. Our well was enclosed by a little shed. Mounted above the shed was a wheel over which a rope had been threaded to create a sort of pulley arrangement for ease in drawing water from the well. A five-gallon bucket was attached to one end of the rope, and the other end was fastened to a windlass. To draw water, all we had to do was drop the bucket, securely tied to the rope, down into the well, and let the bucket fill with water. Once filled, we then turned the windlass, pulling the filled bucket up and out of the well. We always kept a large dipper hanging by the well. Anyone, neighbor or stranger, was free to use the dipper to get water.

When the well went dry, as it often did during the summer months, we hauled water from a spring down the road from us. Having a well nearby meant that we had every luxury of living in the country. Most people may not think of having a well as a luxury, but when our well went dry every summer and we had to haul water from the spring, having a well close by seemed luxurious to us.

And there were other amenities too. One of them was that we didn't have to go to town to purchase very many of our necessities of life. The Watkins man and the "store bus" man delivered them right to our door.

No narrative of my childhood in south Georgia would be complete without mention of the Watkins man. The Watkins man brought his traveling drugstore to our community on a regular basis, and we children looked forward to his visit almost as much the adults did.

The Watkins man drove a large white station wagon, and from it he sold many different kinds of medicines. Mother was always glad to see him come because from him she was able to replenish her stock of castor oil, alum, and several other nasty-tasting medications she used whenever we appeared to be "puny." The castor oil was especially dreadful. According to my mother, the castor oil washed all of the germs out of our body. I must have looked puny often, because I certainly got a good share of castor oil. She would chase the castor oil with a glass of juice, usually orange or grapefruit. Many years passed before I could drink either of these juices because they always reminded me of the smell and taste of castor oil.

Perhaps that's why my favorite peddler was the "store bus man," a big fat white man who looked as if he consumed more treats than he sold. His truck was a veritable candyland to a young boy like me. For a long time I believed he was old Saint Nick without the beard. He came, regular as clockwork, every Thursday evening.

His nickname, the "store bus man," came from the large, bright-orange bus he drove. His bus held any and all consumable goods you would find in a grocery store. My association with him as the bringer of wondrous gifts was not far off the mark, because he sold all types of candy, squirrel nuts, sugar daddies, honey buns, penny cookies, and—my ever-lasting favorite—bubble gum.

I could keep a piece of bubble gum forever. I would chew it the entire day, taking it out only to eat. At night I'd roll it up in a ball and save it behind the bed post. Except for missing a little sugar, it seemed to me that it chewed better the second day than it did the first.

Unlike Santa, the store bus man had certain rules. He wouldn't allow us to climb onto the back of the truck where all of the treats were stored. So all of us, including my parents, would ceremoniously swing open the two large doors at the rear of the truck.

The store bus man came only once a week, and so I usually purchased extra gum with the nickels my daddy gave me for chores. Like any experienced hoarder, I hid the surplus in different rooms in the house.

When we weren't occupied with the Watkins man or the store bus man, we generally found many things to do on the grounds of my first home. The barn at the rear of the house was a favorite spot. That old building displayed a graceful beauty each day as the sun gradually changed the color of the boards from brown to a soft grayish-black. It was built from large, unpainted boards obtained from the town's sawmill.

Although the barn's purpose was to house grain from our harvest and provide shelter for our livestock, it meant much more us children. When we were tired of playing hide and seek, we entertained ourselves by crawling among the bales of hay in the barn loft, rolling in the sweet-smelling straw that had been loosened from the bales.

When our interest in this less-risky play waned, we'd swing from the rafters and pretend to fly by jumping from the hayloft. We flapped our arms as we plunged to the ground. As if in attestation to the sixth sense all mothers seem to have, sometimes my mother's pointing finger broke up dangerous game. She didn't have to say a word because the pointed finger was well respected by all of us. We had all been recipients of the consequences of ignoring its message. If we did not obey, Mother would follow her warning by getting a switch from the peach tree.

The memory of that switch would instantaneously stop us from jumping out of the barn's hayloft, at least for that day. However, no sooner than Mother could turn her back, we were off to find trouble elsewhere.

Our front porch was low to the ground, and immense oak trees shaded it. I was a little wary of these trees. During a particularly vicious rainstorm the previous spring, a huge limb from one of these trees had fallen on me, pinning me to the porch. In spite of the fact that my injuries were limited to small scrapes and bruises, this experience discouraged me from attempting to climb these trees.

My other siblings had no such troubling memories to discourage them, however. Especially Boot, who had become the most courageous of all the stair-step children.

His fearless nature was not inborn; at one time we all thought him quite the coward. My brother Boot was Daddy's favorite; he usually got away with things we would have been punished for. Daddy nicknamed him Boot because boots were my brother's favorite footwear.

Daddy even let Boot start school a year late. I think Daddy let him have his way on this because he felt that Boot didn't have a "close" brother to bond with, since he was born between two girls (Mary Ann and Nancy Sue). My two oldest brothers (Raymond and Robert) were born two years apart; Jack and I were born close together, too.

Jack and I, being younger than Boot, reaped the benefit of having Boot home an extra year, and so we weren't jealous at all of Daddy's special allowance for him. While playing hooky from school with Daddy's blessing, Boot was teaching Jack and me some neat tricks he had learned from the stack of comic books he read daily—especially the comic books about superheroes.

Two utility lines stretched below the limbs of the large oak trees beside the porch and attached to the side of the house. These lines made ideal jumping targets. Boot would spring from the porch, flying through the air like Superman, demonstrating the ultimate in bravado by touching the utility lines with his bare hands just before descending to the hard-packed ground next to the porch. (Don't try this yourself at your home; Boots was a professional.)

Jack and I tried to follow his lead by taking turns after him. Since we were smaller, though, our legs didn't have the strength to propel our bodies high enough into the air to make contact with the lines. Nevertheless, we exhausted ourselves trying and even begged Boot to lift us up onto his shoulders so that we could touch those electric lines.

Boot teased us, poking his chest out with pride in his ability to perform this brave stunt. With a serious face, he warned Jack and me that we had to be flying through the air to touch the utility lines to avoid being electrocuted. He told us that if we touched those lines while touching something on the ground, our bodies would be toasted like a piece of bread. Jack and I stood and listened to Boot, awestruck by his great knowledge of electricity and flying.

In spite of Boot's obvious pride in his bravado, he took the time to caution us quite sternly and frequently about the potential tragedy that awaited us for being incautious. To illustrate, he would roll up his pants leg to show us his scar, the gruesome remainder of a burn he'd received while jumping over the fire under Mother's wash pot.

"I got this scar a long time before you two were born. Now, listen," Boot would say, in subconscious imitation of the authoritative voice our mother used when gently scolding us, "one day when I was little, littler than you two . . . ." He paused, piercing us with a serious glance, " . . . I was playing in the yard on wash day. Mother had built the fire up high under the wash pot."

Jack and I nodded solemnly, knowing that to be our mother's practice when clothes were badly stained and wouldn't respond to the scrub board she used every wash day. These persistent stains succumbed, however, to a bath of boiling hot water and her homemade potash soap. And it seemed that every washday required at least one boiling to render our clothes clean enough to be acceptable to her standards.

"Mother made the fire extra big that day. I guess she was in a hurry, or maybe there was a lot of clothes. Anyway, Mother built up the fire like that and went inside the house to get the dirty clothes. The fire stuck out on the sides of the wash pot. I knew I could jump that fire, and I did . . . at least the first time."

From Boot's vivid description, Jack and I had no trouble visualizing him hurdling over the fire, his legs barely clearing the leaping flames. Boot continued his tale. On his second flight the flames ignited his pants legs, sending him screaming and rolling on the ground in an orange ball of fire. That fire almost burned his legs and his new pair of brown cowboy boots to a crisp before Robert and Raymond, hearing his screams, raced to his rescue from the wood pile where they'd been busy cutting firewood. Boot stopped wearing boots after this incident, but the nickname stuck with him for life.

Even with Boot's "help," keeping the ten of us out of devilment was a major undertaking for our mother. Perhaps that is why she loved her flower garden so passionately. Our work in the fields, while providing vital sustenance and a reward of its own, did not seem to nourish Mother's aesthetic nature. Mother seemed to find relaxation from cultivating her flower garden. Those passive-yet-brilliant blooms did not perversely seek trouble or injury as we children did; they merely required a knowledgeable and tender hand in order to flourish. And flourish they did, quite heartily, as if in outward evidence of Mother's passion for life. Our yard was banked by a multitude of colorful flowers, which she tended carefully and lovingly.

Mother always planted flowers in her garden and changed them according to the season. Each February, as soon as winter's icy, frosty grip on the soil had loosened, small buds of yellow crocus peeked through the earth to herald the approaching spring. Later would come tulips. Come April, the Easter lilies would be just shy of full bloom. On Sundays she'd cut a few of the best blooms to use as a centerpiece for the dining room table, a few more than that on the Sundays we had company for dinner.

Selecting and cutting the flowers was Mother's province alone. We children could admire the flowers in the garden, but Mother did not allow our curious fingers to touch them. Like anything that is forbidden to a small child, this made exploring them all the more enticing. Having become an adventurous lad, I always saw the need to explore this beautiful area, in spite of Mother's taboo against it. That got me into trouble more than once!

In an attempt to dissuade us from disturbing her flowers, Mother was quite fond of quoting Proverbs 23:13. "Don't fail to correct your children; discipline won't hurt them! They won't die if you use a stick on them!"

Although there were many children in our family, and we were quite rambunctious, I suppose we were no better or worse than children of any other family. In fact, I believe we behaved better than some. Our yard served as a playground for many of the neighborhood children. There was Sue Gal, a slender, dark-complexioned girl with pigtails. Sue Gal had a brother and sister named Will James and Freddie Mac, who was also dark-complexioned and had thick, jet-black curly hair.

I remember that Will James was a little bit on the dishonest side. One day after playing in the yard, he took a liking to Boot's BB gun, so much so that he took it home with him.

When we realized the gun was missing, and a search of our house turned up nothing, the next place to look was obvious. Off to Will James' house we went—Sue, Sugarfoot (Allene), and me—all of us courageously following Boot. To my five-year-old mind, the solemn expressions on my older siblings' faces made me certain that I had the honor of participating in an important and possibly dangerous mission. The half-mile across the cotton field and up the dirt road seemed a short walk that hot sunny day.

As we approached the little house on the hill, Will James and Freddie Mae slowly emerged from their front door. They stood silently on their porch, as if waiting for us to make the first move. It seemed that they knew what we were there for. They stood looking defiantly at our group, and I did my best to match my older sibling's intimidating stares. Only the lack of gun holsters and badges separated this scene from a 1950's western movie showdown. Oddly enough, no blow was passed, and no word was spoken.

A minute or two passed. Then, as though an unspoken agreement had been reached between the two on the porch and the group standing on the hard-packed dirt yard, we slowly began to search the area. Not surprisingly, the gun turned up only a few minutes later, in the woodpile. Except for a rock stuck into the barrel, the gun appeared no worse for wear. With a last, withering look towards the porch, the posse gathered together for the long, dusty return journey.

Soon after this encounter, Will James and Freddie Mae moved "up north," and we never saw or heard from them again. In my eyes, Boot was a hero, willing to risk all to take back what was his. Too, we all had proved ourselves; we all had stood at the woodpile in full support of our brother.

I learned an important lesson that day: If you take something that isn't yours, somebody may well come looking for it—and they may not come alone.

6
One Dream Ends

In the winter of 1961 Mother became pregnant. Dr. Bates had warned Mother previously that another pregnancy would be life threatening. Mother's body was seriously worn and scarred from the labor of so many natural childbirths and the lack of prenatal care. Despite this, Mother became pregnant with her tenth child. My few recollections of this period are scanty but intense. My brothers and sisters have helped me to recall what happened, even though speaking of this difficult time was hard for them to do.

The dangerous situation meant that Mother would have to forego Ms. Peavy's inexpensive talents as a midwife and seek medical care in town. As the doctor predicted, Mother developed many complications. The most serious of them was toxemia, which caused severe swelling and an uncontrollable high blood pressure. The doctor prescribed bed rest, the only treatment at the time. Out of fear for the baby's life, Mother complied, but unwillingly.

Being confined to bed dampened Mother's spirits. She was a busy person by nature, and she detested not being able to perform her motherly duties. She dreaded being a burden on anyone. Indeed, because of her dread of becoming bed-bound, she struggled for weeks to hide her discomfort. Daddy, fearful of losing her, forced her to follow the doctor's orders. In spite of his distrust of white men's opinions, he believed Dr. Bates and knew there was a strong possibility that Mother or the baby or both might die.

Keeping Mother in bed was not a small task. Someone had to stay with her at all times because she had already made several attempts to get up and "do a little something around the house." She had an appointment with the doctor almost weekly, and she dreaded this appointment almost as much as lounging in the bed in between visits.

The cost of these extra medical expenses was quickly depleting the family's small savings. Purchasing the one hundred acres was quickly slipping into the shadow of Mother's difficult and expensive pregnancy. The choice for Daddy came down to doing all he could to care for Mother's health and buying the farm he wanted so much. If my daddy ever made a deal with God, this was it. He had to save Mother.

By the end of my mother's sixth month of pregnancy, it was obvious no amount of watchfulness was going to put off the inevitable. We were very near to losing both Mother and the unborn baby. This was apparent even to my young eyes. Something was desperately wrong with Mother. She would try to "do a little something," but she would return to bed almost immediately, breathing heavily and finding difficulty even in speaking.

I did what any five-year old would have done, all I could do. I tried to cheer her up. I'd stand by her bedside, prattling brightly about her flower garden. I remember saying things like, "Mother, Bubba wanted me ta' pick you some flowers, but I told him, Uh-uh! Them's Mother's flowers! We got 'ta leave 'em alone, Bubba!"

But Mother's only response—aside from her smile, which never left her—was a low, tired-sounding whisper. I was frightened by the haunted and drawn expression on her swollen face. Even though Jack and I worked hard at our play as we always did, the increasing silence from Mother's room became more ominous as each day passed.

Dr. Bates gravely informed my father that my mother would have to be hospitalized if there was to be any chance of saving her or the baby. His opinion was that termination of the pregnancy would be "advisable," since this was the only way he could guarantee that Mother would be spared. By then, there was no mention of the baby's chances.

Even as sick as Mother was by then, she had other ideas about that suggestion. So she delayed making a decision to follow the doctor's advice. She had both public and private reasons for her decision to delay, even though it might mean her life. Her public reason was simple and seems rather caustic by today's standards, even though it was well accepted by the people of our town. She said, "You have to feed a white man out of a long-handle spoon because you can only trust them from a distance," she said. When she said this to our black neighbors and friends, they nodded their heads in agreement with this piece of common wisdom.

Even though the black people in our town respected Dr. Bates, he was still a white man. Any man who still maintained separate colored and white waiting rooms must surely have a different set of priorities for his colored patients and their unborn babies.

But I believe Mother's more private reasons were what swayed her the most and kept her strong even when it seemed that she should give in and allow the doctor to end the pregnancy. Simply put, Mother believed that abortion was a great sin against God. She believed that God gave children and that He already knew them at conception.

Mother based her belief on the Bible. In the Bible, God blessed Abraham and Sarah with a child when they were far beyond childbearing age (Genesis 18). Not only did He give them a child, but also He directed them to name him Isaac. God stated to Abraham that He would "establish my covenant with him for an everlasting covenant, and with his seed after him" (Gen. 17:19, King James Version). The fact that God told them the child's name, gender, and date of birth proved to Mother that whenever a child is conceived, it had a soul that was placed there by God.

Mother acted on a wisdom born of faith. Out loud, she pondered, "If Mary, who became pregnant prior to marriage, had aborted Jesus, the world would have been lost to sin. And then where would we all be?" The unspoken implication was that perhaps this baby, the one she was fighting to keep, just might be important enough to be worth the risk.

Mother had procrastinated so long that termination of the pregnancy was no longer an option. By then, Dr. Bates said, Mother's blood pressure was so high that she would probably die during the "procedure." The only other option was to hospitalize Mother for the rest of the pregnancy. But even with that precaution he wouldn't give my father any hope that she or the baby would survive. Mother gave in to this and went to the hospital.

The memory of Mother leaving for the hospital is difficult to describe, even today. Would she be back? I didn't know. What I didn't know, and was perhaps better off not knowing, is that no one in our family knew the answer to that question either, although they did a masterful job of trying to reassure Jack, Boot, and me.

In addition to Daddy's worries about Mother, he had the harvest to think about. The life of the farm continues, no matter what human dramas are being played out. By then it was late summer, and the crops were maturing. This was usually a cheerful time on the farm, a season we looked forward to. It seemed that the entire world was blanketed by white cotton, giving the appearance of a winter snow. The cotton hanging from the freshly-opened bolls emitted a distinctive musty odor as it dried and fluffed up under the baking hot sun.

The cotton harvest and its mass semi-hysteria affected my whole world. In town, where the cotton gins were located, all the store windows were stained with the dust that spewed from the wire vents of Mr. T. O. Conner's cotton gin. The shoulders of all the roads leading into town were littered with soft white balls of cotton that had fallen from the loaded trucks and wagons used to haul the cotton to the gin. The dust in town and the cotton on the shoulders of the roads were all signs of thriving industry.

All of the older children were directly involved in this beehive of activity. This year, Boot was old enough to go with Daddy when he took my two older brothers Raymond and Robert with him into town to the gin. Later, Boot proudly announced that Daddy had bought them "Cok' Cola in a little short bottle." Also that Daddy had let him ride in the cab with him, "all by himself!"

Surprisingly, Jack and I weren't jealous or resentful of this treat. We knew that our day would come, and we, too, would have this honor. So we were content merely to race behind the truck until it reached the mailbox near the road, lumbering under that day's weight of cotton. Through the haze of road dust and cotton lint, I can still see Raymond and Robert, sitting tall and straight as Georgia pines, atop the single bale of cotton that filled the entire, extended, black wood body of the family truck. Daddy said he was teaching them how to become men and how to run the cotton business.

Daddy said this so often that I began to equate "cotton business" with "manhood," and I eagerly anticipated the thrill of learning both—at least until my first visit to the cotton gin the next summer. By the time we arrived at the gin, I must have appeared quite the little man, for I remember being so puffed-up with my own self-importance that I made a general nuisance of myself to everyone there.

The man who ran the gin must have sensed my feeling of self-importance. He directed me to stand "over there; that's where the real action is." Blithely unaware that none of the other "men" were standing there, I also failed to notice that he had indeed positioned me in a very active spot. I was right under the large tube that sucked the cotton out of the truck.

The suction instantly pulled my cap off my head and carried it high, right up to where the cotton to be ginned was tossed out of the tube into a huge wire net. I was frightened and thought my cap was gone forever, but the man laughed, climbed a ladder, and retrieved my cap.

After that experience I was content to stay home when the cotton went to the gin. Manhood could wait a while, too, as far as I was concerned. Of course, by the time we returned home, the incident had been edited for Jack's benefit, and by the time I was finished telling about the experience, he was awed by my "bravery." He relished the time when he, too, could risk life and limb by carrying on this rite of passage to manhood!

Monies from the harvested crops began to flow in this time of the year. Our family settled bills and purchased extras the family needed, like clothing and shoes for school. Too, Saturdays in town began to be filled with the talk of upcoming revivals at the churches and the highlight of our farm life, the carnival. Even Daddy would lighten up somewhat. He seemed to have fewer outbursts of rage as the harvest money rolled in. For all of us, life in general became easier and less stressful.

Except this year. This year uncertainties clouded the family's future. As the heat of late summer fell on South Georgia, the mood in our home was as gloomy, heavy, and foreboding as the air before a cloudburst.

Always irritable, Daddy struggled to maintain a deadpan expression in the presence of us children, and he encouraged us to proceed working as normal. The nine of us were close to our parents, and their moods usually set the tone for the house. If they were happy, then we were happy; on the other hand, silence meant that trouble was lurking nearby. We had learned to govern ourselves according to their demeanor. Those days, we could sense by the look in Daddy's eyes that he was worried about losing Mother and their unborn child.

Instead of improving after hospitalization, Mother's health continued to deteriorate rapidly. Soon something else happened that became the deciding factor in what happened next. The baby was dying.

Without the sophisticated diagnostic techniques of today, the baby's heartbeat was the critical indicator of its health. Dr. Bates became alarmed as he listened. The baby's heart had become quite rapid and irregular. There was no doubt it was suffering severe, perhaps life-threatening, fetal distress. Although Mother's pregnancy had just entered the window of time considered safe, he realized there was no more time to lose. He immediately consulted with Dr. Smith, a young surgeon. Dr. Smith was new to the town, but he had already gained recognition as a competent doctor.

Together, the two doctors decided that the baby must be born now, without delay. Not only quickly, but also by surgery, a Cesarean section, in the hope of sparing the baby any further distress. Despite my mother's earlier hesitancy about Dr. Bates, we were grateful she was his patient, much as we were thankful for Dr. Smith's willingness to deliver the baby.

For the black people of that time, going to town to see the doctor was a daylong process. Even though both doctors were willing to care for colored patients, neither would see any patient in the colored waiting room until the white waiting area was empty. There were no hard feelings about this in that day, no sense of racial discrimination. This was simply the custom of the day. Or perhaps custom prevailed because there was little choice; no black doctors practiced in the area in that day.

The fact is, Dr. Smith and Dr. Bates were the only doctors in town who were willing to see colored patients. We were blessed that not only would they see Mother but also that they were so competent. The civil rights movement, with its foundation of equal treatment for all, was still in its youth and had not yet moved to the small towns of South Georgia.

At any rate, having two good doctors on the case encouraged the family, and we all waited eagerly for the birth. Daddy and the three older children stayed in the hospital's waiting room to anticipate the outcome of Mother's surgery. Mary was left at home to oversee us younger kids. Mother felt that Mary was the strongest of the girls and usually left her in charge in her absence.

I can't help feeling, too, that Mother chose Mary to stay with us because she thought Mary's strength would be needed if things did not go well during the surgery. Even though I had been told almost none of the "particulars" of this event, I could sense a profound degree of tension in the air. Still, it never once occurred to me that the kind, loving person that I called "Mama" was at the mercy of the surgeon's knife and that she could be stolen from me in an instant, marring my five-year-old memory for life.

The next day we found out that Mother and the baby had come though surgery but that their prognosis was guarded. The report was that the next couple of days would be "touch and go." The "touch-and-go" phrase seemed to mean a lot to the older people; all I knew was that Mother was going to be all right.

This news eased some of the tension we were suffering, but the "couple of days" turned into nearly two weeks of worry for the family. The new baby rallied quickly, but Mother's recovery was a very slow process. She and the baby stayed in the hospital two weeks. Mother was in what we now call the Intensive Care Unit. We younger ones missed her dearly, but our home life continued much the same.

Since we had all been trained in basic household responsibilities from a very young age, the older children were able to run the household in

Mother's absence. Mary kept the house immaculate and prepared the meals. I did my part by keeping my "smart mouth shut" and keeping my "mannish butt out of the way." At least that's what Mary repeated to me so many times that her voice sounded like a broken record: "Joe Nathan, keep your mannish butt out of the way! Joe Nathan, will you please get your mannish butt off of that!"

If that was not enough, the rest of the time, Mary was busy making up work for me to do. "Go put this up for me! Go do this! Go do that!" I never noticed then that all the jobs she assigned me required my going outside of the house.

When I heard the news that Mother was coming home, that mannish butt of mine jumped for joy! I was delighted to see preparation being made for her arrival. Mother was a lot more tolerant of my hyperactive behavior and much, much gentler on my backside than big sister Mary.

Mother returned home, but she brought someone extra with her, a baby girl named Gwyn Vancette. "Y'all boys, this is your new sister," Mother said, presenting the baby to us in a joyful but matter-of-fact fashion. Although she spoke to all the children, she directed her presentation mostly at Jack and me. I suppose she figured that because we were the youngest, we might feel some jealousy. At that moment, my excitement about Mother's homecoming outshone any reservation I might have had about the new baby.

The rebellion and jealousy came later. I was used to being the baby. When Jack was born, I adjusted to being called the knee baby. Now, I was not a baby at all. Gwyn stole my thunder. Like any dethroned king, I made sure there were repercussions to my descent as soon as I became aware of the change in my position.

The first change I noticed was when Mother's bedroom became off-limits to Jack and me. Jack and I couldn't even go near the bed where the baby slept without one of my big sisters escorting us away like we were pirates. When the baby cried, everyone rushed to pick her up. When Jack or I whimpered, which we were even more prone to do, we were told to be quiet so we would not wake the baby.

"The baby! The baby!" That's all I could hear around the house. Daddy acted as if he didn't know that Mother had named the baby "Gwyn"! He referred to her only as "The Baby." Oh, no! Oh, for heaven sake! The baby had found a weak spot in the heart of my daddy, old Mr. Grouch! Many times during the next few months, I often wanted to tell him "The Baby" has a name. Her name is Gwyn. I could not believe my eyes. Even old hard-nosed Mr. Grouch had goo-goo eyes when he looked at Gwyn.

Perhaps my family's feelings of extreme protectiveness had something to do with Gwyn's having been born quite fragile. She was very tiny, and her eyes remained closed for weeks after her birth. She slept all the time, always dressed in a tiny white lace gown and lying motionless on the bed. We had decided that that's how she was always going to be. My baby brother and I soon gave up on trying to sneak a peek at that new bundle of joy. With the passage of time our queries about the new baby faded all together.

The baby's lack of playfulness soon caused Jack and me to become bored with our new sister. But without question her presence still affected us quite profoundly. Besides, she was a girl, and we already knew that girls were not any fun. Jack and I, on the other hand, were boys, and we were going to grow up to be strong men like my father and Uncle Jesse. We were hurt and resentful toward this little usurper of our exalted places in our kingdom. Temper tantrums and whining would get us nowhere, we knew. So we planned a sneaky counter-attack that ended up soothing our wounded, childish pride.

My baby brother Jack was three years old and one of my best listeners. I was above the law in his eyes. No matter what I said he would nod his head in agreement. "OK, Joe Nathan!" he'd dutifully reply, knowing that I was older, bigger, and surely more knowledgeable anyway. Jack would give me a half-smile as I cunningly mastered-minded our strategy for dealing with this new invader. I made the situation very real, feeding him some solid information, at least as solid and definite as a typical five-year old can assemble when faced with the unknown.

"You was the baby before Gwyn," I ominously pointed out to him. "Now you the knee baby. That's what I useta be. Take it from me, that's a weak second prize." (I omitted, of course, that I would have given anything to be the knee baby again!)

"Now this is tha' killer," I carefully explained to Jack, looking him straight in the eye. "If another baby shows up around here, you not gonna be a baby at all! And that's when all da fun stuff get taken away. We have to guard the fun stuff with our lifes!" Jack solemnly nodded in agreement, fighting back tears.

"Hey, don't cry!" I said. "That's for babies! Now here is the plan. We ain't gonna' let this new baby girl in on any of the fun games. She ain't gonna be playing cops and robbers with us, and she ain't gonna' play with any of the wire mules and tractors that Robert made for us."

As I outlined this secret information to Jack, I folded my arms and puckered my lips while staring at the sky, trying to think of any other treats that needed to be on the untouchable list for our new baby sister. Suddenly one more thing came to mind. "She won't be makin' no mud-pies with us in our bakery either."

Feeling more like a traitor now than the deposed knee baby that I really was, all my feelings came together in me, causing a hot burning lump in my throat. But I didn't dare cry in front of Jack. I wasn't a baby any more. So, barely hiding my tears, I further explained to Jack, "She's too little anyway, and all she can do is sleep, eat, cry, and wait for someone to change her diaper." Then I had to tell Bubba, who had appeared just as I said those words. Bubba was my imaginary friend.

Bubba took the news much better than Jack had, perhaps because Bubba's position in the family would not change one whit. Jack was a good listener, but Bubba was better. Too, Bubba didn't tell secrets, as Jack sometimes did. Nevertheless, Bubba, Jack, and I were best buddies, and we had promised to stay that way forever. We had sealed this agreement by swearing in spit, a solemn vow that we altered slightly that day to commemorate the seriousness of our bond. We each spit into our palms and shook hands with each other while we repeated, "We are brothers through thick and thin, through blood and spit. We ain't gonna let no little girl make us split."

Although for my sake Jack always spoke of my imaginary friend as though he could see him, he still claimed he couldn't see Bubba. So I just told Jack to pretend he saw him anyway. "If you pretend hard enough on something, then it's just like it's real," I declared. I was starting to get a little perturbed that Jack couldn't see Bubba. After all, as I saw him, Bubba was dressed in blue overalls and standing right in front of us. Bubba just smiled as Jack stood there with a perplexed look on his face. Finally Jack admitted it, saying that he could see Bubba. His hesitant voice was not very convincing. I think he agreed only to see me smile. Jack was one of the few people who knew just how much Bubba meant to me.

Bubba was five years old, just like me, and a fellow daredevil. He also looked exactly like me. For some reason, I was the only one who could see or hear him. In addition to bewildering Jack, Bubba's invisibility got me into a lot of trouble. Bubba would play Tarzan by climbing trees and swinging on their limbs, even though he knew this was against Mother's rules. He more often than not forgot his chores, preferring to chase the chickens just to hear them squawk. This also caused them to refuse to lay eggs. All of this made more trouble for me. Too, Bubba could not resist invading my mother's flowerbeds. He declared that he was picking the prettiest and most colorful flowers for me to present to Mother. Unfortunately, Bubba was a little clumsy and trampled on the roots of the plants in his haste. My mother may have been quite forgiving of Bubba's antics, but she still held me responsible.

Bubba was a true and loyal friend who bravely took the blame for all my wrongdoing. He listened worshipfully as I uttered a command, and he obediently complied. Bubba was the only person in the house besides Jack whom I could tell what to do, and he obeyed my every request. Always, though, when the switchings came for Bubba's misdeeds, he disappeared and left me to take the punishment. I would insist that Bubba was the culprit but Mother would say she couldn't whip what she couldn't see. To my pleadings she would reply with agitation, "If I catch that Bubba he will get the same thing I am giving you, and that is a good old-fashioned whipping!"

Of course, Bubba himself never spoke a word, and he disappeared forever about the same time the new baby got settled in. I missed him then, I miss him now, and I will always be a little envious of any child who has a special, loyal, imaginary friend.

Even though the time spent at this, my first home, was almost magical for me, it was soon to end. Daddy was becoming more and more frustrated with his sharecropping agreement. He started to look for alternatives. Our savings, supposedly to buy our own land with, had always before served as a cushion when the harvests were lean. Now they were gone, used to pay the bill for Gwyn's birth. Building them up again would take a long time. But Daddy was not satisfied to wait, for it was becoming increasingly obvious that sharecropping simply was not producing enough money to support the family.

Instead of making money, we were now borrowing money. Daddy had to get several loans from Mr. Freeman on next year's crop to help meet the current household expenditures. This galled Daddy greatly. Too, Daddy had never given up his desire to own his own farm, or at least work for himself. This made borrowing money from Mr. Freeman even more troublesome for Daddy.

To add salt to this open wound, Mr. Freeman wanted my oldest sister Annie Neil to take a job doing the laundry for Mr. Hop Jo. Mr. Hop Jo was a toothless, tobacco-chewing relative of Mr. Freeman's. He had what some might call "roving eyes." He was always hiding behind trees and peeking around corners, as if he was spying on us. Mr. Hop Jo often chewed on a straw that dangled between his lips. His physical appearance was just as unsettling as his personality. He always wore a pair of faded denim overalls that had holes in places that left certain body parts in danger of being exposed. On the crown of his head he wore a redneck straw hat with frazzled edges. The white folks said Mr. Hop Jo was "special." But in the colored folks' quarters they said, "Mr. Hop Jo has a couple of bricks missing from his chimney" and he "needs to be in an asylum."

Mr. Freeman didn't exactly force my daddy to make Annie take the job. He didn't need to use force, because it was simply understood that a tenant farmer would provide some of his children for help in the big house. This was also during the time when a black man didn't say no to a white man or look a white man straight in the eyes when being addressed by him.

One of Daddy's sisters had previously worked this job, but she had married and moved to another community. Mr. Freeman didn't waste any time making it known to Daddy that he needed someone to replace her. Daddy submissively accepted the job for Annie without negotiation or confrontation.

"Yes, sir, Mr. Freeman, my girl will be proud to take the job," he consented, being careful to take his cap off and look at the ground while standing in Mr. Freeman's presence.

Mr. Freeman's hand moved slightly, but he stopped short of shaking Daddy's hand to finalize the deal. Daddy's stomach turned because he knew Annie didn't want that job at all. But Mr. Freeman's subtle implication was clear to Daddy, hatefully clear. Daddy and his family lived on the white man's land, his family needed the money, and, of course, it was a wise investment to keep the landlord happy.

Annie did what she was told, but her new job did not sit well with Daddy. In fact, the situation sent my father's self-esteem to an all-time low. He hated having one of his daughters working as a maid in someone's home. This was something he had intended to stop before another family member was drafted for a job at the "big white house on the hill."

So Daddy kept working toward buying land of his own, saving every penny he could while asking everyone he knew about land for sale. His initial efforts failed because he had his mind set firmly that he would not buy any tract of land less than one hundred acres. Daddy passed over many offers to buy smaller tracts of land, stubbornly insisting on owning at least one hundred acres.

Perhaps Daddy wanted to follow in his father's footsteps, or perhaps this was an attempt to outdo his father. No matter what evil deed Grandpa Buford had done, he had owned a large amount of land. Because of that, the community had considered him well to do. Owning a lot of land was a symbol of wealth, strength, and power. In this way Grandpa Buford had made an impression on my father that overshadowed some of the sadness and shame we saw in his eyes when he heard Grandpa Buford's name mentioned.

The medical expenses for Mother and the new baby, though, meant that Daddy s dream of purchasing a large tract of land was vanishing right before his eyes. To add insult to injury, a boll weevil infestation damaged that year's cotton crop severely. The scanty cotton crop coupled with Mother's illness and baby number ten finally compelled Daddy to lower his standards a little. He decided that if he could not own one hundred acres of land, renting one hundred acres was the next best thing.

So, in the summer of 1963, our family moved from the sharecropper's house into a house that we rented for a one-year term. Even though our stay there didn't turn out to be very long or particularly happy, it stands out in my mind, because Daddy seemed to be happy, almost joyful.

Indeed, even the move to the new house made for a very exciting day. My parents still hadn't fulfilled their dream of owning their own land and reaping the full benefit of their hard work. But that day, it didn't seem to matter.

As we prepared to move to our new home, my parents' faces gleamed with smiles of confidence. I looked forward to exploring my new home and finding new hiding places and the secret treasures that they held. I remember being concerned that the store bus man wouldn't be able to find us; my mother smilingly assured me that nothing would change. So I would still be able to get my weekly treat of bubble gum! I neglected to ask about the Watkins man, but he—and his supply of castor oil—found us quickly.

Somehow even our pets knew were moving and shared in the excitement. The two dogs—a black hound named Sambo and a red three-legged hound named Beaver—barked frantically and jumped on every available surface. The cat—named Scat— became surly, hissing and bowing her back every time anyone came near her. When the time came to leave the old house, we had no trouble locating the dogs, but the cat was nowhere to be found. Characteristically short on patience, my father called off the search quickly and said, "Let's go. That cat'll be all right." So we children climbed onto the pile of household goods in the back of the pickup truck, reluctant to leave the last member of our family to her own devices. I remember watching the house anxiously for that cat, watching until the house became just a speck on the horizon.

The day was bright, hot, and sunny, as summers in South Georgia usually are. We were all filled with excitement, and not a little anxiety, for we were leaving a home and a neighborhood that had been the main part of our life. The move in distance was only about ten miles, but in our small world, it seemed as though we were moving to an entirely different country.

Daddy drove fast, speeding toward our new home with great joy and promise. Renting a farm meant that he was no longer dependent on anyone for his success. This was a big step up from sharecropping. Now, he didn't have to share the proceeds from his harvest with anyone!

As we drove up the dirt road leading to our new house, the dogs jumped down and raced alongside the truck. The dust from the road drifted like clouds in the sky. My concern and worry about the cat we left behind turned out to be for naught. About five days after the move, I was thrilled to find the cat in our front yard. It had just showed up!

Here we were in our new home—all of us. One dream had ended, but we were on our way to another one. Daddy often told us, "Every tub has to set on its own bottom, and every man has to stand on his own two feet." Working for himself and becoming self-supporting meant the world to my father. Falling short of his dream ate at him like cancer, but it did not slow his aspirations. He believed he could conquer anything through hard work. His sturdy, rough frame and his worn and callused hands showed that he practiced what he preached. His dream was better living conditions for us, his family. He knew that we could only achieve that through his independence. Though the sweat of his brow, he was going to prevent us from being maids and servants in someone else's house.

With a confident face and strong willpower, Daddy was not afraid to change his course in when he encountered turbulent winds. Owning land was the first step toward being able to reach the family destiny. If he couldn't do that, then renting a farm was at least a solid step in that direction.

Daddy and my mother were a perfect couple in making this kind of decision. Like the smart woman she was, Mother usually let Daddy do all the talking, while she supportively steered him in the right direction. Although Mother still believed that education was the key to our family's improvement, perhaps she saw Daddy's dream as a precursor to the fulfillment of her own.

Mother's way with Daddy worked wonders to boost his ego and helped to patch that part of his manhood that had been disheartened by his submissiveness to the white man. Her support and guidance was a tremendous show of love, and all the family benefited from it. We children always knew that our parents loved each other.

Though one dream—Daddy's dream of owning a hundred acres—had ended, our lives kept moving forward. Daddy and Mother dreamed another dream, and we went toward it.

Life on the Farm—
Of Characters and Character

In spite of our joy in moving, it soon became apparent that our stay in the house to which we had just moved would be temporary. The new house was just too small for the dozen of us, ten children and our parents. It was even smaller than the house we had moved from.

My mother heard about a house for sale that was much larger. The selling price, which included the building and surrounding grounds, was low because the structure was in such dire need of renovation. After many discussions, my mother convinced my father that he could afford to purchase the old Lampkin school.

Lampkin School was an old school building that had been used by black folks in the area before they were allowed to attend public schools. At its busiest, the school employed five or six teachers. About a hundred students attended this school at any given time. My older siblings—Annie, Raymond, and Robert—had actually attended this school. Now empty, this building would soon take on a new purpose. We renovated it to be our home, and my father still lives in this house today.

The newly renovated house was square built with an A-frame roof. It had about 1300 square feet of space. It had green asbestos siding, a small front porch, and a somewhat larger back porch. The house had four bedrooms, which we thought of as a tremendous amount of space. Now only two or three kids had to sleep in one bed!

We thought this house was a mansion. It was another step toward our family's dream. The house didn't come with Daddy's longed-for one hundred acres, but the extra bedroom was a luxury beyond our greatest hopes.

I loved this new community; there were so many new people to get to know. I was thrilled to find we had family already living there. My mother's parents, whom we called Ma and Pa, and Mother's sister, my Aunt Rosie Belle, lived nearby. We visited them often. Even better, a kid my age named Melvin lived right around the corner from us.

Having family close by made it much easier for me to adjust to my new home, and like any insatiably curious five-year-old, I soon learned a lot about them.

My mother's father, my Pa, was the son of Sid Battle. Sid Battle had owned a farm with well over four hundred acres of land. According to Annie Neil, my oldest sister, Pa moved from his father's plantation after he married, intending to be his own man. The way he did this was to make quick money in one of the oldest businesses in the world—farming.

Our Pa's name was Essex Battle, a tall, bony man, well thought-of in the community, and a deacon in the family church, Sandridge Baptist Church. He chewed Prince Albert tobacco, always keeping a flat red can of his favorite chew in his hip pocket. Pa carried on the church obligation begun by his father Sid, who had built this church, buying and paying for it with money earned from farming.

My maternal grandmother, Annie Jackson Battle, was a short, feisty lady who dipped Juicy Fruit snuff from a small can. She was stiff and stern, demanding the utmost respect from my siblings and me. She did not hesitate to discipline us when she saw the need. Perhaps she was strict because, through her knowledge of Pa's business dealings, she knew what could happen to people who lacked discipline.

I'm not sure how much money Ma and Pa made from farming. Regardless, they were always willing to share the proceeds from their business with their family. In fact, our grandparents made enough money to purchase the two hundred acres of land that all our uncles and their children lived on. Even in lean years, when no one else could afford to replace or repair their vehicles and often walked everywhere, Pa could always afford a new car every year—even though he couldn't drive. The car stayed parked in the back yard until the couple wanted to go into town and got someone to drive them there.

My Aunt Rosie Belle and her husband, Doc, assisted in the family business. I'd be hard pressed to say they "worked" in it. Although I grew to love them dearly, I knew that neither of them was fond of hard work. Doc was a tall, lean, shiftless lazy man. He ended up mortgaging the property that Pa bought the two of them and eventually lost it.

Still, Aunt Rosie Belle and Doc loved my siblings and me as if we were their own. Rosie Belle was a petite, dark-skinned lady with a big-booming voice that could wake up the neighbors, and she frequently did! A true eccentric, she was a source of endless fascination for me. She usually dressed in layers, and it wasn't uncommon for her to wear two pairs of pants topped by a long dress. Like her Ma, she dipped snuff, always keeping a bit of Juicy Fruit pinched behind her lips.

Aunt Rosie Belle's greatest gift to me was her stories. I wasn't the only child around who was entranced, either. One of them, Melvin, turned out to be one of the best friends I ever had.

I met Melvin not long after we moved into the new house. Melvin's family lived across the swamp that bordered the back of our property. The Jones family turned out to be good neighbors; in fact, they were one of the first to welcome us to our new home. Melvin's mother was a good woman. Even though she was busy raising her brood, she took the time to help us work our fields every chance she got. That was just the kind of person she was (and is).

Melvin was her youngest son, and he had two brothers and one sister. I became friends with all of them, but none so close as Melvin. I guess this was partly because Melvin and I were the same age, but mainly I think because I thought Melvin was the neatest kid I knew!

He had skin so pale-chocolate it seemed translucent, quite different from my own dark-brown. He had an egg-shaped head, with a narrow lower jaw that caused his teeth to cross in the front. But this didn't spoil his appearance at all; he was a handsome kid, and always neatly dressed. My admiration and envy must have been obvious at times, but Melvin seemed unaffected by it, remaining good-naturedly oblivious to either opinion.

Melvin and I bonded quickly, growing to be good friends. So much so that when Aunt Rosie Belle took us on one of her fishing trips, she let Melvin tag along too, just like another brother.

My Aunt Rosie Belle loved going fishing. She taught us how to bait our hooks and to "hold our mouths just right" while placing those squirmy worms and wiggly crickets on our hooks. After several lessons in which we gave our mightiest efforts to do "just so," she made us her fishing buddies and took us fishing almost every weekend. I'd literally jump for joy each time I heard the unmistakable sound of the metal weights and hooks in her tackle box rattling as she marched toward our house.

"Y'all boys! Let's go get 'um!" she'd whoop, and we'd race to see who could get our fishing gear together and get outside the first. Smiling a broad smile that broadly displayed her brown stained teeth, she'd declare, "It's a good day for fishing!"

The sound of her voice caused my face to light up like a light bulb. Jack and I had our cane poles and a can of red wigglers packed and ready to go faster than we'd ever done a chore. As soon as we were assembled, we'd take off in a ragged procession, we kids jumping up and down in glee and excitement, and Aunt Rosie Belle striding along at a fast pace, now and then pausing to spit tobacco juice from her brown-stained lips.

Our next stop would be to pick up Melvin, who would have heard the commotion at our house and would be ready for us, waiting for us at the fork down the road. Along with him would be "You Know," his tan, full-blooded hound with long floppy ears, barking frantically next to him. "You Know" was one strange name for a dog, but Melvin got a kick out of people asking him what his name was. If you asked Melvin, "What's your dog's name?" he'd smile and say, "You Know." It took time for this joke to settle in; on more than one occasion the person would shake his head in disgust after several rounds of questioning and declare that Melvin was a little bit off his rocker.

Melvin in tow, off to the spring we'd march behind Aunt Rosie Belle with "You Know" rambling along at our side. The three of us children marched in a line, literally right in the footprints that my aunt made in the red clay dirt of the road as she walked ahead of us.

We were a dedicated team of troopers, attuned to the slightest change in pace. Soon our timing was so practiced that we no longer even bumped into Aunt Rosie Belle's back end when she'd pause to spit.

Mother loved fishing but not as much as Aunt Rosie Belle did. So most of the time we went with Aunt Rosie Belle. We really appreciated her willingness to take us fishing, because we needed an adult in order to get Mother's approval to go anywhere near the water. Fishing was a lot more fun than any of the games we played in the yard. And there were practical pleasures too, for the catch of pan-sized brim and bass made a delicious meal afterward.

Aunt Rosie Belle could tell a story anywhere, about anything at all, and our fishing trips were no exception. She claimed that the area we fished in, Blue Springs, was just full of "haints" and ghosts. This slow-moving body of water made a wonderful (if creepy) background for many of her tales. The water in the spring was as clear as a just-polished mirror. The boundaries of the spring were thick with tall Georgia pines and live oak trees. The moth cocoons hanging thickly from the limbs of the live oak trees added a sinister touch. They looked like someone's beard that had been ripped off and left hanging there. Through the thick underbrush snaked a path that followed the outline of the many different ponds fed by the spring. There was always the sound of some wild creature racing around in the undergrowth or splashing into the water as we made our way down the path. So when we went off to go fishing with Aunt Rosie Belle, we always stayed close to her. We all knew that dangerous snakes made their home in the water and brush in the spring.

As if knowledge of that wasn't enough to keep us right with her, Aunt Rosie Belle would fill our heads with stories, wondrous tales that both enthralled and frightened us. She told stories about catching a ghost once while fishing, and she once swore she caught an eel that changed colors. If it rained and the sun was shining at the same time, she would say that was a sign of the devil beating his wife.

Aunt Rosie Belle's tales were not limited to our fishing expeditions. When she visited on a rainy day, we children would wait anxiously for her to tell some of her ghost tales. Of course, she visited with Mother first, and we were expected to behave until they had finished their chat. Her stories were worth any wait.

Like everyone around her, Aunt Rosie Belle lived in a house with a tin roof. But being Aunt Rosie Belle's roof, there had to be something different about it. During the summer months the roof would make a popping sound. I supposed it was the heat blistering down on that roof. But no! Aunt Rosie Belle insisted that her deceased mother-in-law, Mrs. Alice, caused the noise. "Mrs. Alice up there walking on that roof," she would declare, fixing the listener with a knowing stare.

When Aunt Rosie Belle went to bed at night, she lined the perimeter of her bed with newspaper and would make a pile of newspaper underneath the bed, near the center. On top of this pile, she would place a thimble. She explained that if a "haint" tried to come up on her while she was asleep, she would hear the haint rustling the newspaper. And if that haint did manage to get into the bed, she could throw him into that thimble, where he would turn into a bug, and she could kill him. She also claimed that sometimes when the ghosts came to visit her they would get so involved in reading those newspapers near her bed that they would totally forget they had come to haunt her.

Aunt Rosie Belle always swore that she could see people who were dead, and it wasn't a big thing. It wasn't anything for her to say, "Well, I saw Pa come visit me last night. I saw him walkin' down the road, right past me. He didn't say nothin', and I didn't say nothin'. He was probably going right over there to the church like he normally goes."

Once when Aunt Rosie Belle was telling ghost stories, I was sitting in my chair and holding my feet up off the floor, worried that something was crawling around down there.

And no matter how unbelievable the story she was telling at the time, her husband Doc, who was a tall thin man, would always acknowledge it as being the truth. Usually she would say, "What about it, Doc?" and he would say, "Tha's right!." That was his usual reply. By the time she got through telling some of those ghost stories to us, I'd be afraid to go to bed and close my eyes, because I knew that, as soon as I did, those "haints" would be on me.

Shortly after we moved to our new home, Daddy sold our mules to John Wesley Dobbins, a prominent white man in our new community. Mr. Dobbins owned several acres of land and used mules as well as tractors for farming.

A larger farm meant more profit; it also meant a great deal more work. So after selling Big Mule, Old Daisy, and Old Blue, Daddy bought our first tractor. This was a technological revolution for us.

It seemed that our family was advancing in other ways, too. In my memory, these years seemed to be years of hope. The neighborhood seemed to bustle with excitement. Of course, Daddy made more profit by farming his own land, but it seemed that the farming profession was itself on the upswing.

What may have helped, though, was that most of the people in the community were geared toward working together. Families were strong in this community. As a further help to our family, the three older siblings who had already left home were sending money to my parents on a regular basis. I didn't realize then just how much it helped us all, but of course I realize now that the clothes we wore and the food we ate would not have been nearly as good had they not been able or willing to do this for us.

My brother Robert had been anxious to leave home as soon as he got old enough. The day he left, we were chopping cotton for Bland McDuffie, a white farmer in the area.

The rest of us thought Robert was just working hard, way ahead of anybody, but he had a purpose in getting to the end of his cotton row. The end of his row was going to be the end of his row as a farm worker! As he put it, he was determined to catch the "first gray dog going south." And when the Greyhound bus to Florida came by, he did! Whatever his reasons for leaving, he returned as often as he could.

When my older siblings left home and then returned driving nice cars, they served as positive role models to the rest of us. Their success motivated us to continue to work hard, stay together, and prosper.

The whole family worked together as a unit. In the spring, we spent our time tilling the soil and planting. Summers, we tended the late crops until they were ready for harvest, and we began harvesting all the early crops. This lasted until fall. In the late fall, we spent most of our time scrapping together the leftover crops and clearing the land for the next season. In winter, the priority changed to gathering wood for heat and for cooking. All year round there were livestock to feed and care for. These farm chores brought our family close together.

Even the animals had responsibilities. Bright and early every morning, we were awakened by a cheerful "cock-a-doodle-do!" from our rooster, Big Red. He would climb up on the fence of the pigpen to serve as our wakeup call. Big Red was fire-engine red, with the tips of his wings and tail like black satin. Occasionally, one of the hens would climb up on the fence and crow with Big Red. This was not a good day for the ill-fated bird, because it was considered bad luck for a hen to crow.

Everything we owned had its place. The cat was responsible for getting rid of mice. The dog was responsible for hunting and for keeping the livestock in. The cow supplied milk, and the pigs supplied fresh meat. Big Red was responsible for providing a ready supply of chicks, and the hens were responsible for supplying fresh eggs. Perhaps the division of responsibilities contributed, in its own way, to the sense of order in our family.

We did our laundry on the weekends. Washing clothes for a family this large required lots of water. The males usually drew water from the well for this task, but if the well was dry, we would have to haul water from the spring. No matter where we obtained it, this took a coordinated effort among us.

We owned a wringer washer, the kind that had two rollers on top for wringing the water from the clothes. But because of my mother's high standards for clean clothes, we also had a scrub board. For safety reasons, only Mother or one of the older girls operated the washer, but all the girls had a turn at the scrub board.

We didn't have a clothes dryer; instead we had a long clothesline out back where we hung the wet clothes to dry. The entire family scurried to the clothesline when it began to rain. And in very cold weather, care would have to be taken to prevent the clothes from freezing to the line. The disadvantage of drying clothes this way was that when they finished drying they became stiff. Mother would have to bring the clothes into the house and spray them with starch to loosen them up. This made them pliable enough to submit to a quick but careful ironing that would remove any wrinkles.

A typical morning on the farm would start with my Daddy saying, "Go on, get up from there." I suppose you could say that Big Red was our alarm clock and that Daddy's call served as our snooze alarm! Since the boys took turns getting the fire going in the morning, he would first call the one whose turn it was. The boy who had been called usually pretended he didn't hear. The other ones would poke him in the side, because they knew that if you didn't answer immediately, Daddy was going to go on to the next name.

Daddy usually went back to bed and didn't get up again until the house was warm. And besides, Mother could not cook breakfast for all of us until the fire was going strong. So there was another important reason not to delay making the fire.

But delay we did, and with good reason. All the bedrooms had wood floors. The floors had cracks in them, and there were no rugs to absorb the shock of the cold. When we got up and our feet hit that floor, it felt as though we had stepped on a sheet of ice!

After about thirty minutes, the kitchen would be piping hot, but the bedrooms would still be icy cold. But the thought of a warm kitchen and breakfast would be all it took for us finally to stumble out of bed.

Once the fire was blazing, Mother would get up and begin preparing the meal. Breakfast always included fresh buttermilk biscuits, grits, and occasionally rabbit or fish.

We milked the cow early in the morning and took the milk directly to my mother, who used some of it in that morning's meal. We used some of the milk for drinking; the rest of the milk was either used for cooking later that day or given to the pigs the next day.

While Mama was cooking breakfast, we completed the other early morning ritual of feeding the pigs. At one time our family had several hundred pigs.

One of my fondest memories of those years is that every time we had a meal, the whole family was there. Only work, school, or an emergency excused anyone. Daddy sat at the head of the table, and Mama sat at the other end. All the kids took their places in between. This was also the time of the day when all the kids hoped that it would be raining. If it was too wet to work in the fields, we would all get to go to school. If you were younger, you got to go to school almost every day. But if you were one of the bigger kids, you were definitely going to the field, especially during the harvest season or spring planting. During those times of the year, you could pretty much forget about going to school unless it was raining. The only other exception was if one of us was approaching the limit on the number of days we could miss and still go on to the next grade. That's when my mother would step in.

We got our instructions for the day at breakfast each morning: Who was going to be going to school that day, who was going to clear a field and get ready for planting, and who would do other jobs.

Our meals consisted of seasonal vegetables, whatever we had been picking in the field, plus cornbread and whatever meat we had in the smokehouse. We would work in the field until about six o'clock or sundown. When we got home in the evening, work was not completed. We had to feed the hogs again, while my mother and sisters prepared the evening meal. After we fed the hogs, we would go out to the woodpile, gather wood for the night, and pile it up near the back door.

An example of the sense of community I grew up in is that once we started butchering the hogs, neighbors would come over and help. Once we finished butchering our hogs, we would go over to a neighbor's house and help to butcher their hogs.

Making our own syrup and growing cane to make syrup was also a family and community event. We grew enough cane to make syrup for our family and for other people, because Daddy was one of the few people who owned a cane kettle. We also owned a cane mill, necessary for syrup making. A cane mill is an instrument used to squeeze the juice out of the cane. Our mules pulled the motor that operated the cane mill.

The cane would be fed into one end of the mill, and the cane juice would come out of the other end of the mill down into a large drum. We would take the juice over to the kettle, where we would boil it and add other ingredients. Daddy or some of the gentlemen helping us would always see to it that a little cane juice was left for fermentation. After a few weeks of fermentation, this cane juice contained enough alcohol to make a powerful brew. It also cost a kid a good lashing (if you were caught) or a good night's rest (if you weren't) if you were shrewd enough to sneak a drink of this potent potpourri.

Cane syrup was a treat for our family. In fact, it was served at most of our breakfast meals. Cane syrup and biscuits and a slab of whatever kind of meat we had in the meat house—not quite heaven, but perhaps a little taste of what heaven might be like!

Usually our meat was preserved by salt, followed by a time in the smokehouse. In fact, our smokehouse was the area we kept the meat. It was a small wooden shack with a tin roof that Daddy had built himself.

Daddy would take the meat off to a company that preserved meat by using salt. We would bring the meat back and hang it on the ceiling of the smokehouse, where we would go out and cut a piece off whenever we needed it.

We grew our own meats, we grew our own crops, we worked together as a family and as a community of caring neighbors. We ate together, we prayed together, we played together. To me it was a joyous time. We did a lot of work, but we always knew that our reward was coming on Saturday. Most Saturdays we did not work. If we did work, it was only on Saturday morning. Saturdays we would load up the truck. Everybody would get on the back, and we would ride into town. On Saturday afternoon, just about everybody in the county that had a truck or could catch a ride would gather in town. The women would dress up, the kids would dress up, and even my Daddy would dress up. My daddy would give 10 cents to the smaller kids and maybe 25 cents to the bigger kids.

Pretty much all we did when we went to town on Saturday was park the truck, let the tailgate down, and sit in the bed of the truck. We'd eat candy while the adults sat on the hood and socialized together. Daddy would go down to the Dirty Spoon (or Nigga Town as we called it). To us, this strip of black-owned businesses had the excitement and glamour of downtown New Orleans. All of the bars, pool halls, and clubs that the colored people frequented were located there, just across from the police station and thus under their watchful eye. Mother did not permit us to go into this area because of the many shady characters slinking around in the shadows of the bars.

The fog of light blue cigarette smoke seeped from the door entrance of the juke joints and curled in the air to the slow sweet sound of the saxophone that seemed to be calling Daddy's name, though. Daddy claimed he was going down to the Dirty Spoon only to get a haircut at Mr. Gene

Smith's barbershop. I longed to be allowed to cross the street and look into the bars to see the snakes they were talking about when I heard someone say "snake eyes."

When a fellow named Pete got shot dead for dancing too closely with someone else's wife, Daddy said that he was "gonna' keep his black ass out of Nigga town. Them fools down there are too damn crazy for me." Still shaking his head and sucking his teeth in disgust he said, "All them fools want to do down there is frolic and kill one another. A man got to stay out from down there if he wants to be somebody." True to his word, Daddy didn't go there anymore.

Daddy continued to take us to town every Saturday, but he stayed uptown with us boys. "I've got to set an example for these little old boys I got," he would say. "I've got to teach them how to be men."

When Daddy said this, my body tingled with warmth inside. Daddy really loved us children even though he never spoke it aloud. He was willing to sacrifice something he enjoyed because he wanted us to be somebody.

Every fall, something happened that caused excited talk months before and months after the "big event." It was the fair, the biggest event happening in most small towns. This event made going to town even more fun. The fair ground was located on the south side of town near a small colored section consisting of small, unpainted, dilapidated row houses. White folks usually frequented this side of town only to pick up rent money from the people who lived in the shacks or to pick up a maid or a field worker. Other than frequent visits from the white police serving arrest warrants, the fair was the only time people saw a white face on that side of town. The fair brought the whole community together, though. Over the loud clatter of the diesel fueled engine you could hear people from all races talking and laughing together.

My childhood combined work and play, and both were good. Though our family's work was sometimes hard, these work experiences taught me to equate work with honesty and affluence. These truths I learned in my family during my growing-up years have turned out to be the very foundation our entire country was built on.

My parents first taught us to work by allowing us to watch them. When Daddy was performing a seemly trivial task such as gathering wood for heating the family home, he took us along, but not just to teach us how to gather wood. He took us along to help us learn to work to provide for the welfare of the family.

Our family emphasized actions that helped the family, not just actions that brought success or achievement to an individual. Everybody had assigned duties, ranging from washing dishes to picking cotton to sweeping the yards. Not a bad idea, not a bad idea at all. In fact, it was a good idea, it worked, and all the family benefited from it.

Mary Goes to College

Something happened in the summer of 1967 that gave me hope. Our family already had much for which to be thankful. We were all alive and in good health. Some older siblings of mine had left home and had begun to be successful. Their accomplishments gave me hope. I envisioned flourishing opportunities on the other side of the rainbow for me.

The only blight on the horizon that summer was that Robert was drafted into the army and was sent to Vietnam. We prayed daily for his speedy and safe return home. Even Robert's service in Vietnam worked to our good, however. Robert wanted to become a police officer. He possessed the confidence, temperament, and discipline required to become a good policeman. The Vietnam War prepared him for his quest to achieve this goal.

The big event of the summer that gave us all hope was something else, though. Daddy had always talked about sending Mary and Boot to college. His thinking was that he might be able financially to send two children to college—one boy and one girl. Mary and Boot became the chosen ones.

I could never figure out how Daddy reasoned his way to these choices. Mary and Boot had good heads on their shoulders, but so did the rest of us. The rest of us had minds and plans of our own. Specifically, we planned to find our way out of the cotton fields with or without Dad's blessing or help.

This year, this summer, was Mary's time. She was the oldest child living at home. To help send Mary to college, all of our work became centered on getting the money for Mary's college tuition. We were up early each morning, ready to head out to work in the fields. The main topic of conversation became Mary's going to college.

On this particular day, I had elected not to accompany the others on the truck to the fields. I had chosen to follow behind the truck on my bicycle. You could not have convinced me that my bike wasn't equipped with a V-8 engine. I felt powerful as I rode my bike.

As Daddy shifted gears in the truck, I duplicated the roar of the engine with my mouth. As the truck's speed increased, the truck churned up a mighty cloud of dust from the dirt road. Then Daddy made a right turn off the main road onto a trail that parted two large fields of peanuts. He downshifted the gears to wade the truck through a puddle of mud and standing water. I slid my bike to a halt to watch the truck move through the mud. Panting like a puppy out of breath, I roared like a car waiting at a traffic light. Suddenly, the rear tires of the truck ahead of me started to spin, slinging huge chunks of mud all over me and my shiny new bike.

The crowd on the back of the truck had been paying little attention to me on my bike. Now they roared with laughter as I tucked my hands over my face to protect myself from the mud. I soon was coated with a thick black concoction of dirt and water. I even had the taste of this grit in my mouth.

"Enough is enough!" I shouted. I began to sling chunks of mud back at the people in the truck who were laughing at me. The truck quickly sped away, though, and I hit no one. Soon we were all out in the fields, working to gain money to send Mary to college.

I have to confess that Mary's actually going to college was no big deal for me as a child. One more person off my butt and more free time for play. I thought for a moment that I might have a chance of getting that big private room Mother had designated for her. "Fat chance," I thought to myself. Too many other children were in line ahead of me for that room.

Daddy, though, was focused on getting the money to send Mary to college. We needed the money in thirty days or Mary would have to defer her college until the next year. Early that year, Mary had gotten fifty dollars from Raymond for her application fee. She had applied and been accepted at Albany State College, a small but successful predominantly black college located in Albany, Georgia.

Daddy's goal to send Mary to college was coming to pass. Daddy was going to come up with the money if it was the last thing he did on earth.

So, as we approached the field on that day, no one cared to notice that I was covered with dried earth. Mary's college education was what was important.

I remember having a conversation with Mother as I dragged a four-foot-long sack partly full of cotton along the row next to hers. I remember saying, "Mama, why do we have to work so hard to send Mary to college? I'm tired of working all the time. My knees hurt. I'm tired of crawling around in this dumb old cotton field."

Since my mother had heard this complaint many times before, she had an answer ready. "Honey, this is where you learn to work. This is where you learn to be patient. This is where you learn to finish what you start. What would we do if we planted this cotton and then decided it was too hard to harvest it when it was time? All our work would be for nothing! We are working to send Mary to college so she can make a better life for herself. A better life for Mary means a better life for this family. With an education she can get a better job and send money back home so we all won't have to work so hard."

I gazed intently at Mother crawling on her knees with her head wrapped in a scarf. She acted as if she didn't see me standing there with a confused look on my face. She never stopped removing the cotton from the bolls as she moved down the row to avoid further questions from me.

My immaturity prevented me from paying much attention to Mother's logic for picking cotton. It would take some years to fully understand what Mother was saying. The possibility that Mary could escape the drudgery of the cotton field by obtaining a college education engendered a new idea in me. This is when I became aware that an education could possibly get me out of the cotton fields.

When I complained about picking cotton, Mother patiently repeated this answer. When I got a little older, though, she gave an additional example that really hit home to me. "Most important," she said, "when you learn these things, you'll apply them to your schoolwork. You'll already know how important it is to work hard toward a goal, and this will make it easier for you in school. And when you succeed in school, you'll do well in the world, and you won't forget to share your success with us, just like the others are doing now." In this manner, Mother taught me that a strong will, hard work, determination, and education would be the path to upward mobility for the family.

We labored the entire summer before we had enough money for Mary's college tuition. We talked together, telling our dreams of what we hoped to do when we grew up. We sang together. "Pick a bale of cotton! What you say? Pick a bale a day. Oh my darling, pick a bale of cotton! What you say? Pick a bale a day!" We would sing on and on with one person taking the lead singing and then another. Singing helped to pass the time. In retrospect, it did much more than that. Everybody seemed happy working together.

By the end of the summer, we had accomplished our goal and had a little extra. Mother used some of the extra money to buy towels, sheets, and a couple of new dresses for Mary.

In the fall, the big day arrived. We carefully packed all of Mary's belongings in a footlocker and put it in the trunk of Robert's white 1963 Chevrolet Impala. He had left the car for Mother to drive before going to the Army. The car could comfortably seat six passengers. Mother decided that she would take only the girls this trip: Nancy, Allene, Gwyn, and, of course, Mary.

As we boys watched them leave, our mood ran the gamut from tears to laughter. One source of our tears was that our consolation prize for our hard work was more work. Daddy loaned us the truck for the weekend so that we could go out into the fields, pick up corn, sell it, and keep the money for ourselves. Although we had a corn puller, which mechanically pulled the corn off the stalks, it was not very efficient, and left a lot of corn on the ground.

Boot was the captain of this job, because he was the only one of us who had his driver's license. Basically Jack and I worked for Boot. We would pick up the leftover corn and throw it in the back of the truck, which Boot drove.

When we sold that corn in town, Boot gave us a dozen doughnuts and maybe $1.25 each, and he kept the rest of the money. He told us that he kept a little more of the money because he had a better idea of the value of money than we did. I guess he was right, because Jack and I usually just used our share of the money to buy snacks!

We were happy for a job well done. Mary had gone off to college. Boot had a little extra money in his pocket from the corn harvest. Jack and I had filled our stomachs with fresh sweet doughnuts paid for with the money we earned. Life was good!

It never occurred to us that Mary would need tuition for the second, third, and fourth years of college. This would mean a repeat each year of the previous summer.

The stress to gather that money seemed to have affected Daddy in a way that I had never seen. When we went to town on Saturday, he started going back down to "Nigga" Town, although he tried to keep it from us children. He would bring Mother and us home just before sundown and head right back to town. The following morning at the breakfast table, his breath reeked with the smell of alcohol and vomit. Usually he would refuse to eat, substituting a hot cup of dark coffee for food.

Not long after Daddy started drinking, the bruises started to show up on Mother's arms, and on several occasions her eyes seem blackened.

Mother did a good job of hiding her hurt from us and avoiding questions about her injuries from us children. Once Daddy, angry about trying to come up with tuition money, went out to his truck, took out his pocket knife, and scraped off the Albany State College seal we had placed in the window. At the time I thought it was because he did not want Mary to go to college, but in retrospect, I think it was more the hardship of coming up with the tuition money.

Even with the difficulties, Mother was a real advocate for this new way of life for the ten of us. She genuinely promoted higher education.

Mary did receive her degree in mathematics from Albany State College and moved to Florida. After she found work, she sent money back home for us, and things were better for the family than they had ever been. With this extra money from our siblings living in Florida, we dug a new deep well and were able to have indoor plumbing. Mary didn't look at the help given her as a right but as a privilege. She returned the favor to our family many times over.

The driving force for us to become educated was stimulated by two factors: my father's strict discipline and my mother's desire for us to do better. Of course, my father wanted one or more of us stay with him on the farm and to operate it when he was no longer able to do so. This caused no little conflict when we, one by one, decided we could do better by reaching out and discovering new horizons. Nobody really had any intention of staying home any longer than he or she had to. Of course, as each of us got old enough to leave home, Daddy always had some conflicting emotions, and there was usually a battle about it. In each instance, he felt that just as we were finally old enough to be some real help on the farm, we were ready to leave.

After Mary graduated from college, Mother applied and was offered a job at the school cafeteria. She excepted the position and started to worked full time as a cook. Afterwards she would come home and muster enough energy to cook supper for Daddy. She also kept the old house immaculate. Cleaning her castle seemed to make her happy, or maybe she just wanted to keep busy. It seemed to make her even happier to see us busy! She would have us up as soon as the rooster crowed. We were doing something even if it was nothing but sweeping the yard. Oh, how I wanted to shoot that damn rooster, if only I wasn't too scared to bother Daddy's gun.

In our neighborhood at this time, it was the custom to have a yard that was all dirt and was swept instead of mowed. We usually swept the yard at least once or twice a week, but it could be done more often if Mother thought we needed something to keep us busy.

If we did not have any brush brooms, we were told to go into the woods and get one! A brush broom was simply several tree branches or a scrubby piece of brush that was bound tightly on one end with several turns of string or wire. A small child could make one, and I made more than my share. This task was especially suited for the child who needed something to do! This chore and a whole barrel of others seemed to be the assignment of choice whenever Mother could see that we were not thoroughly occupied doing something else.

Mother's new job in town got Daddy started thinking about starting a new business of his own outside of farming. My memories of Daddy's entrepreneurial activities came long before I knew the meaning of the term "entrepreneur," but I know now that he certainly was one, at least in spirit. Daddy would tend to go from one business idea to another. He would sit in the swing on the porch motioning his legs just enough to keep the swing moving. He would ramble from one business idea to the next, while tugging on the chain that supported the swing. It was as if he were trying to untangle his thoughts. Mother would listen patiently, seeming to be totally supportive of his dreams and ambitions. As we played in the yard we could hear the intensity of the swinging chains as our Daddy gave strong hand motions and Mother gave her usual consenting nods. It is odd that he did not see his productive and sometimes profitable farm as a real business. He wanted to open a barber shop, and next he wanted to open a grocery store!

With every business failure, Daddy blamed Mother. With time Daddy became grouchy and mean. He had a lot of anger built up in him. The ugliness that had been hidden behind closed doors came flying from nowhere right before my eyes one evening. Daddy made a fist and punched it right into Mother's face while she was preparing supper. The whole family stood helpless as we witnessed Daddy beating and kicking Mother for something as innocent at not having supper cooked on time. She tried to fight back but Daddy's strength was just too overwhelming for her small frame. The six of us children could only weep and beg him to stop. "You ain't nothing but a lazy son of bitch," Daddy bellowed at our mother as he finally let up from the swinging of his fists. His deep expressionless stormy brown eyes had turned red as fire. Mother cried as she shifted her body to avoid putting pressure on her wounded arm. I was petrified as he stared straight through the six of us. He seemed to dare us children to help Mother as she lay moaning for mercy on the hard kitchen floor.

Too young and weak to help, I was simply a bystander filled with fear and quickly learning to hate my father. As I grew older, my position changed from a helpless bystander to a person who feared for my mother's life, but I was still too afraid to tackle Daddy. In his rage, he would call me a yellow-bellied coward and all sorts of degrading names. His four-letter words brought the weight of the world tumbling down on my shoulders.

The man who had been so strong and dreamed of prosperity for the whole family was quickly turning into a person filled with emptiness and hate. I often wished Mother would take the six of us still living at home and run away. However, Daddy always seemed so pitiful after his fights with Mother. He easily persuaded her forgiving heart to take him back.

Daddy's temperament was a little subdued when my older brothers were around, but often even their presence did not matter. He would curse and threaten them with his old twelve-gauge shotgun. We all knew that this old gun of Daddy's had what we called a hair trigger. It could be fired with the least amount of pressure from a trigger finger or from any sudden vibration. Having been well used for hunting rabbits, the gun had a broken handle that had been repaired with silver duct tape. When fired, the gun would kick with such a force that even its user had to endure some trauma to operate it. The gun was always kept in the corner right next to my father's side of the bed, and he would run and get it in a hot minute.

In these situations, Mother's words were always kind and seemed to ease the pain I felt from Daddy's verbal abuse. Mother would always try to make sense of this madness and encourage us to never hate anyone. However, Mother also had a way to frighten us. In contrast to Daddy's unprovoked rages and beatings, Mother kept a fresh green hickory switch on her side of the bed. This was a constant reminder that when she spoke with the switch in her hand it was time to take care of some serious business.

I not sure which one I feared the most. Daddy made threats with the gun, but Mother's curved switch with torn leaves was just as threatening. Needless to say, both weapons encouraged rapid growth and spouted a flaming thirst for a new way of life for the ten us.

Regardless of the anger Mother might have felt toward Daddy, she never let that anger show when disciplining one of us. Nor did she sit and do a lot of explaining of her discipline. She would talk to us during the spanking, usually asking, "Are you going to do this anymore?" Of course, we would scream "No, Ma! No, Ma!" and her reply was "Yes, you are!" We would continue to answer "No, Ma! No, Ma!" Her next reply would be, "Now I guess you are calling me a liar then," intensifying her lashes.

As I grew older, my emotions hardened from holding back the tears from Mother's spankings. Too, I became ever more defiant of both my father's anger and his ambition for me to stay on the farm. I decided with certainty that I wanted a better life for my wife and children someday. I made a silent promise to myself that I would never hurt anyone I loved.

It seemed that Daddy's anger and violent tendencies became worse toward the end of each day. As we settled into the house at the approach of sundown, I could sense the change in Daddy's demeanor. Almost without warning he would change from a hardworking farmer to a violent spouse abuser.

As Daddy came into the house, you could tell by the wrinkles on his forehead and the red in the corner of his eyes that it was going to be a long night of verbal and physical abuse to Mother or anyone who got in his way. Most of the time he directed his anger at Mother, rarely doing any physical harm to us children unless we got in his path.

Daddy managed to mostly contain his anger to the circle of our family. Very rarely did he start fights outside the home with anyone, and definitely not with any white people. He was humble as a lamb around white folks. It did not matter the age of the white person; I saw him humble down to a seven year-old white boy at the wood yard in town one day, addressing him as "Yes, Sir," and "No, Sir," calling him Mister. As Jack and I sat in the truck looking on, the scene made me sick to my stomach. This was how my father had been raised. To me, though, at seven or eight—the same age of the boy—my self-esteem dropped to an all-time low, and my respect for my father also dropped a large notch.

One night Daddy was shouting so loudly that a neighbor, Mr. Paul Mays, heard him. Quickly a call came down to the house, and it was Mr. Paul Mays on the phone. He summoned Daddy to the phone and told him to cut out some of that foolishness down there. That night Daddy cooled off. It was "Yes, Sir, Mr. Mays, Yes, Sir, Mr. Mays." That silenced Daddy's rage for about a month, but he was right back into his same old temperament shortly thereafter.

Mother would try to make sense of Daddy's madness, charting the occurrence of each incident on the calendar. She concluded that Daddy was worse during a full moon, pointing to the scribbles she had methodically composed on the large calendar hanging on the kitchen wall. "Yeah, right," I thought to myself. She also told us that the big yellow cat on the picture of that calendar jumped off the calendar at night to catch mice, too.

Sometime after the fighting stopped, Mother would take Daddy over to Dr. Roche, the "rubbing doctor." Dr. Roche would rub him down, claiming to rub some of the evil spirits away. No matter how hard he tried, that rubbing doctor never could rub all those evil spirits out of Daddy. Even so, Daddy was not about to say anything bad about him, because he was white.

After almost every fight between our parents, Jack and I were hauled off by Daddy to visit his mother's grave at Mt. Aire Baptist Church cemetery. Daddy would lead us through the thick of the weeds and undergrowth down a little rocky path to a grave site underneath an old oak tree. The sound of our steps awakened the lizards and scorpions living within the cracks of the tombstones and the dirt of the old graves and sent them racing across our path for cover. As we drew near the gravesite, Daddy would stand silently for a minute as if to gain his composure. Slowly pointing teary-eyed to the three long mounds of dirt—one marked by a broken blue and white teakettle and the other two with no marking at all, he would say, "That's my grandma buried there, and next to her is Grandpa Ache and lying there buried next to Grandpa Ache is my mother."

Jack and I were scared stiff as we listened to Daddy's voice. The air around Daddy seemed to be motionless as he stood gazing at his mother's grave, grieving as if she had died recently and not twenty years earlier. The fear Jack and I felt came from knowing nothing about the three people buried in these unmarked graves. However, we also knew that someone's grave was missing. Where was Grandpa Buford buried, I wondered silently to myself. I knew I did not dare ask my father because this was someone he didn't talk about.

My family always feigned to outsiders that everything in our household was peaches and cream. Somehow I felt that they could see through this fake image. Perhaps this was the driving force behind my wit, my humor, and finally, my determination to become successful. Perhaps this was the driving force behind the ten of us leaving home and starting lives of our own. Not one of us intended on spending one extra minute there after graduating from high school.

However, I have not let our family history become a barrier. Knowing that my direction is being navigated by God our Creator, I have learned to look beyond my troubles, emphasize the opportunities in the present, and focus on the glorification at the end.

(((((((((((((9)))))))))))))
Dreaming of Better Days

I became a dreamer to try to escape the ugliness that surrounded me. I find myself to have been in great company. John Kennedy's famous quotation states, "Some men look at things and ask, why? I look at things and ask, why not?" Now there was a man with the heart of a dreamer! Martin Luther King, another dreamer, dreamed of unity and equality for an entire nation. My dreams revolved around the future of my family. Out of those dreams came the hope that we would all prosper and be in a position to help others.

In looking back on my childhood, I realize that I was living in a fantasy world. I think I believed just about everything my parents told me—especially my mother, whose dreams sometimes included more than a touch of fantasy. My faith in my mother made me truly believe that little boys were made of puppy dog tails and snails, and that little girls were made of sugar and spice and everything nice. That hooting owl we heard in the middle of the night? My mother would tell us that if we coiled our T-shirts into a knot, we could choke the life out of that old owl. I coiled my shirt many nights in the hope that I could stop that scary creature from howling. There was no doubt in my mind that the spring where we went fishing was the home of all the ghosts and goblins.

At night, if one of us claimed to have a sore throat or other illness, Mother had the cure. For a sore throat, she would tell us to go up to the door hanger, and say, "Door Hanger, I have the sore throat. Door Hanger, I have the sore throat. Door Hanger, I have the sore throat." After you had repeated those words three times, you were to go straight to bed, not saying anything at all after that. If we did this, by the next morning we would indeed feel well.

You think that was just a way to make us hush up and go to bed? No, my mother would not lie! Rather, through rearing ten children she had become very clever. She knew how to get the response she needed.

Being poor caused us to miss out on a lot of the material things other children had, like the mini-bike we would have done anything to own. My mother's vivid imagination had the remarkable effect of neutralizing our disappointment, though. She would tell us to visualize what we wanted and then go after it. She would tell us, too, that if we could not have what we wanted today, then we would have it one day. She made us believe that we could accomplish anything through patience, hard work, and time.

Moreover, she taught us that while having dreams is a good thing, dreaming by itself would not bring us the object of our desire. I still remember Mother assuring us daily that we would obtain everything we wanted in life through hard work and prayer. Our belief in this made many of our childhood disappointments easier to bear.

All of us dreamed. And our dreams were big dreams, some bigger than life. By the time I was eight or nine years old, our front porch served as the setting for my dreams. On weekend afternoons, when morning chores and activities had been finished and the evening chores were a while away, we younger children gathered on the porch to count the cars as they drove by. We made a game of taking turns claiming cars as our own as they drove by. This game was a big part of my childhood. Sometimes we'd play this game for hours, because we kids were not allowed to stay in the house during the day. We were all required to stay out of the house, except for mealtimes. Frustrating as this was to us then, this practice formed the basis for one of my fondest memories. This was the perfect way to pass the time, watching the passing cars and dreaming we had our pick of any of them.

Our front porch was small as porches go, but it held the weight of our world. The floor was made of wood slats that squeaked as we jumped up and down. The edge of the porch was laced with two-by-fours, which also served as the banisters. Near the left side of the porch hung a swing made out of wood. The swing was attached to the ceiling by two chains. This swing was Daddy's favorite place to sit. He would sit there for hours, swinging his feet and bellowing out his own dreams.

At the entrance to the porch was a set of concrete steps. Wedged beside the steps were a single row of a dozen neatly trimmed hedges about knee high. Boot kept them trimmed square like a box. Those hedges helped to hide the ugliness of the bare dry dust underneath the house. Coke bottles sometimes littered the area. On those concrete steps my initials were scribbled, a "J" and an upside-down "N." On the second step, Jack's initials were scribbled, and on the bottom step, Gwyn had scribbled hers. Each of us had given in to an irresistible urge on the day those steps were poured, and the concrete was hard before my parents noticed. The three of us had become a close-knit trio. Only later in life would we learn to appreciate this brief time of innocence we shared. The three of us felt invincible. We pledged in blood to live together forever. You've heard of putting your name in lights? Well, we had our name in concrete! Those signatures are still there today. Whenever I return home, our childish scrawls are there waiting on me, a tribute to the closeness of the three of us—and to our dreams. The three of us played games around those concrete steps. The game always started with Boot, because he was the oldest still at home. Boot pointed at the first car, and shouted, "That one's mine."

My sister Nancy, two years younger than Boot, sat on the porch with her little dress on, and with her hair in two ponytails. When the next car drove by, she hollered out, "That one's mine!" All the while, I anxiously anticipated my turn. But my sister Allene, two years older than me, was next. Her hair was in plaits that day, a precursor to her "big hair" phase. As the next car rolled by, she yelled out, "That one is mine!"

After Allene "chose" her car, I knew that my turn was next. I look back and see myself as I was that day—about four feet tall, kind of chunky but far from being robust. My complexion was fair in contrast to Gwyn's deeper hue. The cars we saw usually included at least one Camaro, and since a lot of the white folks in the community had Electra 225 Deuces, we had our pick among the best cars to be had. Sometimes a Roadrunner would come by, a definite "muscle car."

At the approach of the very next car, I finally had my turn. I jumped and shouted, "That one's mine!"

My brother Jack, although two years younger, also played the game with us. However, he pointed at his car after it passed. We forgave his lapse in protocol, for his enthusiasm more than made up for his lack of timing. My sister Gwyn, the baby, was so busy with other things that she never noticed when it was her turn. So we would just pick her a car when her turn came.

We dreamed so vividly of owning those cars, it felt as if we were driving them down the road. These dreams on the front porch were the earliest beginnings of our desires to have cars and other luxury items of our own.

As dusk fell, we all did the ritual of washing our feet before going into the house to help Mother prepare supper and to follow our routine of chores and homework. After that, then began the ritual that stayed with me until I left home. At around nine o'clock, I took out my transistor radio, a gift from my brother Robert, given to me after I practically begged for it, and placed it next to the electric outlet. It was a fine-looking radio, black, with an antenna that stretched about one-and-a-half feet long. I then turned on the radio.

As though some silent signal had passed between us, we all lay quietly there on the beds in our rooms, listening and dreaming. At least I know I passed that time dreaming. We boys would lie in one room, our sisters in the other room. The third room, Mary's, was vacant at that time. We all listened to the same station. Occasionally someone from the girls' room would say, "Turn it up a little bit," or "That's my song. Now, we need to get that package right there."

We listened to our favorite DJ at our favorite station, WLAC in Nashville. The lead DJ, John R, was famous for playing all the R & B hits—B.B. King, The Jackson Five, and Jerry "Iceman" Butler. WLAC was our station of choice, possibly because it was the only station playing black records that we could pick up with that radio! They played all the black songs, and they also sold records. They sold the records in packages. Each package contained four or five records, and they called them something like, "The Horseman's Special," or "The Randy Records Special."

Usually we took a vote on what package to order, after intense, whispered lobbying for our favorites. By voting, we all were agreeing and working as a team. Everyone was responsible for chipping in on the record package we decided to order, and it was understood that you would chip in according to the money that you had. If you didn't have any money, you still had a vote.

We would all lie there silently, listening to WLAC, dreaming—dreaming and thinking about how prosperous our brother and sisters who had moved to Miami were, how they all had new cars and jobs and were sending money back home to us; dreaming that one day we would get our own opportunity to spread our wings and live the good life.

Although the material rewards served as great motivators to all of us, my dreams revolved around becoming somebody important. By this time I had acquired the habit of reading "Discovery Books." Most of the "Discovery Books" were about people who had first explored different areas of the country. All of these people were white, but that did not matter to me. They were all my heroes. Even though I later found out that some of the discoveries credited to them had first been explored by blacks, I never let that revelation sour me on the wondrous visions those books inspired. My obsession with the "Discovery Books" was another factor that put my mind on the road to a higher plane of accomplishment.

Lying there on that bed, I developed a richly woven set of goals; I wanted a book written by me, about me. I wanted to be famous. I wanted to make a significant contribution to humanity. Like many children who dream immensely, it was difficult to share these dreams with anyone else. That last dream, making important contributions to mankind, turned out to be the dream of all six of us as we slept.

Jack, Boot, and I slept in the same bed. We slept like synchronized swimmers. When one turned over, the others turned in unison. The bed consisted of a tiny cast-iron frame, with wooden slats and a homemade mattress and quilts that Mother had made. Our rooms were not heated then, but the chilly draft blowing through the room seemed refreshing as we snuggled up under our heavy load of homemade quilts.

We could look out the window and see almost nothing but stars, the only break in the silky blackness of the night sky. There were no outside lights of any kind except for the quiet illumination of the moon and stars. Only the occasional sound of a hoot owl, or maybe a bobcat's roar, broke the silence.

It seemed so peaceful at night, a wonderful opportunity to dream. I do not know if what I did could be called nightdreaming or daydreaming—probably daydreaming at night, because my conscious dreams of a better life continued well into each night.

We would listen to WLAC on into the night. We would then hear Daddy's familiar voice saying, "Y'all cut that mess off!" We all agreed to disobey this order, because we knew he was not going to get up and enforce it. Instead, we would turn the radio down just a little and continue listening.

All the songs of that era seemed to have a message for us. We enjoyed the songs of the Temptations, the Chi-Lites, Joe Tex, and of course James Brown, an all-time favorite. Some of the songs that made us feel good inside included "Black Power," "It's a Man's World," and "I Feel Good." These songs motivated us and gave us a taste of a larger world, a world we saw as exciting and carefree, a world where nobody had to sleep three to a bed.

My dreams ranged from owning my own bicycle, to owning a mini-bike, to owning a car, to owning my own business. Each of these dreams somehow led to my becoming famous. "Joe Lester rides his bike (mini-bike) (Camaro) across the country, to accept the Nobel Peace Prize" and so on. You get the idea.

The only problem I remember having among the three of us sleeping so close together was that occasionally someone would pee in the bed.

Usually that "someone" was me, because I would be dreaming that I was outside. Immediately I would get a shocked shout from my brother Boot. As dancers who had practiced well, we would all get up, turn that mattress over in unison, then roll back in and continue sleeping.

I think the station went off at midnight or maybe 1:00 a.m. By that time, we had all dozed off to sleep, and the only sound heard was the constant static-filled moan from the transistor radio.

Me, I would continue to dream. My mother said that dreams are what men are made of. At this point in my life, dreams served as an opportunity to escape what I saw as the stifling boundaries of the farm to visit and explore the land of opportunity. We all lay there peacefully, the boys in one room and the girls in another, listening to the radio on into the night.

The most important thing Mother taught us, and the means my family uses to continue its progression, is to draw strength from each other. That strength has helped us obtain many good things in life, because we are all willing to help each other financially, emotionally, or spiritually.

Our mother's teaching has proven to be more precious than any material thing I own. Teaching us to rely on each other even while following our own path was the best gift she could have given us. This teaching has helped us move toward fulfilling our dreams. Like "stair-steps" we used the one before us to take us to the next level of achievement. There was nothing selfish or parasitic about this. This was just what we did as a matter of course. For example, Mary's completion of college inspired my brother Boot (Leonard) to set a similar goal. His goal was more obtainable because he drew strength from her experiences. And he had the privilege of giving Nancy help specific to her chosen field. Literally, we were stair steps, continually climbing to the next level. Then came Allene's turn, then mine, and then Jack and Gwyn followed. We followed our dreams.

Daddy (and Mama) Don't Allow No Fighting Around Here

In our family, fighting was against the rules, and the rules were firmly enforced. To this day I remember the consequences when Jack and I broke the rule against fighting.

One night a small struggle started between Jack and me. The two of us had played nonstop in the yard that day with our friend Melvin. That dreaded time had come—bedtime. At ages four and six, Jack and I were not happy about this. Jack was still coming down emotionally from a day filled with play, and I remember feeling a little agitated that the day had gone by so quickly.

We picked at each other with words at first, and then things started getting physical. As the struggle between Jack and me intensified, Boot lay in the bed grinning at us ominously, as though he were just waiting for one of us to get hurt so he could run and tell Daddy. As it happened, Boot didn't need to do that. The three of us were so involved in our struggle, we were unaware that Daddy had heard our noisy battle from the other room. He had tiptoed through the girl's room and now was standing right behind us.

"What the hell are y'all doing!" Daddy shouted angrily. Instantly, it was quiet enough in that small house to hear a pin drop. Jack and I could only stare silently at each other. Of course, Daddy knew very well what we were doing, but I attempted to invent something to say to try to save us.

"We was just playing!" I said, trying to stay calm as my heart raced uncontrollably. I cautiously positioned myself so that I could see Daddy's face, being careful to avoid direct eye contact. Then I gazed at Daddy, beginning at his stone face down to his hands. His left eye was raised, and he was clenching his lower lip in his teeth. In his hand rested a brown leather belt, which swayed from side to side. Something told me this was not going to be Daddy's customary threat without action.

Without another wasted moment, he shouted, "No Sir-ee, Mr. Gentlemen, y'all are in here passing licks!" He started to lash the belt towards Jack. "Well, the only people in this house that gonna be passing out licks are gonna be me and your mamma."

I numbly waited, knowing my turn was next. By this time tears had started to flow down my face. I looked over at Boot and saw that his grin had turned into a broad smile, as if to say, This is a whipping well past due.

Suddenly, Mother rushed into the room, screaming "Don't hurt them, Raymond!" The noise had awakened her from sleep. Never before had I heard Mother refer to our father as "Raymond." In the past she had always referred to him as "y'all's daddy." The situation was obviously serious. Mother's voice brought Daddy's rage to an abrupt halt—leaving me untouched by the belt, I'm glad to say.

With relative calm restored, they both left the room. A while later, Mother returned. She sat beside the bed and tried to help us make sense of the confusion in our minds. She pampered Jack a little extra as she talked, I suppose because he was the knee-baby (a term we sometimes used to say that there was one other child younger). As Mother talked, she looked primarily at me. Her usually cheerful eyes were deep and dark and told a message of their own. Although Mother never spoke it, I somehow felt that Jack was her favorite. Out of fear of retaliation, I gazed straight in her eyes as she spoke.

Mother said, "If y'all boys start fighting like this, y'all are going to end up in the 'chain gang.'" Mother was referring to the much-feared group of men wearing white striped shirts who sometimes passed the house cutting grass during the summer. A man with a shotgun guarded them; sometimes their legs were bound with chains.

I was now close to terror. The prison road gang! We often ran away as these men approached the house. To end up like them was one of my biggest fears. My dreams that night were filled with frightening images of those "chain gang men." I dreamed they were chasing me. Worse, no matter where I ran, they kept up with me. First I stumbled through the thick of the hedge near the front porch. Then I ran to seek cover behind the barn near the pigpen. The pigs squealed, revealing my location. The chain gang was always one step behind me, though they never caught me.

The next morning, exhausted from running in my sleep, I could not remember what the fight the night before was about or how it had started. However, the lesson I learned that night stayed with me for life. Acts of aggression against a sibling would not be tolerated in our home.

Jack and I never had another physical altercation. As a matter of fact, I never had another physical altercation with any other family member. The next day the two of us were playing again as if nothing had transpired. Jack offered no apology and neither did I, but it seemed that an unspoken agreement had been made never to fight again. Besides, we found greater pleasure in playing than fighting.

Of course, we kids did occasionally get physical with each other. Once when I was drawing water from the well, Jack and I grumbled back and forth; somehow I had scratched my hand on Jack's fingernails. Mother thought that Jack had hit me, and I think he got a whipping for that. The purpose of that whipping was to teach that him not to fight with his brother. It taught me a lesson, too, even though I didn't get the whipping.

Many, of course, suggest that hitting a child only teaches that hitting is OK. However, the clear message I received from physical punishment was that fighting with my brother was a serious offense, serious enough to require the strictest discipline my parents ever used. Far from teaching me that violence is acceptable, such discipline taught me that acting violently was the worst thing a person could do. Physical discipline in our home was always tempered with clear, loving guidelines and expectations that were easy for us to understand.

Neither my siblings nor I have ever been violent people as adults. Perhaps because we were well disciplined while still very young, we did not require harsher forms of discipline by the time we were teenagers.

School Days, School Days

There is always one moment in childhood, someone has suggested, when the door opens and lets the future in. The incident that did this for me is also the one that came close to dashing my dream. It happened in the sixth grade.

My brother Raymond had come home from Miami and stopped by the school to visit me. Having a family member visit you at your class was considered an honor. I remember having a really good feeling as Raymond walked into the classroom. I figured he would not come to visit me at school unless he was proud of me. The teacher knew him well and welcomed him in. I should have known she was up to something. I'm still resentful when I recall the deceitful smile on her face that day. When my brother Raymond asked the teacher how I was doing, she bluntly told him, in front of the whole class, that I was "one of the dumbest Lesters she had ever taught." Up until that time, I thought I had been doing well in school. Time stopped for me as she described my lack of academic ability. It seemed to me she went on for hours. I could feel my face starting to become wet with tears. I felt helpless. As a child I had no means to respond or retaliate. I had been trained to stay in a child's place, and that meant not interjecting comments into an adult conversation.

Raymond listened on with a half smile, saying "Uh hum," between her sentences. He was congenial, but from his occasional glances at me, I could sense that the teacher's words were making him feel uncomfortable. Somehow he knew, though, that the problem was hers, not mine. The teacher humiliated me that day. My heart was breaking, and my head felt as if it could explode. I was afraid to look at my other classmates. I feared that their reaction would be to agree with her. I felt betrayed in a way that only a twelve-year-old embarrassed in front of his classmates can.

I knew that I was not one of her favorites. She usually seemed much kinder to the students with fair or light complexions. She even confessed one day in class that she gave one classmate higher grades because he was from a well-to-do family. She often made the kids on free lunch—like me—go outside and pick up paper or clean the room to earn our way.

This time she had stooped to an all-time low. As if those devastating remarks were not enough, she also told Raymond that I was dumb, ugly, could not learn, and needed to get my other brother Jack to help me with my lessons because I was "slow" and "knotty-headed."

Raymond never made it completely into the classroom that day. He just stood there at the doorway, leaning motionless against the doorframe. The teacher's harsh comments were more than he anticipated, and he said very little, evidently trying not to provoke further conversation. Raymond was very calm and respectful to the teacher. On the other hand if Robert had been there, he would have told that "old bag" (she was all of thirty years old) a thing or two.

I will never, ever, understand her reasons for speaking about me that way, but that one humiliating incident formed a fierce determination in me. I set my mind that I was not going to be all the things she said I was. I would be everything except what she said I was!

From that point on, I set my mind to doing my best in everything I did in school. The best did not have to mean all A's, but it did mean that I gave one hundred and ten percent to accomplish what I had to do. If I did not finish at the highest level, I made sure that I finished at the highest level I could. The very next year, my seventh-grade year, the schools were integrated. Integration in our small town of Hawkinsville occurred without the drama that I had seem on TV in large cities. There were no policemen with dogs escorting poor little black children through a vicious crowd of white folks shouting racial epithets. We had a couple of fistfights every now and then but no more than usually. Integration was a learning process for both races. Black and white students tested age-old myths and stereotypes and feared each other alike. We knew the white children did not want to go to school with us. We could feel the resentment in their eyes when we caught them looking at us. In retaliation we met them with an attitude of our own. We resented being taken from our school, where the principal and all the teachers and any other person in charge looked like us. Our black principals were demoted to assistant principals, with domain over only us black students.

Slowly some of my classmates got on an assimilation "trip." They began to act white.

As they spoke, they began to pay more attention to the pronunciation of their words. Others, though, expressed themselves in a different way. They began to act like the black hoodlums and gangsters of black movies.

My friend John and I handled the situation in yet another way. We began an endless fight to become better academically than any white person in our class. Unknown to our white classmates, we were challenging them on every test.

During that time my mother worked in the school cafeteria as the dietician planning meals. After integration, Daddy somehow did not think it was right for her to be a supervisor. He had always had a problem with her working outside of the home. When he found out that she was the supervisor for all the cafeteria staff, especially one white employee, that just did not seem right to him. He nagged and nagged her until she eventually decided to take a lower-paying position as a cook to keep peace within the family. This also meant training the only white employee in the cafeteria for her old position.

Even to my twelve-year-old mind, it felt wrong that my mother had to become less than she could be. I forgive my father's actions, because he was acting in the manner of that time and place. He felt that his actions were somehow necessary to keep the family on an even keel. However, I have never forgotten. Experiencing the humiliation by my teacher in the sixth grade and seeing my mother have to fall back from her achievement melded together in my mind. They resulted in a burning desire in me that to this day cannot be quenched with anything less that bettering myself, exceeding expectations, and making a way for my children to do the same. Things really got silly around school. The white people had little knowledge of our culture and we of theirs. One of the most ridiculous rules that was imposed on the black girls by the all-white school board was that none of the black girls could wear their hair platted or braided to school. That had been a tradition of all the black girls up until that point. Our parents quickly acted, and that rule was quickly changed. This seemingly minor incident was a precursor to the subtle but pervasive expectations placed on us simply because of our cultural differences. These expectations seemed to color many of the things I wanted to do in order to meet my personal goal of academic excellence. In the eighth grade, for example, my friend John and I were not permitted to attend one of the higher-level algebra classes. It seems that the teachers and administration felt that the lower-level classes were more in keeping with their perception of our academic ability. As a result, John and I decided to sit outside the higher-level class since we were not permitted to go in. At last the teacher let us take the class. This bold act on my part might have been the first instance of my taking my education into my own hands.

When I was in high school, I decided I wanted to go to dental school. This decision must have been a laughing matter to a lot of my fellow students and probably to many of my teachers, too. However, at this point I had developed a strong trust in God and knew that through prayer and obedience my dreams would prevail. I started to try to enroll in the high school classes that would help me pursue my career in dentistry.

Too, it seemed that things began to happen for me to encourage me to keep believing I could achieve my dream. Perhaps partly because there were only ninety-nine students in my twelfth-grade class, a couple of teachers at last took a look at me and saw that I did have the academic ability and intellect to be successful. Until this point I had been operating primary on self-encouragement and glimmers of hope that came from my mother. Mother should have been a minister. She could hammer words into place with the skill of a blacksmith. She could paint a picture of hope when even hope seemed futile. Regardless of how bad a situation was, after a sermon from Mother mountains seemed like mole hills. Her spirit lit a fire in my heart that inspired me to surpass boundaries I never visualized achieving.

As high school graduation approached, I got an unexpected boost to my self-esteem. My Government teacher, an elderly white woman with hair as white as snow, had been quietly observing my academic strivings. Mrs. Twitty was a big woman in physical stature. Students and staff alike respected her. Since she was well into her seventies, she had taught almost every instructor at our school, including the principal. What Mrs. Twitty wanted, Mrs. Twitty got, with respect and no opposition.

One day as I sat chatting with friends, awaiting the beginning of class, I began to notice that Mrs. Twitty was staring right at me. I couldn't figure out why. I looked away, hoping that she would find another prey. It didn't work. She gave me one last hard look and beckoned me with a crooked finger. Oh no, not the infamous finger, I said to myself.

When I got to her desk, without speaking a word she tapped her hand on the chair facing her, inviting me to sit down. She looked me straight in the eye and whispered to me, "You are one of the smartest colored boys in this school system." She nodded her head quickly, expressing her sincerity. "Well, John Singletary is actually the smartest colored boy here, but he has been out so much lately. Is he as sick as he pretends to be?" she asked.

"Yes, ma'am," I replied, giving her all the respect I could muster. I did not know where this conversation was headed. My best friend John had been afflicted with an ugly skin rash that had spread over his body. Some classmates joked that his rash was a result of his meager personal hygiene habits. Nevertheless, they were careful to keep this tease carefully concealed from John. Besides being credited for having a quick brain, my friend was known for having quick fists, too. My friend John Singletary was not only the smartest colored boy in our class. He was the brightest student in our class, period. Unfortunately, he had been out of school for about three or four months and was jeopardizing graduating on time. So perhaps she thought I was the smartest colored boy because she saw me more often than she saw John.

Anyway, she advised me to take my books and move to the other side of the class, away from the rest of the colored kids on my side. She wanted me to get away from them so I could concentrate on my work. I don't remember a condescending tone in her voice, so perhaps this was, to her way of thinking, a compliment.

My feeling at that moment was not, How dare she imply that colored kids aren't smart! It was, She thinks I'm smart, and if she tells me that sitting on the other side of the class will benefit me, I'm going to do it!

As soon as the other kids saw that I had moved, they started to pick on me. They would ball up pieces of paper and throw them at me or they would reflect a mirror into the ceiling behind my back to make Mrs. Twitty falsely accuse me. Once someone floated a paper plane at me that curved and landed right on Mrs. Twitty's desk. It was as though my classmates saw me as a traitor, and they wanted to convince the teacher I was not the "quality" student she thought I was. Eventually, I saw that attempting to distinguish myself through physical separation was not working the way I thought it would, and I moved back to where I had sat originally.

Still, this teacher's well-meaning if misdirected compliment made a lasting impression on me. People in authority at the school had noticed that I was trying to do the best I could and that I wanted to succeed and even excel in school. This notice gave me the boost I needed to stand up to the attitudes of the other students, even after I went back on "their" side.

I did not graduate from high school at the top of the class; I just graduated from high school. I was, however, the best student in my class who planned to attend college. I was on my way, even though I was well aware that the way was not clear of obstacles. A major obstacle to achieving my dream lay just ahead.

Struggling to Get Free

"Do you know where you are going to?" That question is from the class song selected by my high school graduating class. I definitely knew where I wanted to go and that was some distance from Hawkinsville and those cotton fields. But I found Daddy standing right in my path to freedom.

I would have rather asked the devil himself than to have asked that man about leaving to go to college. I had been just an average student in high school, and Daddy had made it known that I would be helping him on the farm full-time after I graduated. I was thinking ahead of him, though, and started making plans to leave to search out my own future.

In celebration of my graduation from high school, I asked Mother if I could I go to Florida with Robert. Mother replied, "I don't know; go ask your daddy." I could sense that she didn't want the responsibility of making a decision of this magnitude. As I could have predicted, Daddy replied, "Go ask your Ma." I wisely cut to the chase by telling Mama that Daddy said it was OK. So I traveled to south Miami to spend the summer with Robert.

Although I had decided sometime before to be a dentist, somehow I had not yet shared this with Robert. So it was during this visit that I shared my dream with him. I poured out my plans and dreams of the future. I told Robert why I wanted to be a dentist and how I planned to go about it. Much of my planning revolved around faith rather than concrete and objective steps, but my faith was strong, and I had no problem relaying this to my mentor. To his credit, Robert replied kindly, even though the words were hard to hear. "Joe, I don't want to burst your bubble, but I really think you've set your goals too high. College is hard enough, but dental school, too? I don't think you should even go to college. Get a job, and earn a living. That should be all the education anyone needs, anyway."

I cried like a newborn baby when I heard Robert say those discouraging words. I was crying tears of frustration, because I wanted so much more than to just get a job and settle for just getting by. I had always been willing to work hard, but at this point I wanted more than a job. I wanted a career. I wanted to establish my own destiny, to reach frontiers that no one else in my circumstances had ever dreamed of and the one person I needed to support me thought I should not go to college! Robert sounded so much like Daddy saying this! I wanted to be able to choose a profession and not have to wait to have an employer choose me! I wanted to be a professional, a dentist! I knew I could do it! I was willing to work hard, and I knew that my hard work would pay off.

I had grown up listening to grown people talk. It seemed to me they were always saying, "We need more black doctors, more black lawyers." The repetition of this cry now resounded through my mind. No one in my town appeared to be willing to take on the challenge, but I wanted the challenge! There were many who had better grades and a better chance of making it than I did, but I truly believed that I had more intelligence. I knew that I was at least more ambitious. Besides, I knew I was not going to be a farmer like my daddy. That sun was too hot, and to listen to him curse and swear the rest of my adult life seemed to be a death sentence to my very soul. Why did I choose dentistry? The choice was easy because I had only two important questions to answer. First, would I be able to help other people by doing this? Second, would I be able to make a good living at it? Dentistry seemed to fit those questions well for me. In spite of the hurt Robert's well-intentioned advice caused me, my mind was made up. The pain his remarks caused made me even more determined to begin the first step in my journey for success. I began the process of enrolling in college. Years later, Robert explained to me why he had made the comments that discouraged me so. He said it was not his intent to discourage me. Rather, he was repeating to me what our father had always preached to us as the foundation for stability: "Get a job and become self-supporting." I wanted that, but I was also determined to do and have more than that. After returning home from vacation with my brother, it was time to re-focus my attention on finding my way in life. It was time to start working at my dream of becoming a dentist. I sought to find someone who didn't doubt I could accomplish my goals. It turned out that the person I found was the one to whom I had turned since my earliest childhood. Just as I had done as a child when some playmate had done or said some hurtful thing to me, I took my bruised self-esteem to my mother. I risked further hurt by telling her about my dream. Her reaction made the gamble worthwhile, though. Perhaps she saw something in me that others did not see when I said, "Mama, I'm going to be a dentist."

When I told her of my goal, she was standing in the kitchen in her apron making supper for the family. I remember how thrilled she was that her son had decided to become a doctor! She was glad to see another seed that she had planted and cultivated so tenderly growing in the right direction. "My boy's going to be a doctor," she crowed to her friends. She believed in me, and pretty soon I again began to believe in myself as well.

Mother's unswerving faith in my dream did not leave room for any adverse criticism from any family member. So, if my siblings had any further doubts about my ability to succeed in this, they kept them to themselves or at least out of my mother's hearing! In this way, my mother became my staunchest ally. From that time I became determined not to disappoint her or ever lose faith in myself again, and not to let others' words cause me to doubt myself. There would be some hills to climb and some burdens to overcome, but I believed I could do it. The first hill to cross would be at home, as mother and I knew, and it seemed like Mt. Everest to me. It was Daddy. My daddy felt betrayed by my plans. He had expected me to be the one to stay home and help him on the farm. Additionally, he did not see the need for me to go to college. He felt he had done enough to see that my older siblings had gone. With my other brothers gone, I was the senior son at the house. That added another burden, because as determined as I was not to let his opposition stop me, I felt a great deal of guilt about what I was doing.

However, my mother's remarkable insight told her that the key to upward mobility for our family would be education. She came to my rescue. I will never forget her serving as my proxy, bearing the brunt of my father's anger, while I sat in the other room with my bags already packed, certain that she would pull it off.

With each child who left home, the dream my father had of one of his children taking over the farm someday faded a little more. Looking back, I realize that he may have looked at me as his major "last hope." I realize now how much my leaving to go to college must have hurt him.

The week leading up to my departure for college I did everything possible to keep Daddy in a good spirit. I fed the hogs on time without any back talk to Daddy. I worked the field harder than ever before, even on Saturdays. I "yes sired" him to death. Every soul in our house walked on pins and needles that week, trying to avoid a skirmish with my father.

Mother also did her part. She buttered Daddy up by killing him with kindness. She cooked his favorite meals, on time. With my bags packed, I anxiously waited for the right moment. I was not going to bring up the subject of leaving. This was a job that only mother could handle.

I recall sitting on those bags and hearing the conversation between Daddy and Mother in the next room. Daddy raged, telling Mother how, just when I had gotten big enough to help on the farm, I was going to leave and go on to college. He did not want that. Oh, he was mad! Mother pleaded with Daddy, saying, "Raymond, let this boy go on. These boys have got to make their own way. They can't stay around here. They need to be going on to college, to do better things for themselves." She pleaded and pleaded with him; it seemed as if hours went by.

In my faith, I knew Mother was going to win. After all, I had my bags packed already, as though they were a magic talisman to guarantee the outcome. More realistically, I knew that when it came to pleading battles with my father, Mother would usually win. But this was the biggest battle she had ever fought on my behalf. As I sat there listening, I had more than one moment when I thought I might have to unpack those bags and get back up on the tractor. However, as I was sure would happen, Mother won the battle for me, and I was soon on my way to Fort Valley State College— and beyond.

Leaving Home

"You are just starting to find yourself, Son," Mother stated as I prepared to leave home. "What you do with your life from now on is out of my hands. I'm turning it over to the Lord."

I had heard those words before-first when Boot went off to college and then when Nancy and afterward Allene had left home. Mother's words were hard to hear, but they were not cold. She was helping me make the harsh transformation into adulthood.

Mother had her own special way of dealing with our leaving home. She preached to us until we reached the point of leaving home, promoting education every step of the way. After preaching us into responsible adults, she grieved our departure from her nest. I remember feeling ashamed for the sadness I had brought over her, but I desperately wanted to leave home.

I saw her standing on the porch. She didn't see me, and so I just looked at her a while. She gazed peacefully toward heaven, appearing to listen as if someone were whispering to her beyond the clouds. As she stared at the distant sky, I could see her lips move almost imperceptibly as she softly hummed, "one glad morning when this life is over, I'll fly away." The song seemed to come from deep within her being.

The lyrics she sang should have been sad, but the tone and rhythm were joyful and up-tempo. Then she began to stamp her feet gently on the porch floor in a foot-rocking motion like some of the elderly women at church did when the "Holy Ghost got into them."

My eyes turned to the sky, too. If she happened to look my way and see me, I didn't want her to see the tears in my eyes. I cried the tears she could not openly shed—tears of satisfaction for this milestone in my life, mixed with a few tears of sadness for my fast approaching departure from Mother's nest.

In spite of my sadness, though, I felt that the day for me to leave home would never come. In hindsight, I did not realize how swiftly the first seventeen years of my life had flown by—"quicker than the shake of a lamb's tail," to use one of Mother's favorite expressions. In contrast, my departure from home one sunny day seemed endless.

Rain had come down all week, but today the gray overcast gave way to a clear blue sky. It was always a muddy mess in our red clay yard after it rained. I remember taking one final look at my old playground. Jack and I had put up my basketball goal in the front yard, supported by a tree cut from the swamp out back. It leaned forward as a result of the wind and most of all as a result of many failed slam dunk attempts. Hanging from the barn next to the pigpen swung an old car tire held in mid air by a rope suspended from the barn's loft. Jack and I had installed the tire swing, too. Although Daddy complained that it was in the way of the tractor, which he usually parked there, he never made us take it down. This was our home-made swing, long since abandoned for more exciting toys. This old yard had my name written all over it. The swing, the basketball goal, and even the deep trench behind Boot's mobile home now filled with water were my doing. With the help of Jack and Gwyn, I had set out to dig our own fishing pond. We planned to trench our way out to the creek bridge located about a football field to the right of the boundaries of Boot's yard.

I should have felt comfortable standing in the yard among all these familiar gadgets, but instead I felt awkward and ridiculous, choking on my words as my family helped me prepare for my departure. Jack and Gwyn tried to make me think they were anxious to see me leave. In theory, they were happy, but the gentleness that emanated from them made me know that they were also sad. I was their leader, and they were like good soldiers with their emotions penned underneath their skin.

Except for Daddy, the whole family had gathered on the back porch. I could hear Daddy moving around inside the house, and I could see him occasionally at first one window, then another. The planks of the wooden floor squeaked as his heels thumped against it. He appeared to be singing. I had never heard Daddy sing before, and so this was totally against his nature. Singing requires expressing emotion from deep within your soul and Daddy just was not the singing type. I think he was doing some chores-or at least pretending to. Perhaps after the previous day's battle between him and Mother, it was for the best that he could not bring himself to step out on the porch.

I could see Mother's hands, her fingers winding one over the other. Her hands showed her anxiety. She seemed to be struggling to hold back tears as I loaded my long-packed bags into the car, a white '63 Volkswagen.

This car, a gift from Annie Nell and her husband, was supposedly in appreciation for our hard work in their store that summer, but since our work had previously been "its own reward," I suspected that this was simply a ruse and that the car was really to make sure the trip to college was a safe one.

Knowing that space was limited in the car, Allene and I had—wisely, I think!—borrowed Daddy's truck and moved our larger items to school earlier in the week. It is amusing to me now that when we asked to borrow his truck, Daddy never even asked what we were borrowing it for, though he surely must have known.

Even with the previous week's trip, I despaired of fitting all the luggage and last minute things into that tiny car. As we finally wedged in the last of the bags, I turned around for a final check. This is when I noticed a neatly wrapped box, sitting by itself.

At that moment, I didn't feel like a grownup, but like a little boy who has decided he is going to run away from home and never come back. On seeing the box, a flood of emotion and memories threatened to erase the control I was struggling to maintain. I simply couldn't allow myself the luxury of an outward display of affection.

A naturally shy person, I found it easy and often safer to be reserved emotionally. And of course I believed that any outward display of emotion was for girls. I had learned from Daddy that a man is not supposed to cry.

I looked up at Mother and, referring to the package, said with difficulty, "Thank you, this sure will be good a little later." She smiled and nodded, assured that I had grasped the package's importance. I opened the lid of the box and looked in. Inside were cookies, milk, and juice, prepared with the same loving attention with which Mother had prepared packages for Robert during the war. In his, there was always a little extra "just in case he met a friend and wanted to share." And today, too, it seemed as though there was enough in the box for more than just my sister Allene and me. While the items in this package were a little different from the packages Robert had been given, the message was the same. I was on my way to a foreign territory, with obstacles of a different kind, of course, but just as real and life changing. As with her other children, Mother knew that it was now up to me to reach beyond my grasp, to triumph over challenge. She had also given me the tools to do this, not the least of which was the guidance she gave me from the Bible.

Mother had taught me well, but now it was time to go. Being a family of reserved emotion, no one cried openly; we exchanged no kisses or hugs that day. Nevertheless the soft subdued tone in which we spoke expressed the love among us. And, of course, there was the box and Mother's final admonition, "Remember, put on the whole armor of God, Joe Nathan. Put on the whole armor of God. This will protect you the last mile of the way." Those words from Ephesians, chapter 6, meant much to me.

As I drove up Blue Spring Road toward Georgia Highway 129, with my sister sitting on the passenger side, the house faded away in the rear-view mirror, but Mother's voice seemed to never stop echoing. "Joe Nathan, the world don't owe you no living. Son, you don't come from rich folks. You'll have to work for the things you want in life."

My smug self-assurance that I had already worked hard enough fell away at that moment, and I felt somewhat like a person who has stepped off a cliff. Instantly, all my support was gone, and I was free-floating in a space that I suddenly felt unprepared for.

The little four-cylinder car struggled as it climbed the hills of the highway, gaining a little in speed as it went downhill. That little car seemed to be just as determined as we were to reach college and a new life.

College Man

My mind would not rest. It kept going back to the events of the day past, when my mother had to fight my daddy on my behalf for the privilege of pursuing my dream. I prayed silently and earnestly that my absence would not begin anew my father's rage at me for leaving, at Mother for helping me, and at the world in general for staying just like it was.

A forty-five-minute drive placed us right at Jose Hall on the Fort Valley State College Campus. I had made this trip on several occasions with my older siblings. Of course, Allene knew the campus layout well herself. Jose Hall was the senior girls' dormitory. Allene lived there now, and Nancy had lived there before her. Ohio Hall, located at the front of the campus, was the home of the freshman men except for the lucky ones like me who had begged their parents to sign a waver to allow them to live off campus.

Concrete sidewalks stretched out across the campus like spaghetti. I had never witnessed so many black people my age in one place before in my life. The campus parking lots were filled to the brim with late-model cars and pickup trucks packed to the windows with boxes, luggage, hot plates, pots, pans, and small refrigerators. Some of the heavily-laden cars and trucks had appropriated the sidewalks and lawns for parking. Still other vehicles, with open trunks, sat near dormitory entrances. I decided from the look of the vehicles and their cargo that many of the students were just like me—down-home country folks. The fathers wore beige khaki pants, white shirts, and caps like my daddy when he was casually dressed. Mothers wore conservative dresses that reached well below their knees. The excitement of students filled the entire campus. Students stood in bunches. Some sat on the lawn, and others huddled together in groups with ghetto boxes blasting. Girls—hundreds of them, some tall, some round, some short and petite like I prefer—came and went everywhere, busy as bees. I thought I had died and gone to heaven. To my great delight, females outnumbered the males seven to one.

Allene looked at me with Mother's face and critical eyes and said, "Come on, boy, and help me unpack my things. I don't have time for your foolishness." I grabbed a couple of bags and made my way through the parlor into the reception area and past the dorm mother's office. The two double doors at the front entrance whooshed back and forth as girls dressed in tight jeans and tee shirts raced in and out of the building. Some carried luggage and some were empty-handed. Some were with parents, and others were alone. I paid care to differentiate couples from singles. The senior dormitory was buzzing with excitement.

Once past the carpet in the parlor, the high heels of the many mothers clicked on the tile hallway, making music like a troop of tap dancers. Clenched-jawed fathers lagged behind mothers with "I know what's on your mind" stares in their eyes and frozen smiles on their faces. Suddenly I heard a shout from the intercom, "Men on the hall! Men on the hall!" At the sound of the intercom, giggling half-naked girls with towels slung around their bodies raced for cover behind slamming doors. My chest stuck out another half inch when I heard the intercom ring out for a second time, "Men on the hall! Men on the hall!"

I felt like a man as I strained to climb the second flight of stairs, carrying my sister's heavy bags. I swelled up with manly pride and mustered up all the cockiness that I could in a bid to impress the young females I passed in the hallways. I hastened to drop Allene's bags on her side of the small room she was to share with a roommate.

After dropping Allene off at Jose Hall, I headed west about six miles on highway 96 past several orchards of peach trees to Rolling Hills trailer park. I thought of all the fun the students back at campus were having, and I thought of all the students back home who did not plan to enter college. I was sure they did not know what they had missed. The controlled structure of the high school years had led us to believe that school was all work and no play except for athletics. As I dismissed this myth from my mind, I kicked my little car into high gear, and we sped down the smooth black highway so I could unpack my belongings and get on with my new life.

Groves of peachtrees with brown leaves lined both sides of the highway. This was Peach County. Peaches were the lifeblood of this farming community, and Fort Valley, Georgia, was the county seat of Peach County. Two major industries controlled this small town—peaches and school buses. This improbable combination provided incomes for many people.

As I made a left turn onto Rolling Hills Drive, the sand and rocks from the dirt road sprinkled against the fender of the car. The dust settled as I reached my final destination—lot number 109-B. Parked there was my new home, a single-wide white trailer with green trim that Raymond and Boot had moved there earlier. Boots and Raymond had purchased some mobile homes as rental units. Their decision to purchase these homes turned out to be a good deal for me. I shared the mobile home with Greg and Keith, two of my "home boys." They paid the rent to me, and I turned the money over to Raymond and Boot. So at least for the first year, my housing was taken care of.

I was really feeling like a man—living off campus and paying my own rent. The mobile home consisted of three bedrooms, a bath, a kitchen, and a den. I checked the mobile home over carefully. This is where the action will be, I thought for a few lustful seconds while admiring my new home. I claimed the bedroom up front with the private shower and left the remaining two for my roommates to choose from. I dropped my bags on my bed and proclaimed to myself that I had finally arrived. I had made my way to college. I had a new home and all of life ahead of me.

The next morning I gobbled down some corn flakes with milk and juice. I had a taste for some hot grits, eggs, and mother's homemade butter biscuits, but I was on my own and did not have the luxury of mother's cooking. However, I did not have long to pine for mother's cooking, for my hunger was soon overtaken by a very nervous stomach. My first college exam was at 8 a.m. in Founder's Hall. I was required to take a placement test for admission because of my low SAT scores.

In spite of my siblings' considerable help at every step, none of them had ever mentioned that a high SAT score was necessary to be accepted by a college. Even John, my smart friend, hadn't a clue as to its importance. So when John and I went to take the SAT, neither of us had any idea of its importance. We just thought it was a required part of graduating high school. So, we both made the mistake of taking the test totally unprepared, with no "cramming" or special preparation. As a matter of fact, we went joy-riding the night before the exam and even shared a bottle of wine. Believe me, if we had known the significance of this test, that would NOT have been a part of our final preparations!

Even if I had known the importance of the SAT and had studied and crammed, I suppose I might not have scored much higher, though. My upbringing had not given me the necessary exposure to different areas of life.

I have since read of severe criticism of the SAT and other such tests. The criticism is that the questions are not racially balanced enough to allow fair comparisons. I disagree with this charge. Race was only part of the issue. I strongly feel that what happened to me was not a racial thing, but a cultural thing. Whether I had been black, white, or any shade in between, the fact remained that I had never experienced anything outside the small, isolated, rural area in which I grew up.

Even television, the medium that enables many kids to learn about the greater world, was far from me. We did have a television, but with so many kids in the family vying for its use, none of us gained much real benefit from it. The city had recently build a new library—a brick building about the size of two double-wide mobile homes joined together. The colored children didn't often frequent the white part of town the library was located in. Even when we did venture into that part of town , the glares from the white storeowners made us feel uncomfortable and produced a reluctance for us to visit the library.

Crushed by my perceived failure on the SAT, I didn't even consider retaking it. I continued to have the intent of living a life of importance, though. I had one last chance to get into school without having to take remedial classes, and I intended to take that chance.

If a person didn't qualify through standardized testing, an entrance test was given at Fort Valley State to determine the level at which one should start college. If you failed to qualify for even the remedial classes, you could plan on spending your life in a menial job, or, in my case, back on the farm. Neither of these options was acceptable to me. Since I had managed to hold onto my unstoppable desire to do whatever it took to get into college, I took the entrance exam that summer.

After I took the entrance exam, I had to stand in a long line to find out my scores. This line curved beyond the boundaries of the hallway, winding outside the building onto the sidewalk. I took my place at the end of the line, thinking about the stories of the Nazi death camps, how without warning you could be chosen to live or die, based on the utterance of a single word by the one in authority. I saw no gray areas. Here the wrong word would have brought me a spiritual death, which to me would have been the same as a physical one.

These test scores were not mailed to your home or posted elsewhere so that you could read your score in solitude and have the shield of anonymity in dealing with the results. I remember wishing desperately for a different way of learning my score. I feared being held back, and I also dreaded being made aware of my terrible fate in a public setting. If the news was bad, I didn't know whether I would erupt in tears or in rage at my smashed dreams. I would probably have done both.

On the day I stood in line, a hundred students stood with me. Except for one sound, you could have heard a feather fall to the freshly waxed floor in that hall. As you stood in line to get your scores, you could hear a very deep-voiced man say, "098" or "097" or "099" to the student at the head of the line. This number designated the remedial course level the student would take if he or she had failed the test. The student hearing this would then have to turn around and walk back down the line, head bowed and eyes downcast, trying to avoid the glances of students in the line as he or she sped up the pace to exit the hall before losing control of their emotions.

The few students who passed the test would hear this same deep voice say, "100" or "VX". These were numbers for regular college courses. These fortunate ones would turn and walk back down the line, gladly meeting others' eyes with a look that could only be described as a combination of gratefulness, relief, and the sudden return of their ability to breathe.

As every other applicant there did, I surreptitiously counted the numbers of happy glimpses and downcast stares and compared the two. My heart sank a little lower the closer I got to the head of the line, because the sad looks were far outnumbering the blissful.

As I reached the third or fourth spot in line, I did what I always did when faced with a sure disappointment. I squared my shoulders, lifted my chin, and decided that no matter what level of remedial classes I had to take, I was still going to be a dentist. What did it matter if it took a little longer? Even if I failed this exam, I was not going to avoid anyone's eyes on the way back down the line.

I silently said a prayer in which I reminded God of the Scripture Mother often quoted: "Ask, and it shall be given you; seek and ye shall find" (Matthew 7:7). Well, I was asking and seeking, and I certainly hoped God thought I was worthy enough to find. I remembered Mother saying if you prayed without having enough faith your prayers would not be answered. I then prayed, Please, please, please give me the faith I need for you to answer my prayer.

Too soon, I reached the head—or was it the end?—of the line. I stood facing the owner of the deep voice, the man who held my fate on the piece of paper in his hand. What was worse, I recognized him! It was Reverend Simmons, the Dean of Developmental Studies!

At the moment I stepped forward, I could see he was studying the paper carefully, head down. Then he looked up suddenly and, with his mustache twisted, said, "Oh, you're OK," in a tone that actually held a hint of surprise at a student that not only didn't have to take any remedial courses, but who had showed very low scores on his SAT.

Trying very hard to disguise my pounding heart, which felt as though it was protruding through my chest, I went back to what my mother had trained me to do when I received a great gift. I opened my mouth and said, "Thank you, Sir," in as deep a voice as I could muster.

As I was walking away, exuberant, I heard him go back to saying, "098," "099," "097." When I finally reached the doorway leading out of the hall, I turned around for one more look. What I saw looked like an endless chain, moving in a slow rhythm. And even with the great distance and poor acoustics, I could still make out "097," "098," "099."

Once out of the reach of the great and powerful Reverend Simmons, I clinched my fist and pulled my arm down near my half-raised hip like a bowler who had just thrown a strike and shouted, "Yes!" Gray clouds lifted, and the sun shone once again. I made it! Thank you, GOD! Thank you, GOD! With the help of God and Mother, I had not only passed but did well enough on the entrance test to "CLEP" the remedial. Evidently I had picked up some things in high school that had helped me to leap over the first obstacle to becoming a dentist.

I went to Fort Valley because I wanted to attend dental school, but there were other reasons as well. One important reason was that I wanted to develop my own identity. Getting away from home and starting my own life seemed to be the quickest route to developing that identity. What I did not realize until much later was that choosing this college meant that I took that leap into independence I craved, while having my family as a sort of parachute to ensure a softer landing if a bailout became necessary. It was truly the best of both worlds.

Of course, I missed my family, but thankfully I had the kind of family that "looked after" me and kept me from many of the pitfalls that befall college freshmen. If I sat quietly and listened, I could hear my mother's voice saying, "Put on the whole armor of God, Joe Nathan, put on the whole armor of God. This will protect you the last mile of the way."

A College Decision That Almost Cost Me My Career

Difficulties and homesickness aside, my freshman year was a year of freedom and excitement. As we had done all our growing up years, my friend John and I continued to challenge other students in basketball, first outside our trailer and later, our apartment, in the afternoons after school. Whenever John and I moved into a new apartment, the first thing to be installed was a basketball hoop. We were never far from our favorite sport!

College wasn't easy, but I didn't find it to be very demanding in some ways. After all, you only had to take two or three classes per day to finish a full day of school. After classes ended, there was nothing to do in the evening except study and play basketball. This was a life of luxury to me. I had been accustomed to boarding the bus each day at 6:00 a.m. for the trip to school and again at 3:00 p.m. for the return trip home. On arriving home at 4:00, I would work in the fields until sundown. After field work I did my daily chores and my homework. On school nights, I then went straight to bed. So the college schedule was a dream come true. Plenty of time for more pleasurable pursuits! When John and I were not playing basketball, we paraded around campus, looking for girls. Of course, we called it "cruising for chicks."

I don't remember putting a lot of effort into studying or making preparations for any of my courses. I think I went to Fort Valley for two or three semesters before I even knew what my grade point average (GPA) was or even how to figure a GPA. Maintaining a certain grade point average didn't mean a thing to me until my sophomore year.

It was during that year that I decided to pledge a fraternity. A quick trip to the registrar's office gave me these two bits of surprising news: you had to have at least a 2.5 GPA to even start the pledge process and I (God be thanked!) had something like a 2.79, a C+ average.

Grade point averages didn't mean a lot to me, but getting into a fraternity did. I eagerly filled out the letter for the pledge period and turned it in. Soon some of the fraternity members came by to visit and remarked, "Well, you do have the grade point average needed to get into a fraternity." I was able to pledge the Omega Psi Phi Fraternity.

That turned out to be a bad decision. The pledge period was an arduous and perplexing time. This period of my life stands as an example of my desperation to become one of the "in" crowd. The decision to join that fraternity remains a monument to my immaturity and lack of good sense. I lasted the eight weeks of the pledge period, but just barely.

My mother had given me the $125 required for the pledge dues. She had earned that money from her job at the school cafeteria. (My daddy, as you can imagine, had not been approached for the money.) Once she gave me that money, I was committed to pledging the fraternity. I swear that if she had not given me that money, I would have gotten off that fraternity pledge line as fast as I could.

Unfortunately for me, though, once committed I felt honor-bound to follow through on my pledge. But soon, with dismay, I found that the fraternity's ideology grossly differed from mine and perhaps even from the ideology of all that is decent. However, I had never been a quitter, and so I stuck the pledge period out, doing all sorts of pointless and crazy things. New college students and their families need to have some idea of what they might be in for in pledging a fraternity. If recent publicized reports are an indicator, nothing much has changed.

Unlike all other events in my life so far, I was unable to draw on the strength and cunning of my friends or family. I was too ashamed to let my family know what was going on with my fraternity pledge activities, though, and I knew my mother would have come to the school and pulled me out immediately if she had known. I could not have handled the embarrassment.

My original reasons for wanting to become a fraternity member seemed logical—at least according to the logic of an eighteen-year-old boy. I wanted to become a member because I wanted so very much to belong to some organization. I felt I had somehow missed out on a lot in high school because I had to work after school instead of participating in extracurricular activities. I wanted to be recognized as being someone special, a standout.

Omega had the reputation of having a difficult pledge term. Tony, one of the members, convinced me that this would be something good for me, a badge of honor. Tony had married my sister Nancy two years earlier, and I looked up to him and trusted his opinion. The Omegas appealed to me because they appeared to be flamboyant, flashy, and the most decorated of all the fraternities on campus. This was in direct contrast to my personality; however, I felt that a change in my own outlook was well overdue.

My pledge period for the Omega Psi Phi fraternity proved to be one of the most challenging tasks I would encounter during my college years. This endeavor almost cost me my dream of becoming a dentist.

After the first week of the pledge period, I quickly learned I did not need this "honor." Mother had given me her hard-earned money to join this organization, and yet its values seemed to repudiate her every teaching.

From day one the hazing started. The six pledges had been instructed to clean the shower and restroom of the living quarters of several fraternity members. The fraternity quarters looked good from the outside. The inside told a different story, however. The interior looked as if it had been struck by a hurricane. Beer bottles littered the floor, and dirty laundry was draped on every available piece of furniture in the common living area. In the middle of the kitchen sat a table supported on one end by concrete blocks. Around the table sat six chairs. Two of them had broken backs. I surmised that these chairs were probably broken as a result of the wild all night parties that I had heard occurred every weekend. The kitchen sink was piled high with dirty dishes, pots, and pans, and even bits of leftover food. The garbage can overflowed with beer cans and liquor bottles. The whole place had a pervasive stench of dirty clothes, rotten food, and sour liquor that made my stomach turn.

As we six pledges marched one by one into this filthy house, we were told by our pledge director, "Pretty Boy" Johnson, "I want this place polished clean enough to eat off the floors in one hour." He clicked his stopwatch and disappeared behind a closed door without further ado. I tossed at his retreating back a "you've got to be joking" grin and let my eyes follow him until the door closed shut.

Without a word, half of us started working in the kitchen, and the other half began to clean the showers. My fellow pledges and workers were strangers to me. We spoke only when there was a need to communicate something about the task at hand. Although eager to pick their brains for information about the pledgeship, I worked silently, scrubbing away at the metal walls of the shower stalls. There were six shower stalls and two commodes—which ran water continuously—located in the far corner of the room. The showers appeared not to have been cleaned in days or possibly months. Around the drains, green mildew had turned black like soot from a chimney. I could tell from the huge dust bunnies located in the bathroom corners that the place had not been swept in more than thirty days. (I had learned from mama that it took about thirty days for a dust bunny to grow, and these dust bunnies were gigantic.) There were more than a few of these fat balls of dust located in every crack of the entire house.

I completed the wall-washing detail and moved onto scrubbing the floors with a toothbrush the big brothers had so generously supplied. As we proceeded to clean the area, we were called one by one, ushered into a back room, and beaten with a wooden board for no apparent reason except to remind us to have more humility. The big brothers of the fraternity proclaimed that we were too cocky and arrogant. They decreed that we needed to be taught a lesson in true humility and respect.

Although I was still new enough in the pledge period to accept this, it troubled me. The idea of being beaten without an explainable reason was abhorrent to me. I had every intention of retaliating but that did not seem like the time. I was with five people whom I barely knew, and we were all in shock. We looked at each other in disbelief. We silently agreed to let things ride for the moment, but our eyes promised a reckoning at some future date.

Shortly afterwards, the six of us discussed the incident and began to become acquainted with each other. We quickly decided that our survival hinged on our becoming a tight, cohesive group, with our own hierarchy and code of honor.

One of the six was O.J. Jones, a senior business major. O.J. seemed to know more about the fraternity members than any of us, and so we elected him president of the group. Omega pledges were referred to as Lamps. O.J. was the shortest pledge, and so he became "Lamp number one." I was next in height and became "Lamp number two." "Lamp number three" was Keith Brown. He had been reared in an environment similar to mine, and I quickly grew close to him. "Lamp number four" was William (Goon) Jackson, a Fort Valley native. "Lamp number five," Lorenzo Rushing, was not officially included as a pledge for some reason I cannot recall. So the fraternity pledged him "underground," against school rules. "Lamp number six," Ethan Bell, was the most talented and did most of the singing and artwork for the group. The six of us bonded

together, trying to make the best of a bad situation. We became known as
"Six the Hard Way."

My brother-in-law Tony had told me he thought this would be good
for me; he had neglected to mention the physical and mental abuse.
Somehow he knew that I never would have joined the fraternity if he had
imparted that knowledge. He also knew that I never started anything
without seeing it to completion. With this in mind I somehow rose to the
occasion.

During the day we had a list of jobs to do for the "big brothers." This
left very little time to attend classes, and I soon found myself slipping
behind in chemistry and anatomy, two core courses for pre-dental majors.
Failing these two courses would have been devastating, a bigger setback to
my college career than having to take remedial courses.

I went to Dr. Black, my anatomy instructor, and begged for permission to drop anatomy or be given an incomplete grade for his course. In
denying my request, Dr. Black stated that I needed to decide what my primary purpose in coming to school was. Was it to get an education, or was
it to pledge the Omega Psi Phi Fraternity?

I then took my plea to Dr. Canty, my chemistry instructor, whose class
I was also failing. Dr. Canty was a member of the Omega Psi Phi fraternity, and I knew he would understand. Even he had no mercy or pity on
me. His reply was the same as Dr. Black's.

Neither one of these men could have known just how torn apart I was
over this. I wanted so much to pass these courses (what else had I come to
college for?), but I just felt obligated to make the fraternity because of my
mother's financial sacrifice and because of my own stubbornness.

At the end of the semester I found myself in one big mess—two Ds.
Until this point I had never received a "D" in a course in my life! Sure, the
fraternity had study time set aside every afternoon in the library. However
this time seemed to be a prime opportunity for the big brothers to find us,
make threats, and pass out work assignments for that night or the next day.

Scholarship was one of the cardinal principles of the group; however,
very little attention was paid to that. During pledgeship, I witnessed inci-
dents of books being taken away and torn up. We were constantly being
pulled out of class or made to leave the library early.

In an effort to fight back, I became defiant—and cunning. One day
Big Brother Grip asked to borrow my car. I answered, "Yes, Sir, Big
Brother," handing him the keys to the '63 Volkswagen that I shared with
my upperclassman sister. That car didn't take kindly to strange drivers. As

Big Brother Grip drove off, I smirked with a sense of satisfaction, because I knew that the only way to stop that car was with the emergency brake. As the little car sped toward the stop sign I could tell that Big Brother Grip was wrestling frantically to gain control of the car. I could hear shouting as he returned to the house. "Lamp Lester, you're trying to kill us!"

"The same as you're trying to do to me," I thought to myself. I knew that I would be punished severely for this offense, but at least I was being punished for something. The only thing I regretted at that moment was that I had to keep my glee internal. Smiling or laughing at that point would have only made the punishment that much worse.

One of the less-harmful jobs I was assigned was the job of doing Big Brother Grip's laundry for the entire eight weeks. Sometimes I intentionally "forgot," keeping Big Brother Grip's dirty laundry locked in the truck of my car for weeks. I'm not sure how I managed to evade punishment for that, but it gave me a little satisfaction to think of him having to wear dirty underwear.

Once our Dean of Pledges instructed me to wash his car from the bottom to the top and underneath—in thirty-two-degree weather. "Yes, Big Brother," I answered. I made a mixture of Clorox and several other chemicals that did a great job of changing that car from luminous silver to dull gray.

"What happened?" the Dean of Pledges asked.

"Sir, I've always heard that washing a car in cold weather will do that. But it should be just as pretty as ever when the weather warms up, sir." As soon as I got out of earshot, I started laughing. I was finally starting to find myself. I was laughing again. It felt good.

The beatings never stopped. I had been beaten to the point that sitting in class was uncomfortable. As soon as my body and mind adapted to the beatings, the big brothers quickly realized this and resorted to other forms of abuse, such as picking hair from my arm or burning my hand with matches or cigarettes. Once the soreness from the beatings healed, they returned to them. There seemed to be no limit to their abuse.

I stuck it out, though, and I finally became a fraternity member. The satisfaction of this "accomplishment" was bittersweet. I swore that if I ever got out of this, I would do everything in my power to warn others about fraternity hazing during the pledge period. Some things aren't worth the cost.

Meeting Kimberly

In the winter of my sophomore year in college, I met the girl who would cause me to stop searching for happiness and complete my life. That winter I met the woman who was to become my wife.

One Parents' Day, after the event was over and the crowds had dispersed, John's roommate Norton approached me. "Joe, meet my girl, Kim," he stated, smiling with pleasure.

But it was my pleasure! Standing there was a princess. Long, jet-black hair grazed her shoulders, her smile further accenting her beauty as she sat down gracefully on the cafeteria steps. Our eyes met briefly. I was poleaxed. I struggled to keep from staring, because this was Norton's girl, and Norton was my good friend. Still, I couldn't help casting glances at this cool, assured beauty sitting so near me. After meeting her, I simply could not get her off my mind.

Later that night in what had become a nightly ritual, Norton, John, Greg, and I gathered in their room to study, swap stories, and generally "hang out" together. Even though I now had a lot of new friends in the fraternity, I preferred hanging with John and Greg. I had known these two all of my life, and we were still inseparable.

Norton was a welcome "extra" in our group. Norton always had plenty of girls—hence his status as a welcome "extra." He had the gift of being confident around women while not appearing boastful. Norton was what we called "cool." A smooth talker, always well-dressed and well-groomed, his hair was cut neatly, parted on the side, and combed to the back. And unlike my hair, his hair stayed right where it was combed. Despite his not-overconfident demeanor, he was in fact quite proud of himself and was especially proud of being from Atlanta.

Tonight, I had more to do than just "hang," though. I intended to test the waters, to find out just how involved Norton and "that girl" were. "Norton, that girl from Atlanta is nice," I said, testing the waters.

"She's OK," Norton replied modestly.

"You better take good care of this one or somebody's going to take her," I cracked (as if this was a joke!).

"If you think you can take her, go ahead," Norton answered with confidence.

John and Greg started to laugh, and I could feel my hackles rising. John loved competition of any kind, and he and Greg were having a ball with the discussion between Norton and me.

"Les! Les! Big Les!" John laughed, slapping Greg's hand, giving him "five."

"Big fraternity man going to work already," Greg roared!

Uncharacteristically, I felt that this laughter coming from my long-time friends seemed to have some deeper meaning, a meaning I couldn't fathom. Had some change taken place in our friendship that I was not aware of? Their reaction seemed disloyal to me.

Norton smiled at their antics but did not seem to find the same amount of humor in the incident as John and Greg. Neither did I.

I left the room that night feeling somehow betrayed. I thought for weeks about this issue. Had my friends changed, or had I? Since pledging Omega I did feel more confident about myself; I was not shy as I had been in the past.

Gradually, things became clear to me. I had changed, and this change was good for me. I did suffer some angst that, however good the change in me, it might adversely affect our friendship. This was not the case, of course, although things were uneasy with the four of us for a time.

I learned from that incident that life is about change and there is no growth without change. People can change and still be in touch with their goals. As for me, I knew myself now better than ever. I wanted to see Kim, but my conscience would not let me subvert a friendship for personal gain. So I put my dream on the back burner, although Kim was never far from my thoughts.

Winter strolled quickly by, then left with a last gasp of cold and rain. The campus lawn became lush and green, and the trees displayed their spring colors. The birds chirped constantly, and their cheerful sounds confirmed that spring was in the air.

Spring is my favorite season, I thought, a season to plant and grow, my mind automatically moving back to the farm. I didn't know it then, but this spring would be a time of great growth for me. This would be the season that I would again meet Kim.

I did not get around to taking freshman orientation until my sophomore year in college. I had somehow missed it in my freshman year. Since I already felt well oriented, I was not thrilled by the prospect of spending an hour a week learning about Fort Valley State, a place I by then knew better than the back of my hand. Freshman orientation was required, however, and so I resolved to go.

The first class was scheduled on Wednesday, which was also Fraternity Dress Day. So I wore my green prom suit, a gift from Annie Nell from her store in Florida. I can still remember how good-looking I thought I was wearing that suit! I felt like a peacock in all its glory.

It must be true that self-confidence is one of the keys to being attractive. As I sat in class trying very hard to look distinguished and not like a freshman, I felt a soft tap on my shoulder. I turned my head, peeking back to see who was tapping. A pair of sparkling eyes and a warm smile met my look. "Hey!" she whispered. It was Kim, prettier than ever.

"What are you doing in here?" she asked in a low silky voice. "This is freshman orientation."

"What are you doing in here?" I replied.

"I don't know. Looking for you, I guess. You are so c-r-a-z-y," she responded, in a voice that could melt the polar ice cap. With the ice thus broken (melted?), I felt instantly comfortable talking to Kim. This was something of a challenge, though, since we were supposed to be listening to the freshman orientation lecture! During the lecture we managed to share a brief, whispered conversation.

After class, I saw Norton in the recreation center. I called out to him. I couldn't wait to tell him the news. As he walked toward me, I bellowed, "I am in the class with your girl!"

"If you're talking about Kim, she ain't my girl anymore. We broke up," he said with a scowl.

Immediately I thought, Well, when opportunity knocks, one should answer.

To Norton, I said, "Well, I guess you don't mind me talking to her then."

"Whatever," Norton answered, waving his hand in annoyance.

It's an understatement that I looked forward to attending the next week's class. What I wore to this class was more important than what I wore on Fraternity Dress Day, and I tried my best to dress to impress. I put on one of the shirts and ties I usually reserved for dress-up day. I wanted desperately to wear my green suit, but I had just worn it the previous week. So the new shirt and tie would just have to do. I had a little trouble choosing the tie but finally decided that the brown one with stripes seemed to be the right choice.

As I entered the classroom, I was happy to see no one sitting in the seat in front of Kim. Kim was wearing blue jeans that fit like a sock on a soft drink bottle. Her hair was down and curled at the ends. Her roommate Bren was sitting right behind Kim. I got the impression that she had been giving Kim lots of encouragement.

Kim smiled a pleasant hello, and I struggled to reply. It was as though that tie had turned into a noose. I tried not to appear overjoyed that she had spoken to me. Immediately I started trying to nonchalantly find out some things.

"How are you and Norton doing?" I asked.

"Oh, you know Norton," she replied. I nodded in consent. "Well, we broke up."

It felt great hearing this for the second time. "Well, I guess I can come over and see you," I said, being careful to put my question into a statement.

"Sure, I'm in Moore Hall," she answered.

For a second I forgot I was in class. It's no wonder that I got a "C" in freshman orientation, because I paid more attention to Kim than to the professor. However, the relationship I started with Kim was well worth the "C."

From that day it was rare to see one of us without the other. Kim and I were inseparable. We developed a bond that still keeps us very close today.

It seems that Norton and Kim's relationship wasn't quite as "over" as Norton indicated to me, though. Norton came over to Kim's dorm one night to try to get her back. It turned out that both of us had paged her at the dorm. When both Norton and I showed up at the same time, both of us stood there, looking at each other bemusedly, each wondering which girl the other one was coming to see.

Kim came down, blithely waved at Norton, and left with me. The girls in the dorm looked out their windows and smiled as Kim and I walked away from the dorm. "Child, y'all in love. You got him, girl." I'm not sure just what Norton did after that.

Having Kim as part of my life meant adjustments in mine, of course. I was glad to make them. To have room for Kim in my life was well worth it. I was working at Shoney's and would bring her some of their strawberry pie after work. Sometimes I would cook at the trailer for Kim and her friends, especially Bren.

I cut way back on my basketball playing, because Kim and I were now spending evenings together. John and Greg would come to the trailer to get me sometimes though, because the three of us were still a team. Kim and I spent a lot of evenings walking in the trailer park, just walking and holding hands and not saying much of anything. We were just happy to spend time together.

If I had any doubts that Kim felt the same towards me, I soon had them put to rest. Some days Kim would catch a ride to Shoney's to see me at work. She and Bren would come in and order food that they never touched, making casual conversation with me as I flew by their table. It only took me a minute to figure that out! Also, some nights after dorm hours were over, I would sling rocks up at her third-floor window to get her to come out. I did not have to sling many, though, because she was generally up, looking out the window, waiting for me.

Eventually it got pretty difficult to leave one another, even for a few days. Her mother did not have to pick her up at school anymore, because I started giving her a ride home on weekends and summers. This gave us just a few more hours together before we had to part. Even a weekend was getting to be too long to be away from each other.

My fraternity brothers would sometimes tease me, saying, "She's got you under lock and key," but I did not pay them any attention. I knew I had a good thing. I suspected that they were jealous that they did not have a girl as pretty and as faithful as mine.

Kim and I were good for each other. Even our grades improved when we started dating. I helped her with her math, and she gave me inspiration to keep running toward my goal of becoming a dentist. I studied harder than I ever had and finally took my grades seriously.

I introduced her to my mother that spring during Parents' Week. After meeting her, my mother said, "Joe, I think this girl is crazier about you than any girl ever has been."

"And I her, Mother," I remember saying, feeling worldly-wise.

Since Daddy was a constant no-show at Parent Days, Kim and I traveled to Hawkinsville so she could meet him. Daddy thought Kim was in high school. He made some remark like, "What grade are you in, child?" Mother made him aware that Kim was in college, not in high school. I think that both my mother and father were elated that I had brought Kim home. My sister Gwyn was elated that I had just brought a girl home. For once, Gwyn had a college girl to show off, and she wasn't even related to her!

I was sitting on top of the world. Although I had felt attracted to many women and had had that attraction reciprocated, I had never had a special girlfriend before, not like Kim. Now I had met the girl of my life. In addition to that, I had joined a fraternity, school was going OK, and I was headed toward accomplishing my dream of becoming a dentist.

But as things turned out, God had sent Kim to me just in time. Not long after we met, a tragedy struck that would have toppled me off the mountain I was standing on, had it not been for her.

17
We Lose Mother

In the fall of 1978, I got a phone call telling me to come home. Mother was sick. I took this information very calmly because Mother had never really been sick before, except for an occasional headache. I suspect we children were usually the source of that. I really thought my mother was untouchable, invincible. I was sure nothing was seriously wrong with her.

I didn't hurry home that day because I had a fraternity meeting and some other odds and ends to do. I was a junior now and following a path of my own despite Mother's warning to stay in close touch with the family. So it was the weekend before I finally went home.

When I got out of the car, I did as I usually did. I walked straight past my mother's house down to Boot's house, which was right next to Mother and Daddy's house. When I finished greeting and "catching up" with Boot, I came back up to see about Mother.

When I went into the house, Mother said, "Joe, I noticed that you walked right by the house and went to Boot's house for a visit before coming to talk to me. I could have cancer or something."

I pretty much blew that off. I was in the prime of my life, I reasoned. Mother was young and had always been healthy. So there couldn't be much wrong with her. I was carefree, really living, glad to be out of the house. So I pretty much ignored the warning signals that weekend.

A couple of weeks later, I got another call to come home. Mother's condition had worsened, and she had to be hospitalized. The feelings of complacency I had the past weekend came back to haunt me.

Even with the sure knowledge that Mother would never have consented to being hospitalized unless something serious were happening, I continued to work hard until the end of the school day. By this time, I had started working at Shoney's part-time after school and was busier than ever. That day, however, I went to the hospital instead of to work. One of my siblings had told me that Mother had had surgery the day before. I didn't ask what kind of surgery. I didn't want to know.

When Kim and I at last arrived at the hospital, we found Mother sitting in a wheelchair next to the window of her room. Oh, it's just a routine precaution after surgery, I thought foolishly. But I could barely stand to look at her that way. I was so uncomfortable I think I looked at the ceiling, floor, and walls more than I looked at her. What I did see managed to put a cold fear into my heart. Mother looked as though she had lost at least thirty pounds.

When time came for us to leave, Mother said, "Don't leave yet, honey. I want you to rub my legs." I found the lotion and rubbed her legs for her. Somehow I suppose Mother knew that if she didn't ask for that personal contact from me, I would not give it. I just wasn't able to cope with the sight of her looking so tired, frail, and vulnerable in that wheelchair.

By this time Mother must have known her illness was terminal, but I did not know. She must have decided not to say anything about that yet. I don't think she shared the fact of her terminal cancer with anyone except my father and one of my older siblings. In fact, I don't remember her ever discussing her illness directly in my presence. My only knowledge of her illness was gained indirectly, through other family members. Our only sure knowledge came near the very end.

Still, I can't believe how little attention I paid to the signs I saw that day. In hindsight, I know this was a form of denial. Subconsciously I felt that as long as I did not openly acknowledge that Mother was actually dying I could somehow make everything all right again. It takes a little of the sting out of my guilt to remind myself that I had no reason to believe that Mother would ever get cancer. Mother didn't smoke or drink, and she wasn't over-weight. Except for the occasional headache, she had never even been ill. The only thing she had ever been hospitalized for was for Gwyn's birth some sixteen years before. I recalled that the two of them had nearly died then. My mind blazing with such thoughts, Kim and I left and hurried back to school. I had a job and some studying to do.

Now I feel my time would have been better spent at the hospital with Mother. At least I was able to be with Mother the day she came home from the hospital. At least I was able to do that much.

When Mother came home from the hospital, she had my sister Mary help her walk through all the rooms, stopping at each room for a lingering look. In each room she would comment on things she would still like to do in these rooms or talk about the child the room belonged to. In many ways, she seemed to have drawn inside herself, and she gave the impression that she was listening to voices we could not hear. Perhaps even then the angels had begun to beckon her, to draw her into their delicate and comforting grasp.

Although I understood in my head that she was very sick, my heart still had not gotten the message that we were losing her. This was the first time I had seen Mother this way, the first time I had not seen her be the driving force in our household.

When I came back home next was for Thanksgiving. Mother's condition had worsened. She seemed to have aged ten years in the past four weeks. She had to use a cane to get around. Mother had had a really bad time the night before, and Daddy asked me to help him to take her into town to see Dr. Smith, her physician. Since Mother was very weak and was unable to sit up, Daddy called Dr. Smith and begged him to come out to the house to see about Mother.

Daddy explained to Dr. Smith how weak and sick Mother was. He pleaded with him to make a house call so Mother would not have to make the trip in the car to his office. Daddy promised he would pay him whatever fee he asked if he would just "come out and see about my wife."

Hearing my father talk so submissively to that white man on the phone angered me. How helpless we were when it came to taking care of our loved ones!

Even as I heard Daddy's end of the phone call, I knew what the answer would be. I remember thinking, Daddy doesn't know any better, but that white man ain't leaving his rich white patients at his office to come out here in the country to see one of us. And it turned out that that was true. We would have to get Mother to the doctor's office somehow.

I stifled my anger. No matter how I felt about Dr. Smith personally, this man had saved mother's life once—when she was pregnant with Gwyn—and he was our only hope now. So I helped Daddy get Mother in the car and drove them both to the doctor's office. When we got there, I could not help noticing the separate black and white waiting rooms. I had forgotten this, assuming this despicable tradition had changed since the last time I had been in this office. I was very wrong.

We waited a long time to see the doctor. As we waited, Daddy supporting Mother on one side and I on the other, I watched to see whether another old practice was still in place. To my disbelief and silent disgust, I realized that, as usual, Dr. Smith saw his white patients first and took his time doing so, too. After finally being called in, I realized with a sinking heart that our long wait had been a waste of time.

After a brief examination of Mother, Dr. Smith called my father outside the examination room. Dr. Smith confirmed that Mother had indeed taken a turn for the worse. My father asked earnestly, "Isn't there anything you can do?" Dr. Smith could only shake his head in hopelessness. He told us to take Mother back home and make her as comfortable as possible.

Not too long after Mother's visit to Dr. Smith and about two weeks before Christmas of 1978, we lost her.

I was prepared for ridicule about my big dreams and ambition. I was prepared for getting by with little money. I was prepared to work hard. I was prepared for the ugliness of racism. I had even thought of my own mortality and was prepared if I were to be a victim of the sting of death. But I was not prepared for the loss of my mother.

Death was not new to me. I had watched my Mother grieve the death of my grandparents. Many of the older people in our community had died. Why, when Mrs. Sweet Brown died, I remember missing her and complaining to Mother over the phone! When old Mrs. Peevy died, Mama and Daddy went to her funeral, but we kids never stopped playing long enough to cause a bother. But these were elderly women, sick and feeble, and expected to pass on.

I had even gone so far, growing up, as to visualize the death of my parents. Strangely enough, I had always pictured that Daddy would die first because of his evil ways and mistreatment of Mother. I imagined how peaceful her life would be without him around to torment and abuse her. On some dark days, when his mistreatment of our mother was too much to bear, I would have welcomed his death. But nothing could have prepared me for my mother's passing. This was the biggest loss of my life. I could not have realized just how big a loss it was until she was actually gone. To this day I remember her saying to one person in the family or another, "You all are going to miss me when I'm gone," and we never took that very seriously. But she knew—and she was right.

Her admonition to me as I left for college rang in my head. "Put on the whole armor of God, Joe Nathan. Put on the whole armor of God." This is the way Mother had lived her life, wearing the whole armor of God, and I could only think that perhaps God took her because he needed another saint in heaven.

Just before Mother's passing, Keith and I had traveled to the Medical College of Georgia to visit the dental school. Even though I was still in denial about the severity of her illness, I had a feeling of foreboding about this trip, a premonition that I shouldn't go. I told Mother that I would cancel the trip if she were feeling worse. Her reply was so typical of her: "Go ahead on and check out the school." By this time, I think she knew she was not going to be around much longer, and she wanted me to continue to concentrate on my goals, unselfishly downplaying her own future.

If only I had known the extent of her illness. If only I had faced more squarely the fact that her time was so near! I would like to have a second chance to spend more time talking with her about trivial things, things that mean so much to me now that she's gone. I can take comfort in the fact that my mother loved me deeply in spite of my "warts and bumps."

Losing her changed me in some essential ways. Staying in touch with the family became more important to me than ever before.

Although hugs were not a big part of my family's interaction with each other, I find myself wishing I had hugged her more and said "I love you" more often. Memories of those hugs we did share seem so important now. In particular, I dwell on the day I left for college. Had I known what was to come so soon, I would have said to hell with tradition and given her the great big hug I ended up withholding from her then. Yes, I know that my mother knew how much I really loved her and understood my macho attitude that day, but that knowledge doesn't stop the ache or fill the empty void her death left.

Mother's life was snuffed out at the age of fifty-four. Of course, to my nineteen-year old mind, fifty-four seemed old. But Mother died far too young. However, her teachings and her motivation continue to live on and remain the driving force in the family to this day.

I think losing Mother was the second time I had seen my daddy cry. He had always been a brick wall, an invincible battlement. His showing such deep emotion at losing her was visible evidence of what my siblings and I had always suspected: Daddy loved my mother with all his heart.

Mother's death brought us all closer together. True to mother's training, we came together and took care of first things first. There was no life insurance, and so we pooled our money to pay for the funeral service and burial.

After Mother's death, Gwyn inherited the car she had driven back and forth to work. She also inherited the care of Daddy. The only one living at home at the time, Gwyn valiantly tried to pick up where Mother left off. That was a huge, overwhelming burden for a young girl who had just celebrated her sixteenth birthday. We all attempted to pick up our own lives and live as normally as possible, but there was no filling up the empty space in ours lives that Mother's death had left.

After Mother's death, some things started to fall apart. Our house itself serves as a good example of the loss of the binding influence she had on all of us. She had started to paint the back portion of the house and did not get an opportunity to complete it. The mark where Mother stopped painting is still just as it was as when she stopped painting in 1978. I do not think Daddy did any more painting on the back of the house after her death. None of us had the heart to complete the job Mother had begun.

Daddy went through a grieving process during this time, although he never shared it with any of us, not even Gwyn. He also went through several financial crises, which he did at least share with us. To keep him from losing the land that was our family's heritage, my older brothers and sisters put money together to help him pay off his farming and other accumulated debts. Even though the farm as a business did not have any financial value to Daddy or us by this time, none of us wanted to give up the place we called home.

None of us realized how close to the edge our finances had always been until then. Mother had done the budgeting and financial planning. Until her death, the farm had never run into any financial crisis. Even though I was aware that funds were often low, we never really experienced hardship until after Mother's death. And Daddy seemed helpless. Before, I had seen him as harsh, demanding, headstrong, and stubborn. Now he seemed only helpless.

The house continued to deteriorate. Home just was not home anymore. The laughter of mother's enveloping love, the smell of food, the neat look of the clean-swept yard—we lost all these things when we lost Mother.

Naturally, Mother's passing affected the lives of her grandchildren, too. Up until this time, my older sister Anne and my older brother Raymond had always brought their kids to spend the summer at our house. After Mother's death, this stopped, because there was no one there to care for them.

We all missed the hymns Mother used to sing around the house as she encouraged us in those goals she helped us envision and work toward. One of her favorite hymns was, "You Don't Know What the Lord Told Me." I didn't know; but I can surely guess! I think it had to do with her taking such loving care of us and encouraging us all to stay close to God and to reach upward in life as high as we could from where we were.

Getting Down to Business

The years to come would be more challenging with my chief motivator, Mother, now gone. As I grew in an understanding of God's work, I began to realize that God does not put more on us than we can bear. I began to realize that Mother passed to me everything I needed to succeed. The one phrase I continued to hear when I faced a new challenge or set out on a new journey of learning was, "Put on the whole armor of God, Joe Nathan. Put on the whole armor of God." I began to feel ready to meet the challenges of the world, even though some days I felt as though the bottom had dropped out of my soul.

I became more serious about my studies. Unknowingly, I had already met another friend who would take me to the next level academically. Keith McRae had become my friend when he pledged Omega Psi Phi fraternity. He was already a dear friend at the time of Mother's passing.

Keith was a straight-A student, partly due to the fact that he studied late at night while everyone else was sleeping or partying. But he was far from being a nerd. He was a tall, dark, and handsome lady's man. His skin was smooth as silk, with a voice to match. He sported a well-groomed beard and always kept a little money in his pocket. All the girls at school thought he was good-looking. Me, I admired his intelligence and was quite impressed by the fact that his brothers were already well-to-do doctors. More than just being my friend, Keith was the hookup to the future that I needed. He inspired me to go straight toward the dental school door. What helped greatly in our friendship is that he and I shared the same intention—getting into dental school.

On one occasion, Keith told me how he realized I wasn't just a jokester but that I really was a good student. He also thanked me for looking out for him during the fraternity pledge period. From then on, there was a strong bond between us. I used our bond to improve my study habits and my grades.

Keith knew where he was going. He knew he was going to dental school, and he knew he would be accepted to the Medical College of Georgia because his brothers were alumni. One brother was a dentist, one of the first two black students to attend the School of Dentistry at the Medical College of Georgia. Another brother was a surgeon, having been a straight-A student at the Medical College of Georgia. Still another brother was an obstetrician-gynecologist.

Keith had the self-assurance that comes from not having any doubts about the future. I didn't have this advantage. But I did have Keith.

For almost every quarter of the last two years of college, I maintained a 3.0 average. I can partly attribute this to my friendship with Keith. Keith maintained a 4.0 average, but he downplayed his own academic achievement while pulling me along behind him. He even defended me from the other students' ridicule as I filled out my applications for admission to dental school. It seems that a large majority of the other students in my class thought I didn't have a prayer of getting into dental school. However, Keith had faith that somehow, some way, he was going to pull me in with him.

Keith's determination placed the conviction even more firmly in my mind that I was going to make it. Until I hooked up with Keith, getting into dental school was more like a challenge, just an unspecified feeling. How I'd do it, I did not know. Keith's unwavering faith in me helped to transform that dream into a reality, and I am indebted to him for that.

I now feel that God Himself was instrumental in bringing Keith into my life at that precise period in time. I have no other explanation for the fact that I met him so soon after Mother's death. He was truly a mentor to me.

Of course, Kim believed in me. And of course I believed in myself. But the real turning point came when I found someone else who believed in my dream as much as I did and also knew specifically how to go about realizing that dream. This encouragement gave me the impetus to do the best I could.

For the first time in my life, I started to actually study. Before then, I was pretty much satisfied with listening in class, taking a few notes, and then showing up for the next test. A passing grade was my main goal. But it seemed that now I wanted much more than to just "pass"; I wanted to excel.

Once I reached this mind-set, Keith capitalized on it. He began to insist that I accompany him almost every night to the library or to his house to study.

His guidance came just in time. I was on the edge of disaster. I had made two Ds while in the pledge process with the fraternity, because I had not attended any classes during that time. Making things worse, while at work at Shoney's I had done little or no studying, especially during the pledge period, when I had done no studying at all. I just went to class (when I could) and then left.

Although Keith was my main mentor at this time, other "angels" also took me under their wings. It was about this time that I ran into Mrs. Palmer, an instructor at the college. She was about thirty-five, kind of "jazzy" for her age, I thought with my nineteen-year old mind. Mrs. Palmer taught French. She had taken an interest in another friend and me because the fraternity we were pledging to was the brother fraternity to her sorority, Delta Sigma Theta.

So far I had not been able to pass the Regent's test, which was the required exit exam to graduate from college. The exam was separated into a reading and a written part. I had passed the reading part, but I could not pass the written part because my grammar and spelling were poor. I don't believe I could have even spelled the word "dentist" at that time.

At any rate, Mrs. Palmer decreed that she was going to help me improve my spelling and sentence structure. She instructed me to write her a report on the ERA (Equal Rights Amendment). Although I was more than willing to accept her help, I was baffled by the assignment. I had no idea what the ERA was, and I did not want to make myself look foolish by asking her. She must have picked up on this immediately, because she looked at me, shook her head, and said, "Lester, you've got a long way to go, and I think I've got my work cut out for me."

She told me to go to the library, read a couple of articles every day, and find an article I wanted to write about. When I found it, I was to write a three-paragraph essay and bring it by her office. She would critique it for me. I did as instructed, at least once a week.

Another instructor also helped me in my progression as a student. Dr. Whitlock was one of the few white female instructors in the Science Department. She was another angel who decided I was worth salvaging and took me under her wing.

I vividly recall a biology seminar in which the other students were doing work related to the seminar. In contrast, Dr. Whitlock had me learning vocabulary words, unbeknownst to the other students, to help me catch up. Dr. Whitlock also encouraged me to take all of the classes she offered. She gave me extra help in those classes. She even loaned me her car a few times when mine had broken down!

If there are such things as angels, then I surely feel as though I have had my share of them. If there are such things as blessings, surely I have been living off the blessings and prayers of someone.

I became obsessed with going to dental school. I started carrying, everywhere, a little book that had pictures of teeth in it. I was still working at Shoney's, and I took this book and others to work, studying them every opportunity I had. This may have been something of an ego thing with me, too. It made me feel better about things to let the other workers know that I would only be working there for a short period of time. It seems as though I felt compelled to let them know that soon I would be going on to bigger, better, and greater things.

Up until this time, Mrs. Craft, who was the manager at Shoney's, had teased me about my cooking. I'll admit that I wasn't one of the better cooks in Shoney's history. But it seemed that once she found out that I was becoming a better student, she started to slack off on the teasing. After most of the cooks I worked with at Shoney's moved on, I became the Senior Cook. Mrs. Craft actually began to give me a little respect. Of course, I was still trying my best to improve as a cook, and I believe she noticed that, too.

Once the regional manager came by to do an inspection. Mrs. Craft told us that he would also observe our cooking on the line, the "acid test" of my slowly improving skills. That night I worked harder than ever—running back and forth, double-checking to make sure everything was cooked to perfection, and presenting plates that looked identical to the pictures on the menu. I still remember the thrill I felt when I found out what the regional manager's assessment of me was. As he left, he told Mrs. Craft to give me a ten-cent raise, because I was one of the better cooks in that kitchen. I was elated! Finally, I was starting to excel, at work as well as at school.

I mailed an application to just about every dental school in the country, which was a small fortune's worth of paper and postage. I saw it as an investment in the future. Others saw it as a waste of good money.

Keith was right by my side encouraging me to keep applying. The two of us took the DAT (Dental School Admission Test) together. Unlike with the SAT (Scholastic Aptitude Test), this time I prepared for the test. My spirits sank to the ground when I found out the results, though. That test, with pages upon pages of questions, was Greek to me. Neither Keith nor I faired very well, but he already had the advantage of a 3.96 GPA. Mine, on the other hand, was 2.8—nowhere near failing but not exactly confidence-boosting, either. I felt doomed once again.

Nevertheless, Keith encouraged me to continue sending those applications in. He exclaimed, "Look, man, numbers are numbers and don't reflect what you are capable of. Keep sending in those applications because there is a school somewhere that wants more than numbers. Don't give up."

Keith was accepted by the Medical College of Georgia School of Dentistry soon after he applied. He was positive I would also receive an acceptance letter any day.

I didn't give up, but I began to worry. The letter of recommendation I received from the Science Department was somewhat disappointing. With the hope that I could get a more complimentary one, I went to Dr. Green, our fraternity advisor, for help.

Dr. Green, a minister, had an impressive voice and could be very persuasive. He had the right qualifications for the job I had in mind—especially the persuasive part. I started visiting Dr. Green daily, sharing my dream with him. Dr. Green encouraged me to pray. He told me, "Prayer changes things, if it is God's will."

That night, lying in bed at the trailer, I began to think about what Dr. Green had said about prayer. During my college years, I had drifted away from the faith I had as a youngster. To me as to many of my fellow students, prayer was just another trend that had passed its time.

But I wondered just the same. Mother was always praying, but it seemed that I had given this no thought since leaving home. I remembered Mother quoting the Bible verse, "Ask, and it shall be given you; seek, and ye shall find" (Matthew 7:7). And now, here was the same example and advice coming from Dr. Green, a well-educated man who seemed to have no need to pray for anything. The comparison between the two of them seemed to shine a new light on the power of prayer. For a second, I felt the presence of someone else in the room with me. The words, "Put on the whole armor of God, Joe Nathan. Put on the whole armor of God" flashed into my mind.

I quickly passed this experience off, though. I was under a huge amount of mental pressure then, and I didn't want anyone (even me!) to think I was "losing it."

In spite of that, I decided to give that "prayer thing" a try. I desperately wanted to be accepted to dental school and intended to try every resource I had to reach that goal. If prayer was the answer, then I would pray. I knelt next to my bed as Mother had taught me and looked toward Heaven. I prayed, "Dear God, if it's your will for me to become a dentist, let your will be done. Use me as your instrument to heal the poor and under-served. I am asking you as humbly as I know how. I ask forgiveness for my all sins. Mother said that you are always watching and that you know our hearts. These blessings I ask in your son Jesus' name. Amen."

From that kneeling position, I crawled into the bed and meditated the rest of the night. It seemed, however, that this sleepless night occurred because a burden had been lifted from my shoulders rather than because of a burden being on them. Some changes were being made in my life that I never dreamed possible. To this day, I'm not sure how I knew this, I just knew.

I had given up on being accepted to the Medical College of Georgia not too long after Keith received his acceptance letter. I set my sights on my second choice, Meharry College in Nashville, Tennessee.

What I had hoped for from Dr. Green was intercession with the Science Department for a better letter of reference. What I received instead was worth so much more. The next day after my night of prayer, Dr. Green asked me to bring him the phone number for Meharry College's Admissions Office. "Now this is what I call a personal reference, Dr. Green," I said, the astonishment surely showing on my face.

Trying hard to hide his amusement, Dr. Green suggested that it might be good strategy if he used his theological title when he called the Director of Admissions at Meharry. He explained, winking his eye, "Sometimes 'Reverend' can open doors that 'Doctor' cannot open."

To my surprise, the Admissions Director, a Mr. West, was quite receptive to "Reverend" Green's call. He even told Dr. Green that my application "looked favorable." I had called Mr. West myself numerous times and had gotten very little from him, certainly never hearing the word "favorable!"

This new information lit a flame of hope for me. Impetuously, and perhaps worrying a little overmuch while waiting for the "other shoe to drop," I persuaded Dr. Green to check on my application almost every month. I suppose he had had enough of my nervousness, because one day he quietly said, "Joe, I think we have called enough. We need to leave the final decision in the hands of God. If you belong at Meharry, then God will put you there. Have a little faith."

But that good advice didn't settle my anxiety down in the slightest. I continued to check my campus mailbox daily, sometimes even on Sunday, even knowing the mail didn't come on Sunday.

For months, it seemed as if my mailbox was only cluttered with rejection letters from the numerous schools to which I had applied. On the days

I didn't receive a rejection letter, my box was filled only with junk mail. And so it went for what seemed like an eternity to me.

In the second week of February I went to the mailbox, and there it was—a letter from the Office of Admissions at Meharry School of Dentistry. I was almost afraid to retrieve it from the mailbox. I even had an irrational vision of that letter disappearing when I touched it.

When I gingerly picked up the letter, it felt heavy, as if it literally contained the entire weight of my future. In reality it did contain the weight of my future. I had waited for what seemed like eons for this letter, and now I was struggling with an almost paralyzing fear of disappointment at what its contents might reveal.

I slowly teased the letter open and peeked to see how long the letter was. I was accustomed to reading rejection letters. I knew they were very short and to the point, almost always only one page in length. I knew their format from memory, too. They all said the same thing: "Dear Sir: We appreciate you applying to our institution. However, we had many qualified applicants . . . ." After those few lines, I knew the rest of the story.

With the letter from Meharry in my hand, I prayed silently, "Dear God, please don't let this letter read that way! Help me to handle it if it does!"

After carefully opening the letter, I risked a glance at the salutation. It read, "Congratulations."

Congratulations! I had to read the word again to comprehend it. My heart seemed to skip a couple of beats and just quit beating for a moment. I could almost anticipate the next line. Words that I had been awaiting for months, words that my eyes devoured so quickly that I had to re-read them several times to be sure they were actually on that page. "Congratulations, you have been conditionally accepted to Meharry Medical College School of Dentistry. You must complete nine semester hours in physics."

No problem, no problem at all! I was already enrolled in the second quarter of physics and had an "A" average in it. No need to take part three of physics. I think I jumped ten feet off the ground!

In my excitement, I failed to pay any attention to the fact that Meharry was on semester hours and Fort Valley was on the quarter system. All I knew was that I had ten hours of physics, and I didn't care to take any course that I did not need. In my excitement I had blanked that "conditional" right off the letter.

But even later, I didn't care. If they had wanted me to stand on my head and sing, I would have, and I would have done the best job of it they had ever seen. I was in!

Suddenly I realized that people were staring, but again, I didn't care. This was the happiest moment of my life. I didn't care who knew. As a matter of fact, I wanted everyone to know.

I immediately raced to the Science department to share the good news, arriving too breathless to tell anyone. I had to let people read the letter themselves. My instructors were dumbfounded. They never thought I would get in. From Fort Valley, only students with a 3.0 GPA or better had gotten accepted in the past to medical and dental programs. Most students with less than 3.0 didn't even apply. They were usually steered into the teaching field or encouraged to change their field of study. At one point, they had even encouraged me to take some classes in marine biology!

Today was my day. I was the talk of the department.

I hurried to find Kim. She was in class in another building. I hurried to her classroom door and held the letter up to the door's window. She stood up smiling and raced toward me. My face proclaimed the good news that she and I had been hoping to hear for such a long time.

I picked her up and kissed her. "Baby we are in! I have been accepted by Meharry, and you have to go with me." I didn't realize that this amounted to a proposal of marriage. But Kim knew, and, of course, I didn't mind. In fact, later I was glad it happened that way.

I wanted her with me through dental school. I didn't think I could make it through dental school without her right there by my side—and I still don't think I could have made it without her. We stood there in the hallway hugging each other for minutes.

By now Kim was crying tears of joy, and I was doing my manly best to hold my tears back. Now I could allow myself to acknowledge my fear that I wouldn't get accepted anywhere. In my darkest moments I had only continued to push forward because of the support of this woman whom I now held in my arms.

After the first rush of emotions, I said a silent prayer of thanks to God. It was then I remembered that I had more people to thank. I didn't rest until I had told Dr. Green, of course, and then followed by giving my family the good news. Keith was equally excited that we would attend dental school together. It didn't even matter that we would be attending different schools.

What a wonderful day!

⟨⟨⟨⟨⟨⟨⟨⟨⟨⟨⟨⟨ *19* ⟩⟩⟩⟩⟩⟩⟩⟩⟩⟩⟩⟩

One Quick Step—Backward

Of course, this personal triumph still didn't mean that I had all the good sense or maturity I needed. I will never forget the date—February 14, 1980—which was anything but a wonderful day.

That weekend, Keith and I went out on the campus to celebrate our new success. I was invited to a "slumber party" given by the Deltas (our sister sorority). Kim was upset that I was going to go to this party because we rarely did anything apart from each other and there would be girls, girls, girls there. The rules of these parties forbade non-members from attending, and so there was no way Kim could go with me. I wasn't thrilled about the idea of going without Kim, but I felt duty-bound to go. They were our "sisters," and all the brothers in the fraternity were going.

Kim accepted my explanation a little huffily. "You have to go because all of the other brothers are going. I suppose if the other brothers stuck their heads in the fire you would too? You want to go because you think the girls there will throw themselves at you, and they probably will. The world will not stop spinning on its axis if you don't show up. If you go and get skunk drunk and sick, don't expect me to feel sorry for you, and don't expect me to clean up your mess. You will soon be leaving for dental school, and this frat thing won't be important then."

In the end, she said she'd decided it wasn't important enough to keep disagreeing about. At any rate, Kim and Paige, Keith's girlfriend, made plans to stay at my mobile home while Keith and I went to the party.

I certainly wish Kim had been with me in view of what happened. She was right about what happened. By way of celebrating my good news, true to Kim's prediction I got drunk as a skunk. I drank gin, beer, vodka, and anything else liquid that passed my way, and I added a few things I had to go and get.

To put it in the college vernacular, "Boy, did I party that night!" What actually happened, though, was that my world began to spin, and I began to reel on my feet. Keith later said that after I moaned the fourth time, "Man, I don't feel so good," he bodily stuffed me into his car and drove me home. The whole trip he was praying I would not upchuck all over the interior of his car.

When we got back to my trailer, Keith asked Kim to help him get me out of the car. She wouldn't. She was still angry that I had gone to the party, and she was appalled to see the shape I'd come home in.

"You took him there, so he is your responsibility," she told Keith, and not in a very nice way.

Angry because Kim wouldn't help, he said, "That's OK, I'll take care of him myself!" So Keith dragged me on back to the bedroom, undressed me, and placed me on the bed.

Ten minutes later I'm told I was out of that bed, stumbling down the hall of the trailer into the living room, jaybird naked. I fell into the middle of the floor, right in front of where Kim and Paige were sitting on the couch.

Kim had decided to let natural consequences take over. She just rolled her eyes at me and sat there, never lifting a finger.

"The bed's spinning, the bed's spinning!" I kept saying. Kim didn't move a muscle or utter a word.

Paige was completely mortified. She gasped in astonishment and quickly put her hands over her face. She said something like, "Are you just gonna' let him lie there like that? Put him back to bed, Keith! Do something, Kim!" All the while I was moaning and groaning and proclaiming my imminent death.

Kim didn't do or say a thing. She just kept rolling her eyes and shaking her head at the spectacle I was making of myself there on the living room floor.

Keith put me back into the bed and pulled the trash can over near the end of the bed. I didn't know what he was doing, but I figured it out pretty quickly. The vodka and other alcoholic drinks started coming out of me all night.

Kim did stay the night but was very stingy with the pity and attention I thought I deserved due to my great suffering. When she deigned to speak, she alternated between fussing at me for doing something "so completely stupid," and breaking out in peals of laughter at my obvious agony. No sympathy there, no siree! After a while, I stopped moaning and complaining and fell into a fitful sleep.

The next morning, my head felt as though it had been run through a paper shredder. My tongue was on fire. And I didn't even want to claim ownership of my stomach. Of course, it felt as though it wasn't too thrilled to be attached to me, either. Moving off that bed took every bit of strength I had in me.

I guess that's one reason I drink very little today; I don't ever care to repeat the experience.

No matter what had happened, though, I simply could not miss school. There was too much riding on that "conditional" acceptance to Meharry, and nothing was going to stand in the way of my "full" acceptance—not even the fire-breathing dragon that had taken up residence in my body and the demon that was using a sledge hammer inside my skull.

There was no way I could get behind the wheel of a car that morning, and so my brother Jack drove me to school. Kim was sitting in the front, and I was lying in the back seat, grateful that the car had lots of room. My stomach still lurched and complained as the car swayed.

I had just about decided that I'd live when we had to stop for a train to pass. Jack couldn't resist the urge to teach me a lesson. The railroad tracks were situated on top of an incline at that crossing. Jack eased up off the brakes and let the car slowly roll back a little as the train passed by.

"Oh, don't do that! I'm sick!" I moaned, trying to cope with the strange feeling of attempting to focus with the car and the train moving in opposite directions. My hungover mind failed to signal my eyes to close, and I was being tortured with every movement. Every time I moaned, Jack pulled back up the slight incline to the tracks and eased slowly, oh so slowly, back again. "What's the matter, boy?" he'd say, "You need to learn to hold your liquor?" I prayed to live so I could kill him later.

My body was in class that day, but my mind was back in the bed. That demon never stopped pounding my skull with a sledgehammer, and so I stumbled back to bed as soon as class was over, still smelling like a distillery.

That terrible time, bad as it was, made me make some important decisions. Aside from resolving never to drink that much again, I also resolved to never do anything else that would jeopardize my chance of reaching my goal. To add to my shame in that experience, I realized I had angered Kim and risked losing her respect. I'm awfully glad Kim didn't change her mind about me after that weekend. I added another vow to the two I had already made—to always be worthy of Kim's high opinion of me.

Kimberly and I Get Married

Kimberly and I were married on June 21, 1980, with the blessings—if not the total approval—of our families. Our families' lack of full approval didn't mean they thought we weren't suited for each other. In fact, the opposite was true. Both our families thought that Kim and I were good people and that our eventual marriage would be "a match made in heaven." What they were hesitant about was the fact that we were so young and that we both had several more years of education ahead of us.

My brothers and sisters had been gently pressuring us to wait until I finished dental school before getting married. Although I saw some validity in their concerns, I felt positive that Kim was now the driving force behind me and that I would cease to exist without her. I not only loved Kim; I genuinely needed her. I saw Kim as showing the same kind of all-encompassing faith my mother had had in me, the faith that I desperately needed in order to face the huge, unknown challenges of dental school.

I wanted Kim with me, in physical presence as well as in spirit. At the same time, I would not take her away from her dream of finishing college unless I could give her the stability of marriage in return. I would not ask her to risk an interruption in her education unless I felt I had something better to offer her.

Facing this critical decision was difficult for us. If Kim stayed at Fort Valley College in Georgia and I went on to Nashville, we would both be at a disadvantage, because we would be separated. We shared the real fear that we would grow apart. On the other hand, if Kim and I married, and she went with me, there was no guarantee that she could easily transfer her credits to an out-of-state college.

We spent many late nights and early mornings discussing the pros and cons of each path. Then, one day Kim said, "This is silly. I love you, and I'm going with you! I can finish my degree by transferring to Tennessee State!"

Her words literally "made my life complete." I would never, ever have asked her to give up college. But she was willing to change schools because she loved me and because she had faith that I would make it up to her later on.

In appreciation, I made a promise to her that I would pay for any extra classes that she had to take because of the transfer. She would be able to complete her degree without interruption. Thank the good Lord, I have been able to keep my promise to her. There were several times in our marriage when the prospect of following through on my promise to her seemed bleak. But Kim was not deterred. Her life plan always included finishing her education, and she not only met but exceeded expectations when she completed her Bachelor of Social Work degree in 1982.

Apart from our youth and questionable finances, we had no doubt that our marriage would benefit us and would last. We both felt strongly that having two people wanting the same things out of life, with similar views on how to get those things, could only increase each other's possibility of success. We had the ingredients for a successful marriage: family, faith, clear goals, and the willingness to work hard to make it work. Kim's family influences varied slightly from mine, but she, too had come from a loving family that respected what we were trying to do.

Our marriage turned out to be excellent decision. We have had our ups and downs, but certainly we have had more ups than downs. Even the "downs" have turned out to be lessons that helped keep our spirits and our faith in each other elevated.

Once our plan to marry was an accomplished fact, my family turned their energies toward "setting us up proper" in our new life. Any doubts they might have had were put aside, as though they had never existed. The well-meaning but unsolicited advice ended. They shared our joy and worked to help us start our married life together. They gladly recognized the fact that I was entering a new phase in life, both by becoming an adult and by becoming part of a legal couple. As Kim and I set out to go to Meharry, my brother Raymond and his wife Lottie were there. He and Boot helped us to move. My sister Mary had gone with us earlier that summer to help us find an apartment to live in after we were married. Mary, who had taken over for Mother after her death, felt as responsible for Kim and me as Mother would have if she had been with us during this time.

Just when it seemed that the search for a home for Kim and me would take the entire summer, we finally settled on an apartment just outside metropolitan Nashville. We found a modest two-bedroom apartment about a twenty-minute drive from campus. A couple of Meharry students had lived in the apartment before us. This apartment was definitely a step up from the mobile home in Fort Valley.

Raymond moved us in his small Ford truck. With a small U-Haul trailer hitched behind it, he drove our newly joined possessions over the mountains of North Georgia and Tennessee into Nashville—and our future.

In Nashville, Raymond paid the first month's rent for us, gave us $13, and left a honey bun on the kitchen counter. We unpacked the U-Haul and truck, and he visited for a little while. Then he said good-bye and headed back to Atlanta.

Standing there in that living room was the first time I had really felt like a grownup. I knew at that instant, too, that grownups can have moments when they are both deliriously happy and terribly scared at the same time. Kim and I looked at each other, smiled, and decided that we had the finest home in the entire state of Tennessee.

One Little Problem—Where Do We Get the Money?

Now that we were in Nashville, the one pressing problem I had was how I would pay for my dental training. The cost would be approximately fifteen thousand dollars per year.

Daddy didn't have any money. I had not gotten any loans and was determined not to. I wasn't eligible for any available scholarship, partly owing to my "conditional" acceptance. The big plus I had, though, was God. I was still operating on faith. Faith is big, faith is powerful, and I knew I would somehow find a way. I once again found myself repeating the phrase Mother had sent me off to college with: "Put on the whole armor of God, Joe Nathan, put on the whole armor of God."

One thing I needed to do was to get the school to confirm my status, academically and financially. I figured that the best way to do that was to go at it like a sniper—with no warning and without too much thought about it beforehand.

I went to school that day wearing my fraternity shirt, which I called my "lucky shirt." Rain was pouring down, and I didn't have an umbrella. Still, I went anyway and just ran to the Administration Building from my car. I arrived soaking wet and completely winded. Not wanting to pause even for a moment, I raced on into the building.

I was running toward my future so fast that I almost bowled over a woman who was waiting for the elevator. She looked at me and kind of shook her head. She said, "Son, you're too old for that."

Undaunted, I got on the first elevator going up. My body was reacting to the all-consuming desire my mind felt to begin my studies. I was in a rush to find a way to overcome my financial obstacles so I could be assured I would be able to begin my classes. I couldn't endure the thought that I could be this close to realizing my dream and be defeated by money.

By the time I entered the third floor of the building, I had slowed down, but not much. The receptionist seemed quite put off by my impatience—or perhaps by my soaking-wet shoes and clothes. Even though she obviously disapproved of the state I was in, she called Mr. West, the Admissions Officer. When he emerged from his office, I suddenly understood her reluctance. I got the uneasy feeling that perhaps she was not so much disapproving of me seeing Mr. West while appearing so disheveled and impatient. Rather, she was trying to safeguard me from him! Instantly, I "settled down," as a grade-school teacher would say.

I'd spoken to Mr. West over the phone many times but had never met him in person. Even at five feet two, Mr. West was imposing. I introduced myself as Joe Lester. In reply, he said, "So! You're Joe Lester!" His tone was not reassuring.

For a moment I thought he was recalling my numerous telephone calls, and I wondered what the penalty would be for my past impatience. Deciding that "the best defense is a good offense," I held out my hand and said, "It's good to finally meet you, sir."

He said nothing immediately in reply but offered his hand. He removed the pipe from his clenched jaw and said abruptly in a clipped manner, "I need to see you in my office." He spoke with a northern accent, like my cousins from New Jersey.

If my initial reception hadn't already intimidated me, Mr. West's office surely would have. Mr. West definitely had an executive office. An impressive high-backed chair stood behind the large cherry desk. A leather sofa and two brown leather chairs seemed to float on top of the thick, plush, burgundy carpet that covered the floor. The neatness of his desk told me that this man was well organized and on top of things. It was then, standing there wet, still breathing hard, and feeling about five years old, that I knew I had better "settle down."

Mr. West took only a moment to let me know just why he had lasted so long as a college admissions officer. As soon he closed his office door, he quite matter-of-factly bombed me with the news that I still had to take part three of the Physics requirement for admission.

It was only here that I finally understood the tenuous nature of my acceptance to this distinguished school. When I first got the letter, all I really saw and absorbed was that I had been accepted. I was sure I had read the whole letter, but I suppose I just failed to comprehend any further message than that. When the letter said, "accepted," my mind just didn't see the need to go any further.

But now I knew. All the running in the world was not going to get me through the doors of Meharry. There was work to do. It took very little explanation on Mr. West's part to clarify things for me. Only now did it come to me that nine semester hours was the same as fifteen quarter hours. Like the man said, I needed that third part of Physics.

I suppose Mr. West picked up quickly on that dumbfounded look I surely must have had at that moment, because he twirled away from me in that high-backed chair and started to dial some numbers on the phone. All I could see over the back of the chair was the salt-and-pepper color of his neatly cropped Afro. The height of the chair almost engulfed his short frame. As I smelled the sweet maple aroma of his pipe tobacco, my mind began to search frantically for ways of overcoming this problem.

I would not, could not, let panic overtake me. There was too much at stake. So I began what would become my mantra over the next four years: "This will only require work, and I'm used to work." But just as I said that to myself, the panic returned, this time with the realization that I might not have the time to do the work before I missed my chance to get into school that year. I knew what the consequences of failure would be. And I dreaded it, not only for myself, but also for Kim, who had put her education on permanent hold for my sake.

At this point I did the only thing I could do. I began to pray. Please God, again I am asking you to come to my aid. I am seeking a solution to my problem. I am reminded of your instructions, "Ask and it shall be given. Seek and ye shall find." I know that I have prayed this prayer many times since I began college, but please hear my request one more time. Thank you, God. In Christ's name, Amen.

Then I began listening to Mr. West's end of the conversation. I could tell he was waiting for someone to tell him what he needed to do "in this situation." I thought to myself, He's having to ask for an exception! The butterflies—and several other species of animals—in my stomach took turns trying to win a war.

Mr. West would occasionally swing around and give me a stony glance, which indicated to me that he was having trouble getting the person he needed to talk to on the phone. I glanced at Mr. West's stern, silent face as he repeatedly tried another extension. Then I clenched my teeth against my lip to keep them from chattering. The chair I was sitting in began to press hard upon my backside as I tried to hide the fear that must have been plainly visible on my face. I prayed silently that no one would answer. Then I prayed just as hard that someone would.

Mr. West was the only person I had been in contact with at Meharry. He was truly my lifeline right now, and I knew my chances would be better with him than with anyone else. But I also knew that I was on my own in this. If he failed to get an exception granted, I was finished for the year. Kim's sacrifice and our move to Nashville would have been wasted effort. It just seemed at that moment that all of the demons in hell were conspiring to keep me out of dental school. At this point my Mother's words rang loud in my head, and I used them like a good luck charm: "Put on the whole armor of God, Joe Nathan. Put on the whole armor of God. It will protect you the last mile of the way."

After what seemed like hours, I heard his tone go from serious to despairing. He hung up the phone, stared back at me, and said, "You just go on. Get out'a here. Consider this your lucky day."

Indeed, it was my lucky day. I chose not to stay around and try my luck. I sure wasn't going to stay and ask any foolish questions! I flashed out of that office like lightening. I raced off to the financial aid department. When I got there, the financial aid director handed me a package that looked similar to the package I'd received my first week of college. I looked into the package like someone who believes they've just gotten a mail bomb. But I had to look to know what was going to happen to me, to Kim, and to our life together.

I couldn't quite believe what my eyes beheld. In the package was notice of a full scholarship to attend the college. And I was going to get a check every month as a stipend to pay for books. I carefully (and I do mean carefully) read over the entire packet, until I was sure of what I was reading. To add to everything else in that wonderful packet, one of the papers told me that, for the first year, I didn't have to pay one cent! It was my lucky day indeed!

For a glimmer of a second, I began to think that my luck was maybe a little more than just luck. I took a moment to reflect on this, but only a moment. Perhaps God was hearing my prayers, after all, I thought quickly. Looking back, I'm amazed at how hastily I became cocksure, though, about my good fortune by dismissing the significance of my prayers on that long night several months earlier and my plea in Mr. West's office. My upbringing almost guaranteed that I would know how to pray, but since leaving home I prayed only when all else failed. At that moment, all that "religious stuff" didn't matter. Things were going my way, and I just felt that I was the one who had "earned" all this happiness. My heart was pumping with joy, and these thoughts only wandered around in my brain for a second. My long held, almost-lost dream was beginning to take form and become a reality, and that's where my thoughts focused.

I hurriedly signed the paper for the scholarship, raced out of the building, tripped over a couple of people, fell down the stairs, and raced home. When I banged open the door of our new apartment, Kim looked up from the newspaper she was reading, probably wondering whether marrying me had been the right decision after all. My voice broke with happiness.

"Kim, they have given me money! Child, we're going to get a check every month!" She took that paper, threw it up in the air, and shrieked for joy. We hugged each other while jumping up and down for what seemed like hours, giddy with relief and also giddy with the excitement that good fortune brings.

Our joy had its basis in the cold, hard reality that we were broke. The thirteen dollars that Raymond had left us was now gone. We had both just started working part-time, Kim at Arby's and I at Shoney's, but neither one of us had been paid yet. Even with this income, things still looked pretty grim. In fact, we didn't have one red dime! So whether I appreciated it or not, God did answer my prayer. Now, we were off to the races!

CCCCCCCCCCC *22* IIIIIIIIIIII

Guess What?

But our path was not to be as smooth as it seemed at the moment when we learned of the financial support we would receive. Kim became ill, so very ill that both of us were worried. She became so exhausted that she refrained from doing any household chores to conserve her energy for the job at Arby's. She had no appetite either. Not since my mother's illness had I been so afraid for someone I loved.

The minute I got my first paycheck, I insisted that she go to the doctor. She was really frightened because she had never before been so ill. I realized just how frightened she was when she didn't protest about the cost of a visit to the doctor. And that worried me even more.

She came home with a long face. When I saw her looking that way, my worry changed to outright fear. I began bombarding her with questions. "What did the doctor say? Is it something serious?"

"Guess what? " she said hesitantly.

"What?" I said insistently.

"I'm pregnant," she said.

For once, I couldn't think of a thing to say.

Being silent was not the right thing to do, though. Kim took my lack of response as disapproval. And she gave up the wall of tears she'd been holding hostage in her eyes. She was afraid of how I'd react, knowing how little money we had and how excited I'd been at having just leaped a major hurdle.

Seeing her sadness and desolation broke my heart. Now I realized even more how much Kim was depending on me. Kim's security was truly dependent on my abilities and good judgment. I couldn't help wondering whether she was wondering whether maybe she had misplaced her trust.

To try to disperse the pall of fear and uncertainty hanging in the air, I said, "Well, I guess we got a little too overjoyed about that Financial Aid letter and celebrated a little too much."

I was relieved that my pathetic attempt at wit seemed to work magic. Almost immediately, her cheeks dimpled and her tear-flooded eyes began to shine. I kissed away the rest of her tears. We settled on the couch with our arms around each other and began to exchange thoughts about our perfect child who was on the way. We speculated on its sex and thought of all of the names we could choose from. In our discussion we raised our just-conceived child from birth to school, college, a profession, and finally marriage and a family. We wrapped ourselves around each other, truly united "until death do us part." From that point on, we never looked back or regretted the pregnancy. We never have.

During the early stages of her pregnancy, Kim was often sick. She hadn't had much exposure to people who were pregnant, and I came along so late in my mother's childbearing years that I didn't really know much either—except, of course, how such things happen! However, I had gathered from hearing my older siblings talk that being really sick wasn't normal. The thought had occurred to me that I could—and probably should—ask my siblings for advice. I wasn't so sure they'd be as happy as I was to hear about our news, though. So Kim and I dealt with her sickness our own way.

This being a new venture for both of us, we soon began making regular trips to the emergency room at Meharry. We didn't have any insurance or any money either, but I figured that the hospital was the place to go if a person needed medical help. I'm certain that if anyone in our family had known about Kim's pregnancy, they would have directed me otherwise. But it turned out that my poor judgment actually benefited us.

On one occasion, Kim was quite ill. She had been throwing up for a couple of days. I rushed her to the emergency room at Meharry to see what was going on. Although I had still not given God praise for all the good things He was doing with my life, Kim and I were about to get another God-sent blessing.

When we got to the emergency room, it was obvious that there was going to be a long wait. The waiting room was crowded, and some of the people sitting in the chairs were moaning. As we sat there, I could see nurses and doctors frantically rushing past the small windows in the double doors of the main treatment room.

The nurse, whom I'm embarrassed to say recognized us from our previous visits, came over after a while and said, "We are really covered up today, as you can see. Since Mrs. Lester is pregnant, we've called in the OB/GYN on call to see her. She really needs to be under the care of the doctor who is going to deliver your baby, and Dr. Caple is one of the best."

I had failed to grasp the significance of the phrase "going to deliver your baby," because I had fixated on the phrase "Mrs. Lester." Boy, did that sound official. I pondered on that for a moment with both Kim and the nurse standing there. They probably were wondering whether I had at last taken leave of my senses. I finally roused myself out of my reverie long enough to say, "OK, let's do it."

A doctor arrived and strolled into the emergency room a little while later. I was taken by Kim's next remark, thinking to myself that perhaps she wasn't quite as sick as I had thought she was. She said slyly, "I sure hope that's my doctor, 'cause he's s-h-a-r-p!"

I had to agree with her. He was sharp. He was well dressed, professional to a tee. In fact, he seemed the epitome of the professional I hoped to be someday. And he did turn out to be her doctor—P. Caple, MD, one of the finest people I have ever known.

Dr. Caple saw Kim in the emergency room that night and told us to come over to his office later on that week for a follow-up visit. When the time came, we dutifully went to his office. There he gave Kim a more thorough examination. He was able to reassure us right away that Kim was fine, and that the sickness would eventually pass, which it did. But there were other matters he wanted to discuss with us.

He took both of us into his private office and sat down behind his desk. Dr. Caple was a tall man, very tall. I remember thinking he could have been a basketball player. In fact, I found out later that he had been just that. Sitting at his desk, he reared back and templed his long slender fingers together in a position of prayer. I wondered what was coming.

I didn't have to wait long. He looked me straight in the eye and said, "You don't have any money, do you?" Before I could answer, he popped another stinging question. "I bet you don't have any insurance either." As if in explanation of the obvious, he continued, "You two just look like you don't have any money or insurance." By this time, I was hoping against hope that he would be willing to take on these two poor fools for the sake of their innocent baby and trust us later for his fee.

Then he chuckled, and I noticed a gleam in his eye. My spirits lifted a little with his next words: "Well, I ran into the same situation when I was at Meharry. Someone helped me out then, and I'm going to repay my debt to them by passing their favor to me, on to you."

This caused me to sit up in my chair and turn an eager ear to hear what followed. He looked squarely at me—not at Kim, but at me. He seemed to realize I was more than willing to take on my responsibilities as a father, even if I was not able to do so financially.

"I'll take care of her for you. I'll do the pre- and post-natal treatment, but you are going to have to find a hospital you can get into. I can't do anything with the hospital for you. But I won't charge you anything for my services."

Of course I agreed. I did not have any other choice but to agree. He was right. I did not have any money, I did not have any insurance either, and I did not want to call home and ask for any money. I did not want to call my siblings and hand them the burden of taking care of my family. It was a matter of pride.

I was happy and relieved that somehow we had solved the immediate problem of getting care for Kim. Dr. Caple's willingness to help us out boosted my spirits, and I began to feel hopeful about things once more. Again, I had faith that we would find a way to pay for the hospital and some day repay Dr. Caple for his kindness and generosity.

That first talk with Dr. Caple also bolstered my ambition to do everything I could to provide care myself to whomever needed it, regardless of their financial situation. I suppose that following through on that ambition has been in part payment of the debt I owe him.

That summer, right after I completed my first year of school, we went to stay with my sister Nancy in Atlanta. By then, of course, there was no way of delaying the inevitability of telling my family. Their response was exactly what I expected it to be: "You two get back home this minute so we can take care of you!" And for once I was able to squelch my rebelliousness and listen to their insistent advice.

For Kim and me, there was an advantage to going back home, however temporarily. This allowed us to establish residence in Dekalb County, the requirement for using Grady Hospital for the baby's delivery. That worked out just fine. I think the entire bill came to about eighty dollars. We were so broke, I don't even remember paying that!

Sometimes blessings come in disguise, and it was so very true for us when our baby was finally born. Jarvia came to us, beautiful and healthy, on July 25, 1981. From the moment of her birth, I really understood what the phrase "pride and joy" meant, because she surely was my "pride and joy." Prior to her birth I felt as though I had only Kim and myself to work hard for. I now had something even more special to work for. I now had my own complete family unit. I'd never been so happy in my life.

That summer, I worked at odd jobs with Norrell Temporary Services. I had one job tearing down a building and then another at a plastic recycling company. Norrell enabled me to work steadily throughout the months before the baby was born and earn a little money. Kim and I had to pay very little money for the baby's birth, but there were extras I wanted the baby to have. I could not expect other people to provide the extra perks for our baby. Providing these things for her or him gave me a sense of fatherly pride. Therefore, I was willing to work to get those things for our future bundle of joy.

I didn't have a clue as to what those extra perks were, but I figured all would be revealed to me after the baby was born. The Good Lord looks after the ignorant because I had no idea of the magnitude of a newborn's needs!

When Jarvia was only a few days old, it was time for Kim and me to pack up and move back to Nashville. I was stunned when my mother-in-law objected quite strenuously to our taking Jarvia with us. "You and Kim can't take this little newborn baby with you now. You ain't got no place to stay and no money. You are going to be in school, and Kim can't work or go to school and take care of the baby at the same time. New babies need a lot of care and cost a lot. Let her stay with me; you can come see her on the weekends. That way Kim can work or go back to school, and you can go to school. You will know that Jarvia is safe and well taken care of. Please let her stay in Atlanta with me."

We ended up getting into a rather heated discussion. I was adamant that we would not be separated from Jarvia. We wanted her to bond with us. We felt her babyhood was too precious for us to miss any part of it. We wanted to be there when she started to follow movement with her eyes, when she smiled her first smile, and when she gave that gurgle of recognition she would soon be able to make whenever we approached.

I knew that my mother-in-law had Jarvia's and our best interest at heart. She was afraid that our youth and lack of money would prevent us from providing a stable environment for Jarvia. So I said, in my best once-and-for-all tone, "Any child that you do not have with you is not your child; it will become the child of the caretaker, regardless of biological birth. Jarvia is going with Kim and me. It won't be easy, I know, but she'll be fine. We'll all be fine." So, against my mother-in-law's will I loaded Kim and Jarvia into our ancient BMW 2002 and headed back to Nashville.

After getting settled again in Nashville, we put Jarvia into day care. Our relatives frowned on this, but Kim and I agreed that we had to do what was best for Jarvia and us. I did not want the marriage and the family to interrupt my education, and I surely was not going to interrupt Kim's education.

Of course, putting Jarvia in day care wasn't easy for either of us. Jarvia looked awfully tiny in the day care center's big crib. But we did it. Kim went back to Tennessee State, and I continued my studies at Meharry.

From Hell to Heaven: Meharry Days

If I doubted there was a hell, those doubts ended when I sat down in my first class at Meharry Medical School. As I got into my first year of work there, I felt I was approaching the very gates of hell. A few times, I felt that I had actually gotten a first class seat on the bus headed there. The excitement and joy of being accepted to dental school was over. The hard work had begun.

I knew that I had to make good on my promise that if I could get into dental school, I would stay the course. If I had any doubt about being able to stay, though, it was in that first year.

The first year at Meharry was a long series of tests, broken by a few classes. What I wanted most was not to be on the low end of the scale, and I eagerly looked forward to my first test scores. Every test was important because you were continuously evaluated and judged by your class placement. Students on the low end of the score sheets were singled out—and I dreaded being singled out. There was enough pressure as it was.

After the first exam, I hurried down to the board where grades were posted to see how I had faired. Not only were the scores posted by Social Security number, they were placed on a graph. When I looked at the graph to see where I had placed, I found I was at "average" or dead center. "Average" may not look too good to some, but to me, "average" meant that I'd beaten out a lot of the others and that I wouldn't be singled out—at least not that day. But I knew I had to keep it up. And therein lay my motivation. I was encouraged—really, overwhelmed—by knowing that I was solidly in the middle of the best of them. At least others would go out before I did.

The first year of dental school concentrated on the sciences—biochemistry, physiology, and gross anatomy. These would prove to be very challenging. These difficult courses certainly threw a monkey wrench in my family life, for in spite of my good intentions of being a full-time father to Jarvia, I remember very little of her first year, mostly scenes from the day-care center where (thankfully) she was thriving.

The daily schedule at Meharry made college seem like kindergarten. We went to classes from 8:00 a.m. to 12:00 noon, had an all-too-short hour for lunch, and were back in class at 1:00 p.m. on the dot until 5:00 p.m. Of course, that was only when the official classes ended. At 5:00, I'd go home for dinner and then turn right around and go back to the school to do lab work. Even when that was finished, the school day wasn't over. I often was up studying until daybreak. There was something to be done around the clock, and it was always urgent. This was almost a daily ritual. But even with this huge amount of study, we as a class were barely getting by. The tests were challenging, almost mind-numbing in content and expectation.

The laid-back, two- to three-class a day habit I had gotten accustomed to in college was nonexistent. Dental school was a full-time job plus a part-time one, all in one. Nonetheless, I met this challenge just as I had met the challenge of work on the farm—"all you can do is all you can do, and I'm going to give it all I can do." Even though I thought I had put religion behind me I frequently found myself saying short silent prayers before some stressful situation or when waiting for test scores. Even though I had shoved God into the background, God did not abandon me. I did not realize this at the time, but in retrospect I can see that God walked every step with me.

Meharry was a small enough school so that our instructors knew about our family backgrounds, a fact they frequently used to keep pushing us on to excellence. One instructor told me one day, "Joe, I think we're going to have to send you back to the farm." He knew just how to tighten the screws, because I dreaded the thought of ever returning to the cotton fields. He must have known those words would fire up my determination. My sixteen-hour days went back to twenty, and I put my head back in the books. There was no way I was going back to Daddy's house to help him farm. I was finished with the farm. I had come too far to turn back now.

My determination to succeed even included willingly conforming to customs that until that time had no real meaning for me. At Meharry it was customary to wear a tie to class, but up until then I'd rarely had reason to wear one. However, I rushed out and bought a couple of ties, and my brother-in-law, Kelly, sent me a whole box of old ties that he had, which I gladly accepted.

This readjustment of my priorities had its humorous moments. One day I noticed Sam, a slender guy from Mobile, Alabama, wearing this little narrow device, a little bar that held his shirt collars down—a collar bar for the tie. Then I realized that most of the men were wearing them. I think the rest of the fellows copied him, for Sam was a snappy dresser, a trend-setter who always dressed in good taste. His dress was "GQ all the way," I heard some of the fellows say. His pants and shirts were always freshly laundered. He usually wore a belt that matched his shoes, and it seemed that he owned a million pairs of shoes, some made of alligator and lizard skins. All of them were of different styles and colors ranging from beige to black, including some boots and loafers. Today we might call him a male Emelda Marcos.

One day I mentioned to Kim how sharp Sam and the other fellows dressed. Having met most of my classmates on one occasion or another, this was not new information for her. She replied that she had noticed that Sam dressed nicely and in good taste. I soon got the feeling that she had been waiting for an opportunity to "fix me up." She started breaking it to me slowly that my green double-knit dress slacks were a "wee bit short around the ankles and more than a couple of years out of style." A little embarrassed by her candidness, I protested. "Sure they're a little tight around my thighs, but that's because the fabric has stretched out to be comfortable!"

I was on the wrong end of a losing argument. Kim and I made a trip to the mall shortly after I received my first student loan refund check. We bought five white dress shirts, five pairs of pleated dress slacks, and two of those collar bars, one gold and one silver. She even convinced me to buy some new shoes.

I had to admit that the new pants and shirt felt good against my body as I rolled into the classroom the next day. However, I was having a little trouble remembering how those fellows had those collar bars fastened around their ties. I fixed the collar as best I remembered, meaning to check it out as soon as I saw one of my classmates. Well, I forgot, just plain forgot, and I ending up sitting in class that day with that bar over the tie upside down. A couple of the guys in the class strolled over to where I was studying and asked me, "Joe, why have you got your bar over your tie?"

Being a person who did not want people to know that I did not know any better, I said irritably, "Well, it's my tie bar. I can wear it like I want to." Bravado can come in handy sometimes. So I wore that tie bar over my tie for a couple of weeks, just to let them know that maybe that was the way I wanted to wear that tie bar. But really I had never worn a tie bar at all before then. At any rate, as soon as I could do it without anyone noticing, I switched it back the correct way.

My new threads made me feel more comfortable in class and helped to ease my defensive ego. I let my guard down a little. Since I felt less self-conscious, I relaxed enough to become more congenial. I actually started to make new friends, like Terry.

Terry was a white boy from Nashville, the only white student in our class, and so of course I knew about him. But I didn't get to actually meet him until one day when he came up and asked me where I got my collar bar.

It didn't take me long to discover that Meharry had obviously searched until they found the smartest white boy in Nashville and put him in our class. Terry's daddy did the dental lab work for the school. I remember thinking, "His daddy has a deal worked out with Meharry—Terry's tuition for the lab work." But that was before I actually got to know him. In addition to his obvious intelligence, Terry had another advantage. He already knew how to do dental lab work, and so that put him far ahead of us who were just now figuring out how to hold a dental mirror.

Terry must have been feeling the same pressure to conform that finally made me go out and get new clothes, because our friendship began when he asked where I got my collar bar. He didn't exactly say "collar bar." What he actually said was, "I was wondering. Where did you get that thing holding your tie in place?" I told him where I'd purchased it, and the very next day Terry showed up wearing a collar bar, too.

I noted with some dismay that he had his on upside-down over the front of his tie like I had first worn mine! It gave me a perverse thrill to straighten him out. I said in mock horror, "What you doin'? Tryin' to pass? Well, at least do it right," I said. I showed him the "proper" way to place that collar bar, as if I had known how all my life.

He didn't stop at the collar bar either. Terry had traded his white shirt, khaki pants, penny loafers, and fat ties for the same pleated, baggy wool pants and thin ties that the rest of us wore. He was conforming to the "black GQ look," and, notwithstanding my teasing, I respected him for it.

Terry and I maintained a professional relationship that gave him a better appreciation of how it felt to be in the minority. Eventually, Terry became just "one of the boys."

I suppose you might say that we had our own discrimination hierarchy. For example, when Martin Luther King, Jr., Day activities were held at the school, we'd come back to class and say to Terry in a quasi-threatening tone, "We're mad as hell!" He got used to our ways after the first few times, though. He told us we were all in the same boat.

And indeed we were. The rest of the world may have discriminated, but the instructors did not discriminate. Whether you were black, white, Indian, or Iranian, we caught the same hell at Meharry.

Meharry was contained on less than ten acres, and its red brick buildings stood five or six stories tall. Concrete sidewalks tied the buildings together, and the landscaping gave almost the entire campus a conservative feel. The exception was the hospital, a modern building with off-white aluminum siding. It stuck out like a sore thumb among all those traditional red brick buildings.

A visitor to this tiny campus would not immediately realize its value to American society at large. Almost every conceivable specialty was represented—medicine, dentistry, nursing, allied health science, dental hygiene, and many Ph.D. programs.

The road of chance had brought my classmates and me to this tiny campus. It seemed that all of us had a lofty goal in coming here. The students at Meharry all seemed to have dreamed for a long time of going to dental school at Meharry, and they behaved as though it were a privilege.

Crime and poverty, evidenced by broken-down single-family houses, surrounded the Meharry campus. Meharry was a bright spot in this otherwise downtrodden area. Outsiders would never guess that Meharry's students and graduates represented over fifty percent of the minority health care workers in the United States.

If you flunked one course at Meharry, you got an opportunity to go before the Dean to beg and plead to take that year over. This standard was more than enough to put the fear of God into us. There was no such thing as repeating just one course. The curriculum required that all courses be taken in sequence. If you were lucky and happened to have the funds, you might be able to go to another school that summer and take that one course over. Otherwise you had to take the whole year's work over.

Not everybody passed every class every year, of course. As poor as many of us were, failing a course could have been devastating. These required courses weren't cheap. Miraculously, everybody in our class managed to come up with funds when funds were needed. Nobody wanted to be left behind. Without realizing it, the forty-nine of us were growing together as a family, bonding as surely as my siblings and I had so many years ago.

One of our classmates excelled above all the rest of us. His name is Dwane, but we simply called him "The Man." Humble in character, he possessed a wonderful personality that has gone unduplicated in my experience. Accenting his personality was an uncanny ability to master any course work put before him. He was a perfectionist, never leaving a t uncrossed or an i without its dot, and somehow he did this while never drawing attention to himself. When the class had exhausted all efforts to answer the questions in our syllabus, someone from our study group would inevitably say, "Let's ask 'The Man.'"

And when "The Man" spoke, everybody listened, even though he usually answered by saying, "I guess."

We would interrupt by saying, "We'll take your guess. It's better than our best answer."

"Shut up and let 'The Man' speak," you'd hear from the background.

"I guess the answer is 'C,'" Dwane would say in a quiet and unassuming tone.

"'C' it is!" I'd say.

This unselfish person assisted perhaps ninety percent of our class throughout dental school, never demanding any recognition. His help has not gone unnoticed in our hearts, and he absolutely deserved the utmost respect among his peers.

Unbelievably, the work got harder in the second year. Meharry's directive that we help each other was the only thing that held us together. By the middle of the second year, I wished they could just have let me walk on hot coals every day, rather than going to classes and taking tests. Some days my resolve faded so much that I even caught myself thinking once more about the farm, and in a much softer light than I had the year before. In that second year, tests were given almost daily.

I labored through my years of dental school, especially the first two years. However, once I reached the dental clinics where we saw patients, I knew that my feet had reached solid ground. After all, I was used to using my hands. Those years of picking cotton, peas, and cucumbers were about to pay off. More than that, I had developed an ability to break the ice with strangers. So, getting new patients, the biggest challenge of a third-year student, was not challenging at all. As a matter of fact, I never had problems keeping new patients, either. That came naturally to me, and I was one of the few students that year who had "repeat customers."

Kim, my rock and my salvation during those years, didn't just sit around and feel sorry for herself. Anything but that. My fellow classmate Dwight discovered that I lived very close to the school, and he started to use Kim as a baby-sitter for his son D.J. Dwight also discovered that Kim was a good cook, and the word spread like wildfire. Soon almost every male in the class was following me home for lunch.

In a way that is hard to explain, Meharry was starting to change all of us in the class, breaking down all sorts of barriers, even down to food. The school was giving us a solid education, but it was also giving us an education about life, specifically in how to be a professional and get along with others. This proved to be, in later years, almost as essential to being a good health care provider as the class work itself.

This was well reflected, I think, by the philosophy of the school, which was that we had to be well prepared, probably better prepared than our counterparts at neighboring Vanderbilt University. Both schools were to treat all patients. However, we at Meharry knew that our patient loads would be primarily made up of indigent patients. So Meharry was coincidentally training us to get the maximum results and achieve above expectations with less.

At Meharry, you were expected to get the job done, regardless of the circumstances. Ironically, that's the same idea that my daddy had, and so this concept was not as unfamiliar to me as it was to some of my classmates. Also emphasized constantly was that we were all expected to work together. The success of our class would not be measured on individual efforts, but on the group. If you had a weak classmate, you were expected to help him study. If some of the class flunked, the whole class got the scolding. This principle, too, was not new to me. I had learned it in my early years. I think this may be why the good Lord directed me to Meharry, a school that had no room for the spoiled or lazy.

In my senior year, I had gained the respect of a lot of the instructors and had achieved the reputation of being a hard worker, even if only a decent student. Knowledge of this respect was something I had to decipher for myself; no instructor at Meharry would give that information to a student. Even in our fourth and final year, the instructors did not discriminate. To put it bluntly, the only egos allowed on campus were theirs.

Once I had done an excellent job on a denture setup. The instructor said, "You did a good job on that." But he gave me a 3.0, which was average.

I, having a sharp tongue, said, "I thought you said I did a good job on that."

He said, "You did. I gave you a C, didn't I?" After which he proceeded to the next student.

He left me with my mouth gaping open, speechless. Here I had done all I felt I could do, my best work so far. The instructor acknowledged that the work was good, but he had given me only an average score. Still, there was a lesson to be learned from this. When you think you have done your very best, take a closer look; it can be better.

Meharry had a way of getting the maximum potential out of every student—every student who had the intention of staying there, that is. Unlike my undergraduate years, study was both mandatory and exhausting. The danger of burnout was ever present. Even though there were times I cursed the day I'd heard of Meharry, I'm still very grateful for the solid base of education I received there. Even more, I'm grateful for the friendships that have lasted until today—life-long personal and professional links that have enriched my life as surely as my Doctor of Dentistry degree.

Life was far from humdrum during our days at Meharry, in spite of the work required. Some friends, Claude and Tondra, had come to live with us for a few months while they got on their feet financially. One night, all of us were asleep. In addition to Claude and Tondra in their room, my brother Jack was asleep on the couch. Claude and I were exhausted from a particularly grueling day of exams. I awoke to Kim shaking my shoulder, whispering, "Joe, wake up! I heard something in Claude and Tondra's room. It sounded like a gunshot!" Sleep-fogged, I was tempted for a moment to tell her to ignore it, when I heard it, too—a sharp thud.

Instantly awake, I mumbled, "You stay here. I'm going to check it out."

At that idea, Kim became frantic, begging with me not to, because we didn't know what was going on in that room, and we didn't hear anybody moving, and that it sounded like a gun. "What if it's a burglar? What if the burglar already killed Claude and Tondra and is coming to get us next?" Some imagination, that Kim! Or was it her imagination? In the neighborhood in which we lived, it was hard to be sure.

Kim suggested that we get underneath the bed instead. That way, if the "burglar" opened our door, the room would appear to be empty. Since that seemed like the path of least resistance, I agreed, and we did. In unison, we did a slow roll off either side of the bed, and like a soldier in combat, I elbowed and kneed my way to the center. Just as Kim slid under the bed, too, we both looked up at each other and said "Jarvia!" as the top of our heads connected with the bed slats. With that, Jarvia stirred and whimpered, "Ma-Ma?" With my head singing and stars in my eyes, I still must have broken some record, getting out from under the bed and picking Jarvia up before she could get too loud. Thankfully, she wasn't fully awake and was not really aware of what was happening.

Just as quickly, I hustled back under the bed, patting Jarvia and whispering, "It's OK," at the same time. My head started pounding in earnest about the same time Jarvia drifted back to sleep.

So there we were under the bed, feeling both frightened and a little foolish at the same time. We huddled under the bed for a moment, and then I remembered the gun. I had an old .22 pistol that had belonged to my mother. Although I abhorred guns, I had tucked it in my bag when I set off for Nashville. I was hoping desperately that the sight of it would be enough to scare off an intruder. I just prayed that I wouldn't be put into the position of actually shooting that thing! I got the gun and returned to my place under the bed with Kim and Jarvia, feeling a little silly and at the same time apprehensive.

From my position, I was able to see the door. As the moments passed, all I could do was stare at it, too apprehensive to take my eyes away from it. If someone had opened that door, I think someone could have gotten seriously hurt, because my reactions would have been on a hair-trigger.

When nothing happened right away, Kim had another idea: we should put Jarvia outside the window so that if somebody was indeed in the house and came in to hurt us, they could not hurt the baby. I wasn't in any position to think about the logic of it, for my head was now reverberating like an entire brass band from striking it on the bed slat a few minutes earlier.

So, abandoning all reason, I took the baby and put her outside the window. Miraculously, she continued sleeping. I wrapped her blanket around her tightly, praying that she would just keep on sleeping.

Then Kim had another idea. Apparently I was out of ideas by that time. "We need to call the police, Joe! They are probably stealing us blind while we're lying here!" So I crept to the extension phone, one of the few luxuries we had allowed ourselves, and quietly called the police. The beeps the phone made sounded almost as loud as my heart beating, which was far too loud! I hurriedly whispered that we had an intruder in the house and to come right away. I returned to the burrow under our bed, and we waited, almost afraid to breathe.

The police arrived quickly, with their siren off. As soon as we heard the car pull up at the street, Kim and I took off like startled rabbits, bounding through the window, narrowly missing Jarvia, who was still—amazingly enough—sleeping on the ground outside.

"I guess I should've told you that I thought there was an intruder inside, Officer," I said, still whispering. "I'm still not real sure."

"Well, something's going on!" Kim whispered even louder. And so we told him about hearing possible gunshots and about Claude and Tondra in the second bedroom, and Jack on the sofa. The policeman looked at us curiously while we were talking. I supposed that he hadn't seen too many people coming out of windows before.

I shouldn't have spent any time wondering what stealth tactics the police would use when they arrived. The officer went straight to the door and knocked firmly on it. In a few moments, Jack came to the window in his underwear, groggy, rubbing sleep out of his eyes. The sight of me, Kim, and the policeman all standing out in the yard must have really woke him up, because his eyes got as wide as two Kennedy half-dollars. He stared out in bewilderment, not really knowing what to think. Still in a trance, he stepped back and opened the door wide, letting the policeman step in. We whispered to Jack that we thought something was going on in Claude and Tondra's room and that we had heard a couple of sounds that sounded like gunshots.

The officer, not impressed at all by this point, said, "Well, get behind me and I'll check it out." He motioned Jack out onto the porch and went into the living room, gun drawn. He turned back to us, pointing in the direction of Claude and Tondra's room, as if to confirm its location. I nodded, fearful of what he would find. Then he carefully turned the knob and slowly opened the door.

He entered the room gun-first, and his loud and commanding voice split the air. "Who's there?" the policeman demanded.

He got an immediate reaction. Claude jumped up, whooping, threw his legs up in the air, grabbed Tondra, and stuck her in front of him in a shielding position. You could barely see Claude behind Tondra. Kim, Jack, and I couldn't see what was happening, and so we started our own chorus on the porch. "What's happened? Are they all right? Claude, Tondra, are y'all OK?"

The policeman lost his stern composure at that moment. He started guffawing so loudly that it woke Jarvia, and she started her own wailing to add to the cacophony of noise on the porch. Kim raced to pick her up and returned to the porch. By that time, we were all laughing hysterically at our obviously unjustified terror and our relief that nothing had really been wrong.

We quickly learned that there'd been nothing unusual going on in the house at all.

We had just overreacted. The policeman declined to stay and continue to share our joyous, if embarrassed, celebration. He soon left us to our own devices. We continued to stand on the porch, talking and laughing in our relief and getting over our shock.

Since it was dark, we were about fifteen or twenty minutes into our celebration before we realized we were in our underwear. But even though we were all modest people, this realization didn't spark the usual reaction. We merely started to laugh even harder, stopping every few seconds to point at each other.

I graduated from Meharry in the spring of 1984, surprisingly in the upper ten percent of my class. Even more surprising, I received several awards at the Student Awards Banquet. But I almost wasn't there to receive them.

As the date for the banquet drew closer, I debated whether I should bother to go. No matter how hard I worked, it seemed as though my efforts were consistently below the expectations of my instructors. Even with decent grades, I came out feeling that my performance over the past four years wasn't good enough to warrant any special recognition. I was grateful just to have graduated.

But when I told Claude and a few other classmates that I probably wouldn't be going, they said, "Well, you need to go. I think they've got some awards for you, man."

Not even questioning just how they would know something like that when I didn't, I believed them. In fact, I became elated, excited at the thought of being rewarded publicly for those four years of sheer hell.

Since it appeared the instructors might be saving a little surprise for me, I wanted to be ready for it. So I headed for the mall. My first purchase was a new pair of shoes. Ever thrifty, I knew that the smaller-sized shoes were a little cheaper. So when I found a size-seven pair on sale, I ignored the fact that they were a bit too snug. They were nice shoes and a good deal. So I bought them. Part of what I'd saved on the shoes financed the purchase of a new suit. It was navy, pinstriped, and double-breasted.

I arrived at the banquet in those tight shoes and new suit, just full of myself, but trying to appear low-key, as though I did this kind of thing every day. I was walking a little gingerly because of the tight shoes, but I was so elated about winning the awards I was willing to ignore just about anything.

Thankfully, my classmates didn't ignore me. I stood in the reception area, mingling, trying to keep my ego from encompassing the whole room. A classmate of mine tapped me on the shoulder and said, "I see you got you a new suit for the awards banquet."

Attempting to maintain my regal demeanor, not wanting anyone to guess that I'd bought new clothes just for this event, I told him, "No, this isn't a new suit."

To which he replied, bluntly, but not unkindly, "You still got the tag on it."

Mortified, my ego thoroughly deflated, I hurried off to the restroom and tore that tag off. When I returned from the men's room, I noticed that everyone else had already been called into the banquet hall. I strolled into the hall as casually and quickly as my shoes would allow and took my seat, hoping that James had been the only person to notice the tags on my new suit. Even though I had been forewarned, I was still astounded when I did receive several awards at the banquet. I received the Nashville dental award for outstanding patient management, the periodontal surgeon award, and the Dean's honor roll award for being one of the top ten students in the class.

As I had done on learning of my acceptance to Meharry years earlier, I partied to celebrate my graduation from Meharry. But not in the same way. I had learned my lesson well. This time I wisely avoided the vodka and O.J. (and other libations) that flowed freely at the house parties occurring all over Nashville.

Family and friends came from everywhere to help celebrate this special occasion. Since Kim and I were still officially residents of Nashville, our own celebration lingered on for quite a while. In fact, we'd planned to stay on for a while after graduation, just so we could see what Nashville was like when we weren't exhausted by work and school.

We had a wonderful time there, almost vacation-like.

Late evenings, my best buddy Larry would swing by in his sky-blue convertible Volkswagen, and off into the town we'd glide, with the top down. In the flush of graduation our egos were as big as the state of Texas, and to me Larry was driving the classiest car in the state of Tennessee. "What a way to live," I thought contentedly as we sped down Charlotte Pike.

We'd stop at one house, party awhile, and then drive on to another house to party a while longer. Regardless of the house, the mood was the same. Everyone was jubilant that we had reached the end of our training at Meharry. We sang songs of joy and made one toast after another, promising never to forsake the sacred bond we had cultivated during our tenure at Meharry.

One night after a long celebration on the town, Larry and I decided to go cruising through Belle Meade, one of Nashville's finest neighborhoods. The car's headlights illuminated the elegant homes in this community. Every square inch of ground was manicured to perfection. No beer cans or stray pieces of litter marred these impressive lawns. There were no bent or torn window screens, and no peeling paint or broken brick could be seen on these homes. Just elegance and luxury, through and through. This scene was in stark contrast to Jefferson Street on our side of town, which was noteworthy for its constant parade of prostitutes and for the broken liquor bottles that littered the landscape.

"Roady, this is the way to live," Larry muttered quietly, almost reverently. And I agreed with him. Belle Meade was so peaceful; even the air seemed fresher.

But something troubled me about this serene and beautiful area. I wasn't comfortable here, even though I had every right to be. "Larry, something is wrong, man," I said, not really by way of reply. I paused for a second, trying to let my thoughts solidify, and then went on. "Money can buy a lot of things, but it can't buy peace and happiness. But I do want money. I want to make enough money so I can live in a neighborhood like this if I want to. I don't even want to be identified with the people on Jefferson Street. I don't want to be anything like them."

"I am not talking about buying anything, Joe," Larry explained, "I was just thinking." Then, taking on the haughty tone that we both perceived that the owners of these fine houses must have when speaking to the lower classes, he said wryly, "Y'all need to stop throwing junk out on the street over in y'all's neighborhood."

"Yassuh, Mr. Larry," I postured in reply. Then we both laughed and changed the conversation to less serious subjects—Larry's plans to move back to Memphis with his wife and two sons, and my plans, which were no secret either. I was going back home to Hawkinsville, where I would start a private practice to serve the under-served population of my community. "And maybe," I thought with a grin, "to make enough money to build me one of those big fancy houses."

Then I started looking back at the obstacles and challenges I had crossed to get to where I was now. I also thought about the potential I had. I was sitting on top of the world, and I couldn't imagine myself failing. I had a strong, close family behind me. I also had a strong faith in God, because I had witnessed several miracles already. Too, I had an education and, through that, a profession. I was suddenly seized with the thought that unrealized potential is truly one of life's great tragedies. I intended to use what God had given me. In preparation, I'd already been to Atlanta before my graduation and had taken and passed the Georgia State Board. Now, I had my degree and the skills necessary to do a good job. Just as important, I had an unselfish, unwavering desire to do my best for any patient I might treat. I had learned from Meharry that you must have the knowledge you need to treat the patient, but second, and more importantly, you must care enough to deliver that care accurately.

"So here I am, graduated from dental school. I've beaten the odds," I thought.

Now I know that there weren't any "odds" to beat. The only obstacle in any person's way is that person's lack of faith in himself or herself. Once you set your mind to something and become willing to work at it, there is no stopping. True, I've had to slow down a time or two, but I have never stopped. I never intend to; I intend to keep going, achieving my God-given dreams.

Beginning My
Dental Practice

I was ready now—for most things. Eight years of advanced education had prepared me fully to become a competent health care provider. However, some of the lessons I still needed to learn were not taught in any curriculum. As I began my dental practice, I soon found myself drawing heavily on skills obtained much earlier in life. Some of the things still left to learn, I learned through my own error; some lessons were merely granted to me by an all-knowing and all-loving God.

Reflecting back on what I was like on graduation day in May of 1984, I really thought I had the world in the palm of my hand. When I compare myself at age twenty-six to people today at that age, I now realize how young and inexperienced I was. Even so, I wasn't swayed from my determination to conduct my practice with the mission that had burned inside me for many years. I was determined that the priority of my practice would be serving the underserved. I had faith that I'd be able to do this without having to neglect my family's needs or other financial obligations.

In July 1984, I opened my dental practice in Fort Valley, Georgia, with one hundred thousand dollars of borrowed money and a steep monthly payment of one thousand five hundred dollars. This was a large undertaking for a twenty-six year old. Risky, too. In an instant, I was elevated from my childhood years into a grownup, with all the responsibilities of a business and a family. There were four of us by then. My second daughter, Tiffany, had been born to Kim and me on January 10, 1985.

All of this I had worked for and dreamed of all my life, but I soon came to realize that becoming an adult was not as glamorous as I thought it would be. The practice of dentistry was not a game. The responsibility of running a business was not a game. I was faced with the challenge of building the image of a successful medical professional, and I had to do it as soon as I arrived in Fort Valley.

Before we had even unpacked the U-Haul truck at our rented two-bedroom apartment in Warner Robins, Georgia, a military town located five miles north of Fort Valley, I was met by an entourage of bankers who were willing to loan money to me. I found it easy to get credit cards and to make auto loans. So, with the money, I leased and renovated a suite of offices, hired staff, and at least gave the appearance of a prosperous practice.

Of course my preference would have been to eliminate the "borrow" and "repay" parts, but at that time new medical practitioners generally started their practices by going into debt. I was no exception. In fact, I opened my office grateful that I was not already heavily in debt from student loans, as many of my colleagues were.

Following my dream, I started treating patients in Peach and Pulaski Counties. However, I learned very quickly that treating the underserved was not as lucrative as I hoped it might be. I had plenty of patients but, as they say, "not the paying kind."

I can laugh about it now. I don't know what I'd been thinking. The fact is that a dentist who treats people with little money will get just that—little money. I treated hundreds of people with little or no ability to pay me. For a while, I luxuriated in the thrill of being able just to do something for somebody. I felt quite powerful, because people came to me for advice, for treatment, and even sometimes for money that I did not have and did not know that I did not have.

Of course I was paid, in a way. The people of the community did pay me, but not in ways that the bank considered currency. In rural Georgia, bartering was common. So I received some things in trade for the work I did. Once I even received some catfish in trade for services. I couldn't take them to the bank, but they made several wonderful meals for us. Another time, I received a bushel of purple hull peas and a couple of yellow-meat watermelons. I made some dentures one day for a little old lady who was as sweet as she could be. She never paid me one penny, though. When I told her the price of the dentures, she just said, "Go ahead, Ms. Sadie will give you something for your work." I understood that "something" to mean money. To my surprise, thereafter she brought me home-cooked meals at noon daily. Every time I instructed the staff to asked her for a payment on her dentures, she would come stepping through the office door with some of her homemade sweet potato pie, turnip greens seasoned with smoked ham hocks, fried chicken, and cornbread. Included would be a gallon of homemade lemonade. She'd say, "Y'all children doin' all right today? Your mama and me was real good friends. She'd be so proud of you if she could see you." Then she'd smile and hand me the plate wrapped neatly in aluminum. The smell of that food would fill the entire office. Of course she brought extra for the staff as her way of paying them off, too.

After those meals I just didn't have the heart to ask her for any money. I'd hear myself saying, "Thank you, Ms. Sadie. I see you're doin' well today. You sure are a good cook."

Out of the corner of my eye, I could see Kim and the rest of the staff grinning and elbowing each other. I 'd hear them whispering, "I thought he said he was going to ask her for his money regardless of what she brought for lunch today." Ms. Sadie never paid me one dime in currency, and I never asked her for one dime either. I consider her debt paid in full.

It wasn't long before those easy payments I owed to the bank turned into a staggering load of debt. But it felt good having the opportunity to give back to the community, because this was why I had gone to school. I had planned to get the training and return to treat people in my own neighborhood. It took about six months before I realized that my finances were sinking fast. I was barely making my loan payments. So I began to ponder my situation. I refused to even think about giving up my practice, and so I took a part-time job at a nearby primary health center to offset some of the expenses at the office.

The job at Plains, Georgia, turned out to be quite an experience. Even the interview for this position turned out to be a challenge in an unexpected way. As I drove from my home in Warner Robins to Plains, I was anticipating the types of questions I might be asked. I formulated possible responses to those questions. Little did I know that some of the questions would have nothing to do with my training and experience as a dentist. Those questions, though, were just as important to my doing the job as what degree I held.

When I arrived for my interview, I was met by an all-white staff. They were very cordial, but they obviously were nervous about the situation. They were concerned that I might be the first black dentist to work at their center, whose primary clientele was white. Such a concern never occurred to me.

The midwife, who also served as the director for the clinic, expressed her concerns to me in the interview. She spoke frankly and openly about her concern that "some patients might have a problem with this transition." After confirming my qualifications and experience as a dentist, she actually asked if I would mind if she could "call and inform" the patients in the area that I was a black dentist before they got to the center, to "head off any embarrassment for me or for the patients."

I wanted this job. In fact, I needed this job quite badly. I could have chosen a quite different response to her "request," but thankfully the joke-ster in me came to the fore. My response to her was, "Go right ahead, because I'm still going to be black when they get here!"

Whatever the director's doubts about my "acceptance," I felt very sure that I wouldn't have a problem treating any patient that came into the clinic. I was not raised in an environment where I had been taught to hate, dislike, or mistreat anybody. Besides, I was eager to treat and care for patients, and there was also the not-so-small issue of desperately needing the income.

Thus, I became the "first black dentist in Plains, Georgia." It felt good being the first. I had been second—and sometimes eighth!—for so long, that it was great to be first. Of course, I don't think there was another den-tist in Plains anyway, except for the dentist I replaced. So people in the clinic didn't have a lot of choice but to work with me. This was not the most comfortable way to start a working relationship, but it worked nonetheless.

Before long, I was "on my way," doing a first-class job and known for it. The director's worries had been for naught. The staff and I jelled just fine. I was laughing, telling my jokes as usual, and rendering good treat-ment to the patients. I remember very few awkward moments.

Oddly enough, my patients were far more accepting and receptive of me than the staff had been initially. Proof positive was when the dental clinic, never overly busy before my arrival, became booked up six months in advance. Evidently the word had spread that it didn't matter what color a person was; what mattered was that each patient was treated well. I had the ability to deliver in all those categories.

When I went to work each morning, there'd be a line of patients wait-ing for dental care. The line stretched out around that little wooden build-ing. Since the clinic operated on a "first-come, first-served" basis, this line generally remained the same length until the middle of the afternoon. We had so many patients that in order to find time to eat lunch we had to lock the door of the clinic.

One particular morning, when the receptionist went to the door to lock it, a tall, sunburned Caucasian man, a farmer in the community, stuck his mud-streaked brogan in the door and hollered back to me, "Doc, I know you got to eat, but please don't leave me like this. Just give me a shot of Novocain or something to get me out of my discomfort, and then you can go enjoy your meal. I'll wait for you. Please don't leave me hurtin' like this." I looked at him and saw a man in need of my services. He saw me as a professional who had the capability of helping him. Nothing more, nothing less. I made sure that his pain was lessened before I ate lunch.

That part-time job in Plains soon turned into a full-time offer of employment with the clinic. This offer was tempting. A full-time position would have meant job security, a steady income, and a virtual end to the struggle to retain my private practice. However, accepting the offer would prevent me from being able to give enough attention to the private practice to make it worthwhile. I ended up declining the offer, though I got decision-making assistance through a most unusual circumstance.

Not too long after the offer from the clinic, I found the clinic had two famous patients—President and First Lady Jimmy and Rosalyn Carter. They had appointments with the dentist I had replaced. He had continued to work on Fridays to finish some cases he had in progress. Once I heard that the former President and First Lady were going to be at the clinic, I jumped at the opportunity to have them as my patients. I canceled the appointments at Fort Valley and made an extra trip to Plains for the opportunity to meet them. I reasoned that since the clinic was now mine officially I would be the dentist to treat them if I were there. That proved to be true.

When President Carter came into my treatment room, he was wearing blue jeans, a flannel shirt, and the same wide grin he had sported while in office some years before. He seemed as plain as Plains, Georgia. Rosalyn came in with him and chatted with me while I examined him. She also dressed casually and wore a headscarf.

While there was nothing exemplary about their dress, their character and approach exemplified that they were exceptional human beings. As my mother would say, "They got a light soul. They shine like a Christian." They exuded a sincere warmth and genuine interest toward those of us in the clinic.

I doubt very seriously that they remember meeting me in the clinic that day, but my memory of meeting them will last a lifetime. The contrast in where I started and where I was now was staggering. To move from the cotton fields of Hawkinsville to the campuses of Fort Valley College and Meharry College, to owning my own practice, and now to meeting and treating a President and First Lady—it was unbelievable, like delicious icing on an already-tasty cake. In some ways, the Carters were ordinary people who had done extraordinary things. In my mind, I was an ordinary person, too, but that was my ambition—to do extraordinary things. I gained much from meeting them, most importantly the impetus to keep pushing on, no matter what the obstacles. They will probably never realize what an inspiration this short visit was to me. There is no way they could have known that meeting them served as God-inspired encouragement that bolstered my weakened resolve to continue doing everything I could for the underserved. It seemed truly fateful that their visit came during what was for me an ethical dilemma. The unpretentiousness of these two powerful but unassuming people inspired me to keep away from the demon of money-love that seemed to have consumed many of my colleagues. In other words, it helped me keep my priorities straight.

The people in this primary care center had accepted me for my ability to treat patients, relate to other people, and be productive. Their concerns about my being a black dentist soon evaporated.

I changed, too. The experiences I had growing up were coming back to me, and I was using them in developing personal wisdom. This happened on an unconscious level, of course, but this process left an imprint on my personality. I was going about my business, doing things I knew I was good at and very much wanted to do—practicing dentistry, of course, but also developing friendships and professional relationships and telling a joke or two. Although my beginnings in this clinic were somewhat adversarial, I had the extraordinary opportunity to become a productive professional in this new and different community. I knew that I just wanted to have the opportunity to show the staff and potential patients that I was as human as any white dentist was and if given half a chance could become a very competent and respected member of this professional team. I was absolutely determined to become a respected member of this team. I wanted to be judged by my own merits and not by any preconceived notion of what black people were like.

Is not that what life is all about? What a person is and what a person contributes to society are more important than such external matters as the color of one's skin. This was something I already knew, but I suppose it was starting to become a part of my character.

I believe that my trip to Plains was destiny, just like all the other life experiences I learned from. I came out of that experience feeling I truly was destined to make a contribution to society.

I once heard a minister say that a blessing is when preparation and opportunity meet. That is true. I continue to be blessed because opportunities continue to present themselves, and I continue to prepare myself for whatever comes.

The experience at the clinic in Plains was my first real encounter with racial issues on the job, and it turned out to be positive. I feel that when a person speaks openly about his or her concerns, and you give an honest answer, the expectations then become predictable. When you have predictable expectations, the fear level also decreases, paving the way to a more harmonious relationship.

During this time, Kim and I were careful with the money I earned, and pretty soon we no longer needed the income from the clinic to meet our obligations. So with some regret, I ended my job in this small town and returned to my private practice full-time.

But I was soon to learn that the success of my practice was dependent on the success of that year's harvest, and a couple of years later, an excessively rainy summer ruined many of the crops in South Georgia. So I once again looked elsewhere for supplemental income. This search led me to a job that, while quite secure, also allowed me to continue my mission of serving the underserved. Certainly my clients there were among the most underserved in society. I took a position as a staff dentist for the Georgia Department of Corrections. As with my experience in Plains, this encounter matured me and altered my life significantly.

(((((((((((((*25*)))))))))))))

My Life in Prison—As a Dentist, not an Inmate

It took many months for me to become used to the appearance of the prison, which was officially called the Middle Georgia Correctional Complex. A stark, low-lying set of buildings situated on several acres of otherwise useless land, it gave the appearance of having no life, no spirit. The same could be said of many of its unwilling occupants.

On parking your car, you were almost compelled to see the Georgia flag flying, displaying its large Confederate emblem, boldly popping its tail in the wind just below the American flag. The flag's Confederate emblem seemed to serve as a constant reminder to the "good old boys" of the way it used to be before they lost the war to "them Yankee Niggalovers up there in the North."

As I began working in the prison system, I encountered incarceration of the worst kinds. In a way, not just inmates were incarcerated, but also many of the staff. Even though staff members were able to walk out of the doors at the end of their workday, many of them were imprisoned as well. The worst kind of incarceration is to be, not only bodily imprisoned, but also mentally imprisoned. When your mind is locked or fixed, and you're not willing to diversify your thinking, then you're "mentally" in prison as certainly as others are physically in prison.

The prison was home to sixty percent of all the felons in the state. Oddly enough, behind the steel fences and treetop-tall razor wire, I was not among total strangers. To my dismay and embarrassment, a goodly number of them were casualties from the streets of Hawkinsville. There was "Big Tank" who sang in the prison choir and was now near the end of a life sentence for murder. I heard that "Satellite," the big tough dude who had murdered old Mr. Pete, had been though these gates. Both "Big Tank" and "Satellite" were from the small town of Hawkinsville and were doing time for being a fool or killing some fool.

Some inmates were victims of their circumstances. My very own first cousin—nicknamed "Catfish"—was among the first I recognized wearing the white cotton uniform with a blue stripe running the length of the side of his pants. I could trace the beginning of my cousin's troubles to an unusual incident. Ironically, they seemed to have begun when he was bitten by a rattlesnake during a fishing trip on Big Tawachaee Creek. His survival of that bite from that rattlesnake made him the talk of the town for months and boosted his self-esteem to an all-time high. He became quite egotistical and developed an attitude that he could do no wrong. It's intriguing to me that such an event could change a person like that, making him feel aggressive and confident enough to risk breaking the law. I must admit that I was one of the ones who were enthralled by his life-threatening experience. I was quite envious of his honored status among our town's "tough guys." Sadly, though, soon my cousin found himself compromising his values in an attempt to identify with the values of his peers. This proved to be far more harmful to him than the trauma of the snakebite.

Physically, "Catfish's" wounds mended, the only lingering after-effect being something that actually increased his social status among the brothers. The snakebite caused Catfish to have a slight limp as he walked. But a little limp in a brother's walk wasn't a bad thing among the brothers around Hawkinsville. All of them had perfected a little limp or bounce in their walk. We called this "the pimp walk." But no matter how vulgar its name, this walk represented self-pride and respect. This little limp was the only thing we owned that the white boys didn't try to take credit for.

Sporting his new walk and new attitude, Catfish started hanging out on the corner with the boys in "Nigga town," shooting crap and talking trash from sun-up to sundown. Mostly because they did, he started smoking a little "pot," and pretty soon he turned to selling some, too. He made a lot of fast money selling "pot" and even had the luxury of getting weed for his own use at a bargain price. I think the weed that he was able to obtain for his personal habit was more precious to him than any money he earned from selling it. Perhaps the concept of "getting something for nothing," was the attraction there.

The money he made from his sales he spent lavishly on fast women and cars, but it was the "high" from drugs that seemed to help him escape the littered streets of Nigga town to a dreamland of fame and easy fortune.

I said "seemed" because this "easy money" lifestyle in reality earned him a quick trip to prison. Just as with the other young black faces, I often saw him "marching the hall," tugging at his crotch, protecting his "balls" as if those were the only things he had left to hold onto. Such was the result of the life he had lived.

Catfish was only one of the many unwilling citizens of this small village called a prison. The prison was indeed like a small town in many ways. The warden served as the mayor of the town, but this was no democracy. It was more like a feudal village and even bore some physical resemblance to one. The double chain-link fences served as the walls of the city. Even the guard towers had an eerie resemblance to the turrets, or watchtowers, of medieval times. Of course, these watchtowers were used to keep people in, not out! And like the villages of the Middle Ages, there was a not quite obvious, but nonetheless well-defined, class system. There were victims and predators, peacemakers and instigators, servants and lords, and even a few court jesters! And just as in the "free world," where an inmate stood in the "pecking order" had a great deal to do with the quality of his life and in how staff members and other inmates dealt with him.

I quickly learned about the class system in this peculiar hierarchy. At the highest level were the "prison philosophers" and "jail-house lawyers." They were the articulate, literate, quick thinkers who used their minds to maintain the respect of and dominance over the other inmates. Some inmates carried both roles. Knowledge and wisdom were powerful currency here, even more than sheer physical strength. The jailhouse lawyers were revered because they knew the most about the ins and outs of the legal system and thus could help an inmate regain his most treasured possession—freedom. The most physically intimidating inmate protected them, at least until that inmate decided that the advice they gave had lost him a legal battle.

Prison philosophers were highly respected, also. Their musings about prison life and life in general helped to break up the mind-numbing boredom and hopelessness of the average inmate's existence. Like the storytellers of old, these men carried the history of prison life in their minds and kept many myths and truisms alive.

"Modern-day slavery for the black man" is the prison philosopher's favorite way of describing the makeup of the prison population. To casual observers, and to me, this phrase contained the sad ring of truth. The inmate population was composed of a large percentage of minorities, especially when compared to the percentage of minorities in the general population. I'm not sure whether minorities were committing most of the crimes, or whether we were in a system where minorities were penalized more frequently and severely for their crime. That is a determination I gladly leave to those who are learned in statistics and sociology.

Nevertheless, I thought instantly upon my arrival in the prison, "For all the sisters who are having problems finding a brother, well, here they are." In every dormitory (or housing unit, as they were called), young men my age and older were locked up in cages and told what to do every minute, every hour of the day. The isolation from family and friends was unimaginable to me, for I had never experienced it or known anyone who had. I thanked God that I had used my talents in a more positive manner than Catfish had, for I could see myself easily fitting the role of inmate philosopher or jail house lawyer. My quick tongue and willingness to share my views on life with others would have made me an excellent prison philosopher.

While I was still orienting myself to the eccentricities of prison life, I ran into an inmate I'll call "B.B." He was a dark-complexioned brother from Hawkinsville who was riding out a life sentence for murdering a shiftless young light-skinned thug named "Moo" (short for Moore).

Moo was a member of a gang led by a charcoal-black "Nigga" everyone called "Ray Cool." Cool and his group of small-town bullies wreaked havoc on almost every decent human being in Hawkinsville. "Cool and the Gang" seemed destined to become criminals. They began young, stealing Afro picks and combs from the pockets of kids in high school. It was a common sight to see "Ray Cool" and his boys swaggering around the schoolyard with their pockets filled with stolen red, black, and orange Afro combs.

Obviously, they didn't need all those combs; selling them wasn't the reason either, because everyone had two or three combs of his own. No, "The Gang" stole them just to let people know how bad they were, for bravado's sake. "Black Ray Cool" would steal an Afro comb and walk right in front of his victim with the comb stuck in his own nappy Afro, as if daring the victim to speak up.

This was only the beginning, the "training ground" for the gang. Most of them dropped out of high school at age sixteen and graduated to the more-lucrative business of stealing tape players from cars. A stolen tape player could be sold for around twenty dollars. That was a bargain considering that the same thing sold for over fifty dollars at the local Western Auto store. Most people in town, especially the youth, were so intimidated by the gang members that they were hesitant about reporting the theft of their tape players. So the gang never lacked for either "mer-chandise" or "customers."

The gang was well versed in intimidation tactics. When they weren't busy stealing, they'd come to the basketball court and "bow-hog" the court, taking other player's turns "down" as we called it. Eventually my friends and I would just leave the court whenever we saw them coming. We knew from experience that they didn't play fair. They fouled people on purpose and on occasion took basketballs forcibly from the younger kids, sending them home squealing. It was a long time before any of us got up the nerve to face up to them, but face them we did, each in our own way.

In my senior year of high school, my brother-in-law Tony, my friend Milton, and I beat Ray and his gang in a basketball game. Then Tony did something that not many others did, something that infuriated Ray Cool. Tony refused to back down in the face of the gang's threats to "kick his butt!" It wasn't long before they started messing with me as a way of getting back at Tony.

Tony was a visitor on the basketball court and had no respect for Cool and his gang. The fact that Tony was a visitor made him an unknown entity to them. That made them cautious in how they approached him. Besides that, Tony was big, standing six feet one and weighing two hundred pounds to Cool's squatty five foot, six inch frame that carried less than one-hundred-and-twenty pounds. After the day he faced them down, they didn't mess with Tony anymore.

But I was another story. I didn't have the advantage of size, and I didn't naturally relish open confrontations the way Tony did. To make things worse, I was "marked" as kin to someone who had faced them down. So I had to get creative if I was to survive, and I went to Daddy for help. Daddy got permission from the local sheriff for me to carry my shotgun in the trunk of my car to scare those fools away from me. Daddy and the Sheriff also managed to let the word "leak out" that I was thus protected, and there wasn't any more harassment from any of the gang members. In fact, they tended to steer clear of me, especially if I was driving my car. Luckily, I never had to use that gun, but I believe I would have if they had been dumb enough to push me. It takes me aback to think that I could easily have ended up just like B.B., incarcerated for life for killing one of those thugs over something as trivial as a basketball game.

Considering himself the "baddest" of the Ray Cool's gang, Moo had developed a bad habit that was to cost him his life. Anytime Moo found himself on the losing end of a gambling game, he would huffily pick up his purse and walk defiantly away. Everybody knew "Moo" was a crazy "Nigga" and usually let him have his way.

But one night, B.B. evidently decided he had had enough. He shot Moo just after Moo had picked up his money and turned to walk away from the craps game there on the streets of "Nigga Town." I could see clearly that there was a very thin line separating B.B and me. But that line was significant. B.B. used his gun, and I didn't.

When B.B. recognized me in the prison, he tried very hard to draw that invisible gap even closer together. He swore "with his right hand on the Bible" that he and I were related. I didn't know if we were related or not. Chances are we probably were related somewhere along the line, because every black person in Hawkinsville was probably related in some way, whether close or far away. It wasn't easy to find someone to date in Hawkinsville! But the blacks were not unique in this quandary. It was no different for the whites living in this small town. It seemed that they, too, were always dating close to their bloodline.

Being B.B.'s "cousin" (literal or otherwise), I served as his connection to the "free world." Being associated with someone who was doing something with his or her life raised an inmate's value in prison. This was somewhat similar to the kind of emotional substance that I had gained from being a good basketball player. It was similar, too, to the eminence my friend John gained when he beat up Ricky "Boxman," a sixth-grade school bully whose hard, square profile gave him a boxy appearance. Ricky "Boxman" was a tough character, and he had earned his reputation by beating down little guys like me. However, John had "put knots up-side his head like a mad hornet!" After that fight, John gained the utmost respect for out-boxing "Boxman" and rarely had to defend his "rep"— reputation—after that.

That one incident stands out in my mind because it finally helped me recognize that self-assurance can be gained through something as simple as being a victor in a school brawl. Hawkinsville brothers grabbed at anything that would make them seem tough or cause them to gain respect in the eyes of their peers. If you had a "rep" of being tough, it kept the bullies "off of your ass."

Unfortunately, being a "bad ass" sometimes required acting like an even bigger "bad ass," which often led to prison. John and I were lucky; we were blessed with strong families. John only had to use his fighting skill to defend himself. My family took what they believed to be the best course to help me do the same.

I found out from B.B. that all the members of Ray Cool's gang were in that prison, dead, or locked away at some other institution. Unfortunately, Ray Cool never made it here. Someone killed him at a party one night. The investigation has dragged on so long that it is unlikely that his killer will ever be brought before a judge. Likely the police are glad to be free of Ray Cool, too.

Some things change, and then others just stay the same. Likewise some people change, and others never will. The mistakes of my childhood counterparts behind bars at this complex appeared to nibble at their souls like a cancer. They can't seem to get rid of it, either. Ironically, prison seems not to be a deterrent from committing crimes for so many of my brothers here. The Georgia Department of Corrections maintains almost a fifty-percent recidivism rate. The reality is that parolees return to the prison system as if the iron gates out front were one big revolving door. Many African-American brothers find themselves so comfortable with the system that they become "institutionalized," as we call it around the "pen." Instead of prison molding these men into productive citizens, incarcerated men here are reduced to drones totally dependent on the system for all their necessities. Responding to the voice of a corrections officer to tell them what time to sleep and eat and pee becomes automatic. This ritual alone is enough to steal a brother's manhood without even mentioning the demeaning living conditions in which open toilets sit in the middle of the cell floors, with no walls to shield others from the stink or to provide privacy.

Of course, there are specks of "white" or some other minority here, but I speak solely about the brothers because by birth I have a special kinship with them. This is not to make light of any other race's "problem child," but it appears that we brothers have more than our fair share of dirty laundry.

Once I overheard a young convict of maybe twenty-four or twenty five shouting in panic as he marched down the concrete sidewalk to "the chow." He was saying, "Y'all, this chain gang done broke me. Mr. Man done whip me without throwing a blow." He went on to repeat these lines the entire distance of his walk to the dining hall. He was not speaking to anyone in particular, just to anyone in earshot. It disturbed me to see one of my own kind, a human being, in such an oppressed—or depressed— state of mind. As I observed this brother traveling the distance from his cellblock to the inmate dining hall, a faded "pimp walk" was the only clue of condescension in his demeanor. Watching this brother, I got a brief insight into why society pictures the black man as a shiftless, lazy thug who doesn't support his own children but instead steals from his own kind.

Yet, these brothers are only dead in spirit and need only to repent of their sins to save their souls. They need only to accept Christ Jesus, God's beloved and perfect Son who died on the cross and took all of our sins as their personal Savior and be spiritually born again. To be born again assures our soul everlasting life. In this new life of the saved, one's nationality or race or education or social position is unimportant. Whether a person has Christ is what matters, and He is available to all, even to my brothers in prison.

Changes—But the Dream Goes On

Our lives were about to change again. I had heard of an opening in a new prison north of Atlanta, one that was being built to replace an older, much smaller facility. The new prison would be quite large, ensuring the need for a Dental Director, which would be a step or two up the pay scale.

I liked the idea, but our decision was not easy to make. In fact, there were many reasons not to move. A big one was that I loved being a "hometown hero," even with the desperate finances in which Kim and I sometimes found ourselves. Despite my best efforts, my private practice continued to lose more than I was able to financially cover with my part-time position with the state.

The move to Atlanta would be advantageous to us on several fronts, most of them financial. It would open the opportunity for Kim to find full-time employment in her chosen field of social work, an opportunity that was scarce in our hometown or adjoining cities. Too, by transferring to the prison in the Atlanta area, I would be able secure a full-time position, continuing my employment with the Department of Corrections with no loss of benefits or seniority.

To make the deal even sweeter, I had the option of beginning a new private practice on a part-time basis. When my research determined that there was a scarcity of good dentists in Atlanta, it seemed that it would be easy to carve out a niche for myself there.

So making the move seemed like a good thing to do. What tipped the balance was that Kim and I weren't afraid of a challenge. Our lives so far had involved nothing but risk and hard work. So we decided that no matter what the disadvantages, we could deal with them as they came along. So we set our minds and hearts on the move.

I had a personal reason for wanting to make the move. For as long as I could remember, I had worn at least two hats—working and going to school, and then essentially holding down two jobs since earning my dental degree. My children were growing up without me, a situation I abhorred and wanted to change. And although I hated to admit it, I was tired. The risk of burnout is always present in a professional career, and mine was no exception. In addition to allowing Kim to realize her own dream, her working might generate enough income so that my holding only one job would be enough. Or at least my real dream might come true; I could have a private practice lucrative enough to pay the bills, with my work with the prison inmates as a sideline.

With all the planning and preparation, I never forgot to pray. As I planned for this move to Atlanta, I prayed for Kim's dream to come true. I prayed that my children would be happy in their new home. My most negative thoughts concerned the potential effects of moving them away from the only home they could remember. I prayed the hardest about that. My final prayer was for God to let His will be done. And God's will was done, but not in the way we had expected.

I moved in with my brother Jack and his wife in Lithonia, near Atlanta. Kim had already been researching the job market in Atlanta prior to our move. She had placed her resume' with several schools, but she had not yet been interviewed. Still, we weren't worried. Kim was very qualified, personally and academically, to work in a number of fields. Once we had moved, we were sure it would only be a matter of a few months before Kim was settled in a solid career path.

True to our expectations, Kim found a job soon after our arrival in Atlanta, one for which her skills, ability, and education had prepared her. But it was quite different from what we had expected. This job called on her never-ending capacity for love of family. Kim became the primary caregiver of my baby sister Gwyn, who had been diagnosed with a serious illness that would eventually prove fatal.

What made Gwyn's news even more abominable was that, shortly before the diagnosis came, Gwyn had given birth to a son, named Roy after his father. She quickly became too ill to look after the baby. In fact, she was in no shape to even take care of herself.

Gwyn's diagnosis redirected the lives of our entire family. Our brothers and sisters pulled together. That was good, for the closeness of our family was about to be tested in ways that none of us could have ever imagined.

It is tragically ironic that this illness happened to the youngest of us, the baby of the family. Whereas only a few generations ago, it would have been accepted that a family as large as ours would have lost one or more siblings in childhood, now we were facing the possibility that we might lose the youngest of us first.

To add to this irony, Gwyn had been in very good health, plus she was an optimistic person, the type of person who deserved to have a lot of life ahead of them. Even as the baby's birth approached, she finished her master's degree in social work and had just obtained employment in that field. If a positive attitude leads to a long and good life, Gwyn should have outlived us all.

In the face of this trial, Gwyn came as close as I had ever seen her to losing her belief in a kind, just, and loving God. In her anger and disbelief, she questioned "Lord, why me? A person who's never intentionally done anybody wrong, a person who's worked hard to have a better life for my son and me? Is all my education in vain?" She would spit out in anger, "Lord, did you bring me this far just to leave me?"

My heart would seize up with anger when I heard her tearing herself apart like that. But what help could I offer? I was angry too! A big part of my own anger was that I had not one good answer or piece of wisdom to offer her. I felt helpless. I had no answers. For a while, there was only rage.

But Gwyn did not give up any fight easily. True to her nature, this period of outward anger and questioning was fleeting. She eventually channeled her anger, changing her priorities to concentrating on getting better. Her passionate spirit turned toward defeating this devil that had so viciously invaded her body. What the doctors prescribed or recommended, she did without question, and she struggled daily to maintain her positive attitude.

There was another tragedy to deal with as well. Along with the loss of her health, Gwyn lost her marriage. As Gwyn grew sicker, it seemed that support from her husband grew weaker. I tried very hard not to question Gwyn's husband's actions, because I firmly believe that judgment belongs to God and should be reserved for Him to dispense. Still, I was angry to see it happen

Perhaps this distancing between Gwyn and her husband was for the best, though. Gwyn needed around her only the people who would help her in her fight for life, without any emotional detractors. I finally came to recognize that any animosity I felt toward her husband would have to wait to be dealt with after her battle was over. With great effort, I was able to stay out of their marital conflicts—for the most part at least.

As Gwyn grew sicker, it seemed that the miles separating our brothers and sisters grew shorter. The telephone became our collective lifeline. Phone calls were an almost daily ritual among the ten of us, the connections between Texas, Florida, and Georgia reverberating with our words of anger, fear, encouragement, and optimism. Too, the baby, whom Gwyn had already nicknamed "Little Roy," became our baby. Our countless conversations included snippets of information on his progress. His first smile, his first step, the first time he sat up on his own—all his "firsts" were celebrated by us as though no distance separated us. In reflection, having Little Roy to celebrate and rejoice over helped to offset some of the darker emotions that we were all trying to deal with.

Kim and I became closer, too. Under the stress of Gwyn's disease, we bonded together to fight this unwelcome intruder in our loved one's life. Gwyn's battle became our battle, with Gwyn's heart enmeshed with ours in some mystical way. Kim and I came to see our move from Middle Georgia to Atlanta almost as destiny and quickly realized that Kim's not having a job had really turned out to be a blessing in disguise. Gwyn and her baby needed a full-time caretaker, and Kim took on that job willingly, instinctively.

This is not to say that it was easy for Kim. In addition to Gwyn and Little Roy's daily care, Kim was responsible for administering large and frequent doses of medication. Kim transported Gwyn to endless medical appointments. She also was a counselor and a motivator and was there for Gwyn when the medical news became more and more disappointing. Gwyn began to trust and depend on Kim for her every need.

This was a source of great internal conflict for me. I wanted so much to be with Kim, the children, Little Roy, and my dear sister as much as I could. But I knew that as the breadwinner, I would have to go and do the job I was paid to do. To an extent I never had before then, I was constantly torn between doing right by my family and doing right by the people I had sworn I would serve to my fullest ability—my patients.

At work, I did my best to hold up as well as I could. No matter how difficult the situation, I tried to hide the fact that my baby sister was seriously ill and might die. I had always believed that people generally don't know what a person is going through unless they know that person well—unless they shared the same common experiences, culture, and, yes, even racial similarities. I soon learned, however, that I had underestimated my co-workers.

One day I was going about my daily tasks, seeing patients, handling requests from other medical staff and the correctional supervisors, all of whom seemed to want me to try to fit in "just one more, could you? I don't think this inmate can wait until tomorrow." Gwyn had just called me and told me that she was about to have a blood transfusion and that she just wouldn't allow it to be done until I arrived at the hospital. I could hear the anxiety and fear in her voice. My presence was not medically needed, but Gwyn's fear of the unknown made her insist on the presence of her big brother. Just as when she got hurt or sick when we were children, only "her Joe" could make her feel better.

I assured her I would be there as soon as I could, and I went back to my next patient, knowing in truth that it would be at least several hours until I could be with her and she could have the transfusion. My eyes simply poured water as each patient sat in the chair. I was not crying exactly, but the tears would not stop. Nor would my thoughts, although I tried valiantly to quell them so I could give my full attention to my work. I realized with a start that it was not so much that I was torn between my dedication for her and the dedication I had for the inmates in my care. Rather, I was just plain scared that the next visit to the hospital might be my last visit with my sister. And it was the purest agony to continue pretending that everything was fine.

An officer who was working in the Medical Unit at that time, a white female, came into the dental clinic. I don't know how but somehow she just knew what was going on with me, and she spoke softly in my ear, softly so that only I and not the inmate lying near could hear, "Doc, you're not alone. I have a brother who is dying from the very same thing." Her kind words relieved a ton of the burden I was carrying that day. I was able to turn my attention to the immediate task of finishing my day's work. My eyes still poured, but my heart was a little lighter. It became a little easier to turn my thoughts to the task at hand. These words, coming from a person of an entirely different race and, I thought, an entirely different circumstance, delivered a message to me far bigger than the words she spoke. That message was "We're all alike. Red, brown, black, or yellow, we want to help shoulder your burden. We are all with you in spirit."

We tried to keep Gwyn's days as nearly normal as possible in spite of how hard it was. To this end, we planned to take the baby to Crawford Long Hospital so that Gwyn could see him in his Easter finery. Little Roy had been living with Kim and me for some months now because of Gwyn's frequent hospital stays. So Kim and I felt most responsible for what happened next.

Earlier, Gwyn had picked out and purchased a handsome white satin suit for Roy to wear for Easter. It had seemed so important to her to have the final say on this, perhaps because by then she had the final say in so few things. We were aghast when we discovered that the suit had been left at her mother-in-law's house, too far away to retrieve in time to make the hospital visit. Kim did the only thing that could be done; she rushed out and purchased a replacement suit for Roy.

We were hoping against hope that Gwyn wouldn't notice the switch. Little Roy wouldn't be able to go to her room anyway, we reasoned, and she might not notice the difference from her window. Too, we even hoped that she might not even remember purchasing the suit.

We were wrong. Kim carried Roy out to the street and held him up to the window so that Gwyn could see what he looked like for Easter. She was so happy to see him there, all dressed up, smiling and wiggling in his brand new outfit. Gwyn did notice the suit, of course. And it was heartbreaking, later, to have to explain why he wasn't wearing the white suit she had purchased for him. Of course, she said she wasn't angry and that she understood. But the look in her eyes told a different tale.

I could tell that this visit had been hard for her. I knew this for certain when she later asked us not to bring Little Roy back to the hospital to see her again. The reason she gave was that she didn't want him to come one day and find her gone. As a matter of fact, she said she didn't feel as if she would be around very much longer anyway. It broke my heart to hear these words coming from someone who lived and breathed for her son, but I told myself that this was part of her process of grieving.

We were all in agony, our self-recriminations mounting. Did Gwyn's seeing Little Roy in an outfit she had not picked out cause her to make that decision that day? In another time and place, this might have been a small matter, but we agonized even though we knew we could not go back and change things.

As the end grew nearer, Gwyn started to grasp more tightly those things that identified her as an independent person. Perhaps it was because, one by one, she was losing them. Her reactions, normal and natural as they were, tore at our hearts as we had to make decisions "for her own good." It was an emotional struggle for us to move Gwyn from her home to my sister Nancy's house. It was also a struggle to stop her from trying to drive her car. Her illness had made her too weak to drive or even to get around easily on her own.

It became almost a mission for her to try to pay every bill she owed, even though the family had banded together to make sure she did not need to worry about money. Our reassurances were not enough to quell her independent pride in paying her own way. Even though Christmas was months away, Gwyn even insisted on buying Little Roy's Christmas toys herself, despite our constant assurance that Roy would have all his heart desired waiting for him under the tree on Christmas morning. It was as though she had a compelling urgency to make all those preparations before leaving this earth. She seemed determined to make sure she had absolutely no unfinished business.

If I thought that Mother's death was one of the most difficult losses I would ever have to come to grips with, the anguish of losing Gwyn was almost unimaginable. Lying in this hospital bed was a person, so dear to me, who was full of youth and who had so much ahead of her. This was the girl I had taught to ride a bicycle. Only the year before, she had been brimming with joy, so full of charisma that the tone of conversation brightened merely from her walking into the room.

Her life had paralleled mine. Her dreams paralleled mine. How and why did Death choose her? Why was she lying there with needles stuck in her arm, an oxygen mask covering her mouth and nose, with her life force pouring out, even as I watched over her? She did not, could not, have done anything to deserve this fate.

By this time she was fevered and weak, but one thing about her character remained—her sense of humor. One day when a friend came to visit, the family circled around Gwyn's bed, as we had begun doing by then, as though we were unable to give up any interaction Gwyn had with the outside world. When the friend asked, "Gwyn, how are you doing?" Gwyn smiled a ghost of her former winning smile and said, "Oh, I'm making it." That weak attempt at humor was enough to put us into gales of laughter. A stranger looking at us would have seen only pathos, while we saw a little remembrance of the spirit that Gwyn had once turned on the world.

At one point, the doctor inserted a tube down her throat to help her breathe, but we requested that he remove it. We realized that the tube had taken away the last vital function she had, the last function she could identify with—her ability to talk, to communicate. We felt that this loss was causing her far more suffering than her shortness of breath, as terrifying as that was to watch.

By this time, the family felt frustrated and helpless. Before now, our strength in numbers had made us seem invincible. We had always been able to call on one another to pull us out of a bad situation when necessary, but our invincibility became just another illusion that had to be stripped away in the cold, hard reality of Gwyn's suffering.

As Gwyn's condition worsened, I had the opportunity to watch Dr. Steinberg, Gwyn's physician, examine and treat her. It did not take me long to recognize him as a doctor who shared my passion for the kind treatment of the sick. Never frustrated, he was consistently compassionate and gentle with my sister. As I watched him care for her, a part of his bedside manner started to affect me deeply. Dr. Steinberg had a way of displaying hope when even the most casual observer could tell there was none. Even as a fellow medical professional who knew the end was surely near for Gwyn, I found myself hanging onto his every word. His words gave me the small comfort of being able to deny the inevitable for just a little bit longer.

On the evening of August 16, 1992, as Kim and I lay sleepless on a hospital cart next to Gwyn's bed and as my father sat quietly in a chair at the foot of her bed, Gwyn left us. Her passing was so quiet, so gentle, that for a moment we did not realize Gwyn was gone. It was almost as though Gwyn had purposely waited until all the visitors had left and the room was quiet to make her exit.

Kim had the first inkling that something had happened. She tapped me on the shoulder and whispered shakily, "I think I just saw her take her last breath." Almost instantly, Daddy, Kim, and I were standing beside Gwyn's bed, afraid to touch her, just listening for what we knew we would not hear. Soon we became certain that Gwyn's spirit had passed on to the heavens to start a new beginning, a heavenly life.

Prior knowledge does little to prepare a person for an event like that. We were grateful that her suffering was over but still astounded that she was actually gone. So it was with shock and grief that my father, Kim, and I began notifying our family that the end had come to Gwyn's earthly life.

Those first few days were especially difficult, I think, because our family had to be called from far away. No telephone can hold a hand or wipe tears away. All of us, the ten of us, seemed to be connected at the soul, and Gwyn's death forced us all to think about our own mortality. It made us think of how vulnerable our own lives were and how precious the gift of life really is. Gwyn left us with this thought—that you have to live every moment, that you cannot wait to start living. In the past, we had all worked so hard, our inspiration being that one day we would all be able to stop working and retire. Now we knew that one cannot wait for retirement to start living. The time that we have to live is now.

Several months after Gwyn's passing, Kim, the children, and I traveled to Miami, where Kelly and Mary arranged a feast for us at one of the most lavish restaurants in Fort Lauderdale. The rest of our family joined us there. To me this seemed to be a closure for the death of our sister—a celebration in honor of her. We as a family had held together under the most difficult circumstances, and we had came out of those circumstances stronger. The strength we had was in a different form this time. Our strength was not the strength to work and gain material wealth or the strength to make a mark on life, but the strength of loving, giving, and enjoying life now.

The restaurant was a magnificent stucco building. Mary and Kelly had arranged a seafood buffet, with every type of seafood imaginable. We had our choice of any wine or beverage you might think of, and there was a veritable bounty of fruits, salads, and vegetables. The waiters and even the manager were at our every beck and call. A man sat in the corner playing a grand piano, and a violinist accompanied him.

As we assembled at the table in our private room, it seemed as if an angelic light shone above us from the ceiling. Although I had never been there before, this place seemed familiar to me. Perhaps I had visited it in my dreams! I remember thinking that it felt as if Gwyn and my mother were somehow there with us too.

During the dinner, no one discussed what we had been through so recently. However, I knew Gwyn's passing was in the back of the mind of everyone there. Gwyn's death had transformed us all.

As the musicians played in the background, we all ate and talked of things that families usually talk about at family gatherings, everything from how big the children have grown to "how's business?" Characteristic of our family, we found humor in the conversation. We talked among ourselves; we told jokes. My brother-in-law Rick, a connoisseur of fine food, ate as if he had never eaten before.

By then Little Roy had gone to live with Nancy, and she brought him to the dinner. At the dinner, we passed him from person to person to person. Jack's little boy, Jack Allen, was there too, and we did the same thing with him. Everybody held these little ones for a while and fed them bits of food from their plates, giving each child a kiss and a hug before passing them to the next person. It was as if we were sharing and passing on our family's love as we passed these children from one to another.

As the violin played, I had a sudden inspiration. I took Kim's hand and walked with her to the dance floor. We danced alone. As we danced, I whirled her around. Becoming bolder, at one point I turned to the table where my family sat and sent a small wave to "the crowd." Accompanied by the music of the piano and violin, Kim and I danced gracefully into the night. As we danced, I thought about the American dream, the pursuit of happiness. For me, pursuing happiness means reaching for the heavens. Whether or not one actually reaches the object of desire, it is the act of reaching out that gives vitality to the human spirit.

Gwyn's death has not been in vain. I have grown from losing her. From out of my grief, I have learned to live, to laugh to the fullest, and to enjoy every minute of every day. Although Gwyn is not here today, our family continues to rejoice and marvel at the memory of her ambition and energy. Remembering her continues to teach us, too, that all a family really has is each other. And in a strong family, no amount of trial and tribulation can break them apart.

Every other year, all of our family make time to gather together. Some would call this a family reunion, but I like to think of this as simply a "family union." Gwyn and my mother, both of whom I am certain are very busy in Heaven, must surely stop and smile at our collective antics. We gather together, laugh a lot, hug a lot, eat too much, spend too much money, and leave thankful that we had the opportunity to do so.

And my own dream continues. In fact, I've vowed never to stop dreaming. Now, though, I have one more dream—that in addition to the relentless pursuit of goals, I will take the time to cherish where I am now. Rather than waiting until I reach the top of the mountain to rejoice and feel good about life, I will stop on any narrow crag I find, turn around, look to see where I am, relish how far I have come, and thus renew my dedication to reaching the mountain's peak.

As I continue my climb to reach the mountain's peak, I feel I can hear my mother's voice saying the words she spoke so long ago, "Put on the whole armor of God, Joe Nathan. Put on the whole armor of God. It will protect you the last mile of the way." Mother was right.

((((((((((((((( )(( ))((((((((((()))))))))))

Afterword

Annie (Nell) Lester-Thomas
Attended Paine College in Augusta, Ga.; successful self-employed business-woman, currently comfortably retired in south Florida.

Raymond Lester Jr.
B.S., Florida Atlantic University, Boca Raton; M.B.A., University of Miami; J.D., Atlanta Law School; Ortho McNeil Pharmaceutical, 24 years.

Robert L. Lester Sr.
B.S., Barry University; M.P.A., University of Miami; graduate of Southern Police Institute, University of Louisville; Vietnam war veteran; Miami-Dade Police Department, position, first lieutenant, 28 years.

Mary A. Lester-Jacob
B.A., Albany State University; M.B.A., University of Miami; co-owns a Burger King franchise with her husband.

Leonard (Boot) Lester
B.B.A., Fort Valley State University; self-employed financial analyst, Hawkinsville, Ga.

Nancy Lester-Bailey
B.S., Fort Valley State University; M.S., Clark Atlanta University; Ph.D., Clark Atlanta University; school counselor, Henry County Board of Education, 23 years.

Allene Lester
B.B.A., Fort Valley State University; M.A., Amber University; software engineer, EDS, 15 years.

Joe N. Lester
B.S., Fort Valley State University; D.D.S., Meharry Medical College, School of Dentistry; currently practices in Conyers, Ga; published writer.

Jack Lester
B.S., Fort Valley State University; D.D.S., Meharry Medical College, School of Dentistry; currently practices in Atlanta, Ga.

Gwyn V. Lester-Jordan (1962-1992)
B.S., Fort Valley State University; M.S.W., Clark Atlanta University.

(((((((((((((/(((((((((((((((((((/(((((((((

About the Author

Joe Lester grew up on a farm, but now he is a dentist in private practice in Conyers, Georgia, near Atlanta. In addition, he renders dental treatment to troubled youth detained in the Georgia Department of Juvenile Services. He provides guidance, insight, and hope in addition to dental services.

Dr. Lester formerly served as a Dental Director of the Georgia Department of Corrections, where he provided dental services for nearly ten years to men and women incarcerated in Georgia's prison system. During this time, he also served as President of the Georgia Correctional Dental Society.

A native of Pulaski County, Georgia, he earned his Bachelor of Science degree in zoology from Fort Valley State University and his dental degree from Meharry Medical College School of Dentistry.

Dr. Lester speaks at various events and is active in his church. Dr. Lester and his wife, Kimberly, reside near Atlanta in Lithonia, Georgia, with their three children.

INSIDE
BETWEEN ARCHITECTURE AND LANDSCAPE
OUTSIDE

ROCKPORT

INSIDE
OUTSIDE

BETWEEN ARCHITECTURE AND LANDSCAPE

GLOUCESTER MASSACHUSETTS

ROCKPORT PUBLISHERS

Anita Berrizbeitia and Linda Pollak

First published in the United States of America by
Rockport Publishers, Inc.
33 Commercial Street
Gloucester, Massachusetts 01930-5089
Telephone: (978) 282-9590
Facsimile: (978) 283-2742

Distributed to the book trade and art trade in the United States by
North Light Books, an imprint of
F & W Publications
1507 Dana Avenue
Cincinnati, Ohio 45207
Telephone: (800) 289-0963

Other distribution by
Rockport Publishers, Inc.
Gloucester, Massachusetts 01930-5089

ISBN 1-56496-631-3

10 9 8 7 6 5 4 3 2 1

Designer: Stoltze Design
Cover image: Frontcover
          School at Morella, Morella, Spain, Carmen Pinós and Enric Miralles, Architects
          Backcover
          Top left: Villa Dall'Ava, St. Cloud, France, Rem Koolhaas, Architect
          Top right: Etienne Dolet Public Housing, Issy-les Molineaux, France, Catherine Mosbach, Architect
          Bottom left: Municipal Ocean Swimming pool, Leça de Palmeira, Matushinos, Portugal, Alvaro Siza, Architect
          Bottom right: Querini Stampalia Foundation, Venice, Italy, Carlo Scarpa, Architect

Printed in China